MECHANIX ILLUSTRATED
HOW-TO-DO-IT
ENCYCLOPEDIA

Edited by the Combined Staffs of MECHANIX ILLUSTRATED
FAWCETT BOOKS and ELECTRONICS ILLUSTRATED

IN SIXTEEN VOLUMES

VOLUME 8

COMPLETE CONTENTS
AND INDEX IN VOLUME 16

No part of the text or illustrations in this encyclopedia may be used without the written permission of Fawcett Publications, Inc. All rights reserved under Pan-American Copyright Convention and the International Copyright Convention.

COPYRIGHT 1961 FAWCETT PUBLICATIONS, INC.

Well-known reader services of Mechanix Illustrated are extended to readers of this encyclopedia to the extent of blueprint and plan offerings as indicated throughout the various volumes. Inquiries relating to such services and communications regarding the editorial material in this encyclopedia should be directed to Fawcett Publications, Inc., Encyclopedia Service, 67 West 44th Street, New York 36, N. Y. Printed in the United States of America.

GOLDEN PRESS • **NEW YORK**

FIREPLACES

ADD A FIREPLACE

FIREPLACE construction has been greatly simplified in recent years by the manufacture of pressed steel fireplace units which serve as the heart of the heating system. At one time it required a skilled mason to construct the smoke shelf, throat, and damper mechanism; now all these things are built into the pressed steel unit. Today it is simply a matter of setting the unit on a prepared foundation and building the fireplace around it. As one contractor said, "It's difficult to build fireplaces that *won't* work when factory-built units are used."

However, this does not preclude the necessity for exercising care when installing one of these units. It is important that the fireplace be properly situated in the room. Remember, a properly built fireplace has plenty of thermal muscle, so the room should be a large one. Those bright, crackling flames you love to watch contain a surprising

DECIDE on dimensions before starting work. **FLOOR JOISTS support hearth's foundation**

STEEL RODS strengthen hearth's concrete. **HEARTHSTONES are of uniform thickness.**

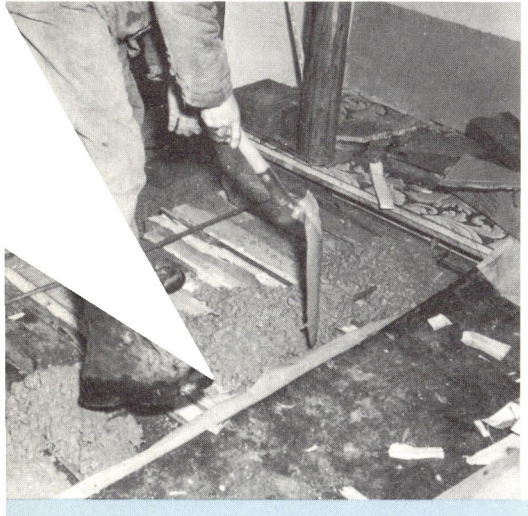

amount of heat and if you build up a roaring fire in a small room you will find your guests fleeing in self-defense. For this reason you should always build your fireplace to face the length rather than the width of a room, unless the room's width exceeds 15 feet.

Make provision for a large hearth. Unless the hearth is wide, your floor covering may scorch or even burn. The hearth should be at least the width of the fireplace masonry (usually about six feet) and not less than 30 inches deep. An eight-foot-wide hearth extending one foot beyond the masonry on either side and 43 inches out from the firebox is none too big for a roaring fire.

The average fireplace unit shapes a hearth about 20 inches deep. The additional depth is made up of masonry. If you skimp on masonry and build it to the minimum four-inch depth you won't be able to burn larger logs. So make the width of the masonry at the fire-

FIREPLACES

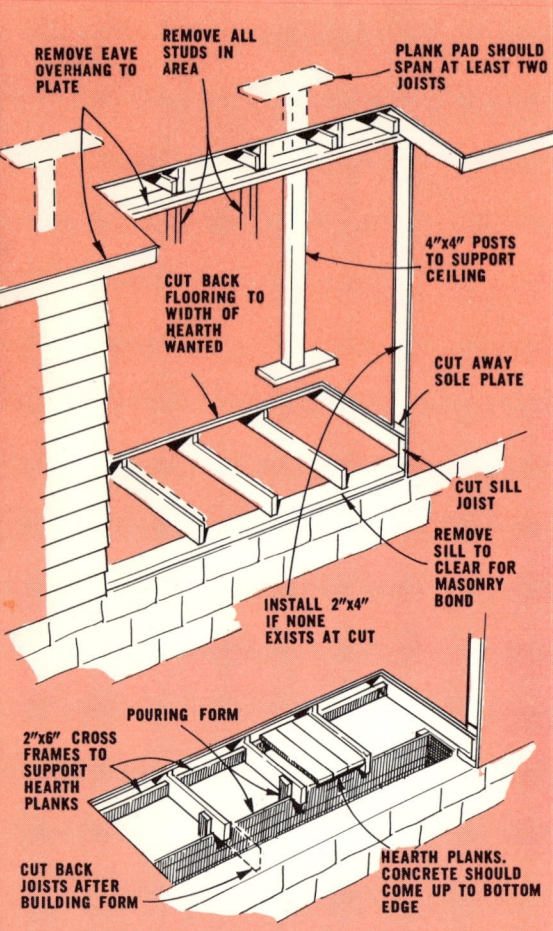

CEMENT BLOCKS frame exterior foundation.

box opening at least eight to ten inches.

Build your firebox deep enough to accommodate those old stumps you'll bring back from the country, otherwise fire may spill out on the hearth or smoke escape into the room.

Don't let the mantelpiece climb too high. Keep it low enough to permit even a short guest the comfort of leaning on it with his elbow.

Raw Materials

Gather up plenty of rocks and fieldstones. An average fireplace will use about 20 tons equally divided between face stone and rubble stone. The face stone will form the exterior of the fireplace. The rubble stone is used to build up a solid masonry interior.

Cutting Through The Wall

Cut a hole in the side of your house the exact width of the fireplace. Remove the inside and outside finish to expose the studs. Then brace the ceiling above the hole with a 6x6-inch crosspiece strongly supported by uprights at each end. Don't place these too close to the working area but set them back a foot or so from the opening to give yourself room to work. When the crosspiece is in place, remove the studs.

Do not take out the plate, but cut off the roof overhang. Remember that the masonry will come flush to the plate and will support the plate in place of the

ASH CHANNEL is covered with flat stones.

1348

FIREPLACES

STEEL UNIT is centered over fire hearth.   **RUBBLE STONE** is the fireplace's muscle.

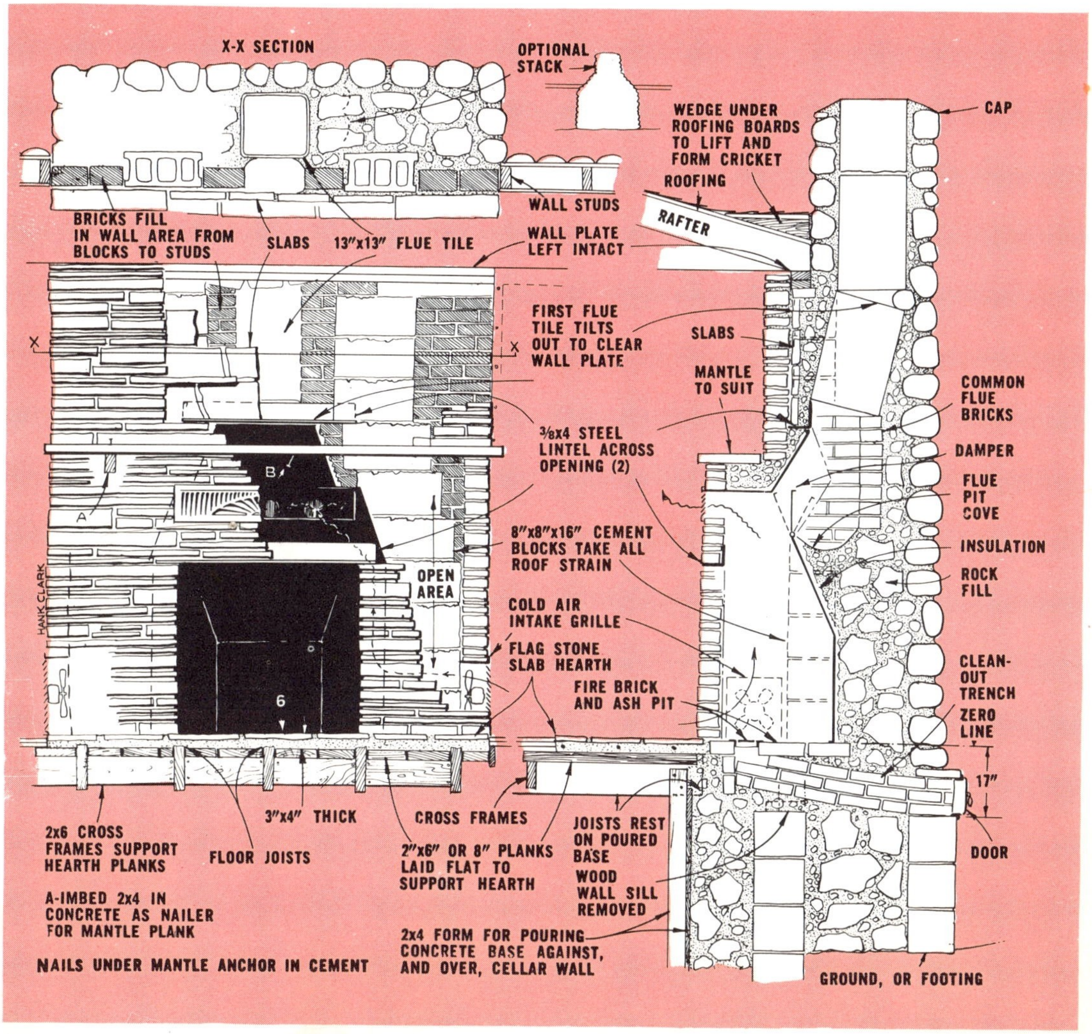

X-X SECTION

OPTIONAL STACK

CAP

WEDGE UNDER ROOFING BOARDS TO LIFT AND FORM CRICKET

WALL STUDS

WALL PLATE LEFT INTACT

ROOFING

RAFTER

BRICKS FILL IN WALL AREA FROM BLOCKS TO STUDS

SLABS 13"x13" FLUE TILE

FIRST FLUE TILE TILTS OUT TO CLEAR WALL PLATE

SLABS

MANTLE TO SUIT

COMMON FLUE BRICKS

3/8x4 STEEL LINTEL ACROSS OPENING (2)

DAMPER

FLUE PIT COVE

8"x8"x16" CEMENT BLOCKS TAKE ALL ROOF STRAIN

INSULATION

ROCK FILL

OPEN AREA

COLD AIR INTAKE GRILLE

FLAG STONE SLAB HEARTH

FIRE BRICK AND ASH PIT

CLEAN-OUT TRENCH

ZERO LINE

17"

HANK CLARK

2x6 CROSS FRAMES SUPPORT HEARTH PLANKS

3"x4" THICK FLOOR JOISTS

CROSS FRAMES

2"x6" OR 8" PLANKS LAID FLAT TO SUPPORT HEARTH

JOISTS REST ON POURED BASE

WOOD WALL SILL REMOVED

DOOR

A-IMBED 2x4 IN CONCRETE AS NAILER FOR MANTLE PLANK

2x4 FORM FOR POURING CONCRETE BASE AGAINST, AND OVER, CELLAR WALL

NAILS UNDER MANTLE ANCHOR IN CEMENT

GROUND, OR FOOTING

1349

FIREPLACES

BRICK forms pocket for the smoke shelf.

CHECK WORK frequently with level, plumb.

VARY inside stonework to suit your taste.

FLUE LINER tips out to clear the roof line.

ERECT scaffolding as chimney work rises.

SLOPE MORTAR around flue liner to finish.

studs. You can erect a small tarpaulin now to keep out weather and insects until the masonry closes the hole.

Outline the hearth and remove the flooring from that area. The supporting floor joists will be at least 2x6s and more likely 2x8s or 2x10s. The hearth should be at least four inches thick. If you have to slice off that much from the floor joists, build up cement-block or masonry pylons from below to give added support to these weakened timbers. These problems differ according to varying house designs and the correct solution in your own case should be apparent as soon as the joists are exposed.

The Foundation

Build up the outside fireplace foundation. This must be a firm base for those tons of rock it will support and should be somewhat larger all around than the dimensions of the masonry over it.

If the house stands on well-drained soil and if there are several feet from ground to floor level it may be possible to lay the foundation flat on the ground. Inquiry about building practices in your own community will determine if this is feasible. However, the safest method of anchoring the foundation is to dig a hole to a point below frost penetration. This will vary from a few inches to a few feet depending on your local climate.

Build up the foundation with mortar and rock. Set a mixer alongside the excavation and dump in alternately a layer of concrete and a layer of rock. Ready-mix concrete will save work at this point of the project.

You are ready now to start installation of the pressed steel fireplace. Some tricky measurements are involved here so work carefully. The floor will be level with the hearth and firebox; call this point zero. If you are installing an outside ash dump you will have to figure on setting the outside door at zero minus about 17 inches. This allows for the distance of the drop from firebox to ash channel (about 14 inches) plus a gradual three-inch down-slope along the ash channel to the outside exit.

The modern decorating trend nowadays is to use custom-fitted fireplace screens instead of the heretofore conventional stand-up kind. Custom screens have the advantage of occupying no floor space and, of course, the hazard of falling is completely eliminated. Their installation is a comparatively easy job. The Bennett-Ireland Company of Norwich, New York, can supply you with a kit which will fit your fireplace opening exactly. •

FASTEN brackets with self-tapping

SUPPORT BAR is lowered into the brackets.

FISHING BOX

Fishing Box

Keep that tangly gear in order with this easy week-end project.

WHEN you are out by that peaceful stream, you don't want to waste "catchin' time" searching for the lures and sinkers that will help you snag that big one. And what could be more frustrating than to be all set to go and discover the thing you need is back home someplace!

You don't have to experience such calamity if you provide yourself with a means of keeping all your fishing equipment in one compact case—all set to go, anytime. And this easy-to-make tackle box is exactly the right answer. And if you have a fishing trip coming up soon, don't let it worry you. You can build this item in just one or two evenings.

The box has a lift-out tray, compartmented for small items, and a good size storage area below which you can use for bigger items like reels. Two suitcase-type catches snug down the top cover.

We used a high-density type overlaid fir plywood to make the project because it's very hard and smooth and will take a lot of abuse. You don't even have to protect it with paint. But conventional type fir plywood could be used especially if you choose a waterproof type.

Check the drawing before you begin construction. Then lay the component parts out on the plywood to utilize the material to best advantage. Where mitered

Everything is right at hand when the fish bite.

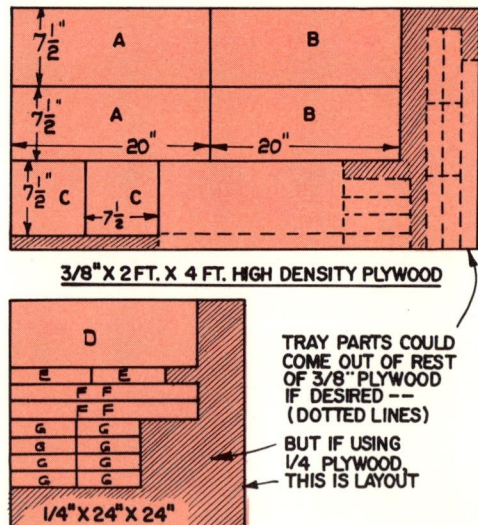

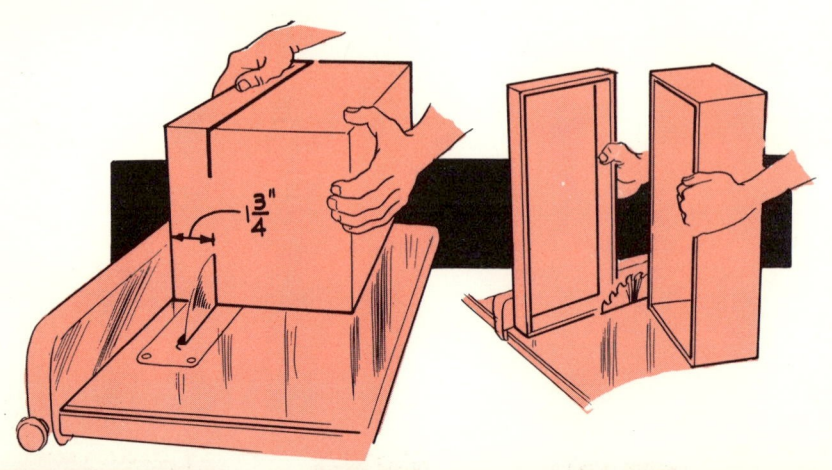

1352

FISHING BOX

joints are called for, it will be easier to cut parts slightly oversize to begin with, then trim down to exact size as you match one piece against the other.

The job will be much easier if you make the project as a closed box, making the cut which separates the lid from the body after the box is completely assembled. First cut to length and fasten at the corners of sides "B" the pieces of ¾"-quarter round molding which support the lift-out tray. These will also help to position and hold the two ends (parts C) as they are being nailed. Attaching the top and bottom, using glue and ¾" brads, then put the assembled box aside until the glue droes.

Assemble the tray by nailing and gluing the ends (part E) to the bottom and then adding the sides (parts F). Cut the dividers to correct length and fasten in place as indicated.

To remove the lid from the box body make a cut around all four sides 1¾" down from what will be the top. This is easily done on a table saw by setting the rip fence the required distance away from the saw blade.

All that remains now is to attach the hardware as indicated on the drawing.

If you've used the high density overlaid plywood the job is done except for some little sanding on cut edges. If you're going to paint, first brush on a flat undercoat. Sand lightly when dry, then apply a second coat which can be tinted slightly in the tone of the finish color. Finally, apply the finish coat. Bear in mind that the box is going to get a great deal of rough handling and weather, so use the best quality of outdoor finish that is available, both inside and out. It should last for many years. • *By R. J. DeCristoforo*

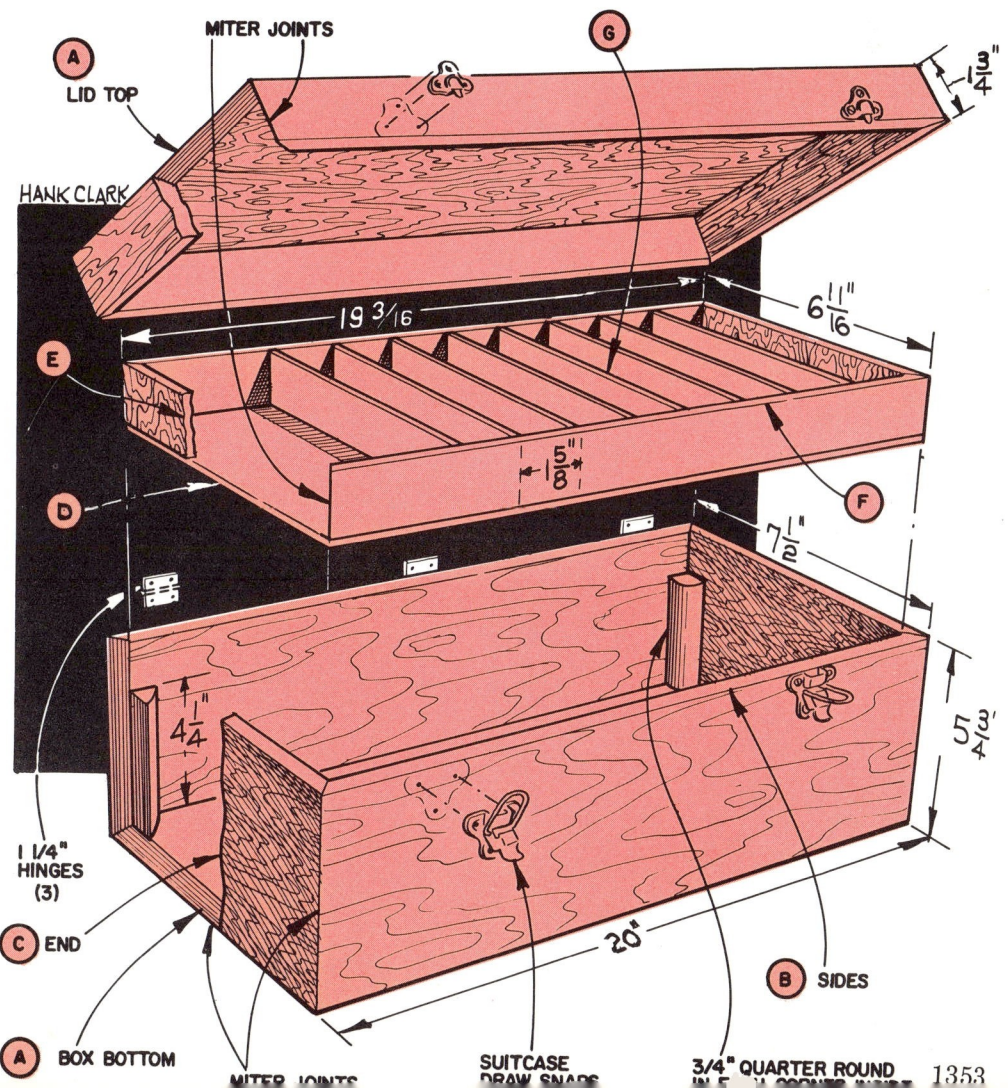

FLAGSTONE

how to handle flagstone

Results are dramatic whether you set them in cement or lay them on sand.

FLAGSTONE IS A TRADITIONAL favorite as a terrace surfacing. The stones come in a variety of colors, thicknesses, and shapes. Easiest to work with are precut flags in exact, squared-off, ready-to-lay sizes. These are also the most expensive. Typically, rectangular flags 1-inch thick cost about 50 cents a square foot, 1½-inch 60 cents. Irregular flags are 28 and 40 cents, for these two thicknesses. If you buy over 500 square feet, you can expect a quantity discount. Prices are often lower, too, if you pick up your own stones

To move heavy stone stand it on edge, rocking it from corner to corner. A wheelbarrow is a help.

1354

FLAGSTONE

at the yard. Stones are measured by their minimum thickness.

You can lay flags on sand, or on well-drained earth by merely cutting out sod and leaving grass joints. You can lay them on a gravel or cinder base, or over concrete. On concrete, the thinner flags can be used, but anything less than 1-inch is inadvisable otherwise.

In rectangular stones you can get all sizes from 12x12 inches to 54x54 inches at 6-inch intervals; that is, 12x12, 12x18, to 12x54, etc. Actual sizes of the stones are ¾ inch less in each direction as allowance for joints. Usually, the larger the stones the easier they are to lay.

Pattern and shape. To make a patterned paving, use ten or eleven different sizes of stones. Work out your pattern to scale with colored paper squares on cardboard. A scale of 1 inch to equal 1 foot is easy to handle. Break the joints, trying not to have more than 3 stones (never over 4) in a line in any direction before taking a step. Shift the squares around until you get the pattern that pleases you most, then copy it on

Measure diagonals for rectangular terrace. Make sure they are equal or terrace will be lopsided.

Where drainage is problem, remove existing soil, replace with six inches of sand or a porous fill.

Use flour or lime to mark curb around perimeter and use a backhoe to dig along lines indicated.

Without mortar, lay lower row of blocks in a 16-inch trench on sandbed, use long level to align.

1355

To cement upper row, use Sakrete Mortar Mix or six parts sand, one of lime, one of cement, little water.

Have sand for bed dumped as close to terrace as truck can get. Save the lawn by spreading tarp.

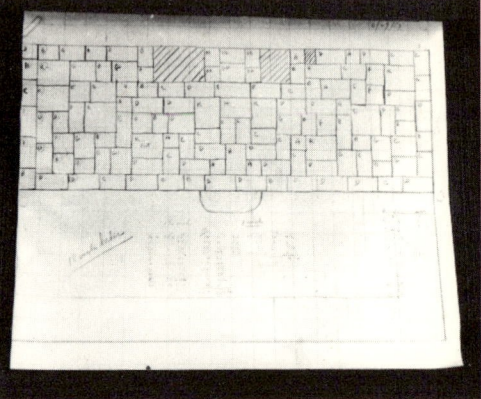

Level sand and tamp or roll firm. Curb protects against frost and it keeps base from washing out.

Tack your terrace pattern to nearby wall. Above pattern has letter of alphabet to key flag size.

As shown here, flags are laid along terrace edge. Small stones are used to fill cavities in blocks.

To make joint proper width, shift flag with tire iron or metal bar; also use it to pry up stones.

FLAGSTONE

paper, keying each size stone with a different letter. For uniformity, the same pattern sequence should be repeated on each half of the terrace.

A rectangular terrace is easiest, for it can be made without the necessity of cutting any stones. However, if you don't mind a little extra effort, you can make the shape round, oval, or irregular. Don't arbitrarily select a shape because it pleases your fancy. Sketch the plan of your house, grounds, walks, principal trees and planting beds to scale on paper, and try to work out a terrace shape that makes sense in your scheme. If your plan doesn't look good on paper, it won't be any better when you build it. Plan to pitch your terrace away from the house ¾ to 1 inch in 10 feet.

Preparing the base. A terrace laid on sand requires no foundation, but a curb around it, extendng 12 to 24 inches below grade, will help curb frost action and can be a help in keeping your sand in place. In the construction illustrated a 16-inch trench was dug for a curb made of block. A backhoe to do the digging was hired for an hour. Just enough sand was used in the bottom of the trench to get a level bed, and the bottom course of blocks was laid dry on the sand. Only the upper courses were cemented together.

Sometimes, instead of blocks, wooden headers are used to hold the terrace edge in line. Use wood that is naturally rot-resistant, or treat other wood with a water-repellent preservative such as Woodlife. Stake headers well to hold them in place. One-inch boards can be curved gently to match a rounded terrace edge. To make the boards bend more sharply, cut saw kerfs at 1-inch intervals along its outside.

Where ground is well settled and frost is no problem, flags may be laid directly on leveled soil. Where there is frost, use a sand bed of from 2 to 6 inches, depending on the quality of drainage in the soil below. If it's clay, hardpan, or otherwise poorly drained, use 6. You may find it desirable to dig out the poor soil before replacing it with sand. But don't put sand under only *part* of the terrace. A uniform bed under the whole terrace is important so that it will react uniformly to frost. Clay, loam, and sand in different parts will react unequally and the paving will roll.

Save by using dead sand. This is very fine sand, containing some clay. Its cost is likely to be $1.75 per yard, as compared with about $6.00 for building sand. You can also save with road sand. This also contains some clay, but is ¼-inch screen, and contains particles up to that size.

Construction pointers. Begin laying flags at a corner or along a wall. Prepare the bed for each stone by tamping it well. The sand should be damp. Spray it if necessary to keep it damp.

Temporarily set the stone in position and firm it there, then lift it and inspect its bed. You'll be able to spot high and low areas

When sand is damp it packs easier. A fine water spray is used when sand looks like it is drying.

Prepare base to match varying thickness of stone. Base should match irregular bottom of flagstone.

1357

FLAGSTONE

Place stone on prepared bed. Then, allowing for pitch of terrace, check level from side to side.

To check for a high spot, try standing with one foot on opposite corners. Adjust if flag rocks.

Lift stone that is not level. Note dampness on stone. Look at level of sand to find high spot.

FLAGSTONE

by the way the sand has been compressed. Make adjustments by adding or taking away sand until you get the stone so it fits its space level in both directions and is supported by its bed over its entire bottom.

By standing on opposite corners of a stone and trying to rock it, you can tell how well it is seated. By running your toe along two adjacent stones, you can stub out discrepencies in leveling which must be corrected.

You don't have to lift heavy stones. Hold them on edge and "walk" them along by rocking them from one corner to the other. A tire iron or other flat piece of metal is good for shifting stones and adjusting the space between them, as well as for prying them up enough for a handhold.

To cut a stone, rest it on a bed of sand. Score it with a chisel along the line of cut. Notch well at each end of the line and chisel along the line repeatedly until the stone parts.

If, when your paving is complete, you fill the joints with sand, you may find the sand splatters out when it rains. Many prefer mossy joints. If you can get fine black dirt from the woods, in which moss is already growing, you're assured of quick success. Otherwise you can use any ordinary soil and sour it, starting the bacterial action, by pouring on buttermilk.

Alternately, you can fill the cracks with top soil and plant thyme or other plants which grow low and stand bruising. Plants soften the hard look of masonry, take away its raw newness. Where joints are very tight you may want to chip away corners to make room for plants. Check with your local nurseryman as to which do best in your area.

Flagstone on concrete. The slab, preferably, should have a rough finish to insure a good bond. If it has a steel-troweled finish, it is necessary to use metal lath to reinforce the mortar bed you place under the stones. Fit all flags before you begin permanent laying.

A ¾-inch mortar bed is usually satisfactory. You can use Sakrete Sand Mix for the purpose, or mix your own using 1 part sand, 3 parts portland cement, and ¼ part lime. You may find it advantageous to add about ½ shovel of lime to a bag of Sakrete.

Put down only enough mortar for one flag at a time. Twist each flag back and forth in its bed to settle it firmly. Level all flags equally by setting a straightedge across them. The mixture for the joints is a little richer and drier than for the bed. Use a minimum of water, pack the crumbly mortar into the joints with a flat jointer, scooping it off a trowel held close to the joint. Brush off dropped mortar later. •

Scrape away high spot with trowel. If stone is low then add sand. Replace stone, check again.

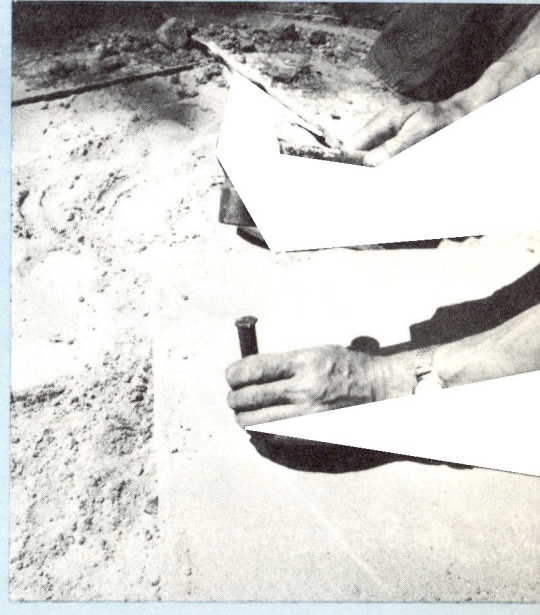

To cut stone: rest it on sand, scratch a line; chisel notch at each end and then along the mark.

1359

Flashing

THERE is more to flashing than meets the eye. A professional flashing job has roofing paper or felt under the exposed flashing, whether it be some kind of metallic sheeting or roll roofing. And not all flashing is visible. Shingles may cover the ridge, or peak, of an asphalt-shingled roof but there will be copper or other flashing underneath.

Seasonal changes in temperature and the elements in general are rough on the roofing cement frequently used at the edges of flashing. A new coating of the cement or flashing compound may seal the edges as good as new. Small holes and cracks can be treated in the same way.

The replacement of old flashing with new is not a job to be undertaken lightly by the average handy man. Shingles or other roofing material will have to be removed first to get at the edges of the flashing where the nailing has been done. If you have embarked on such a project, the old flashing can serve as a pattern for the new Where one piece of metallic flashing touches another, the two must be of the

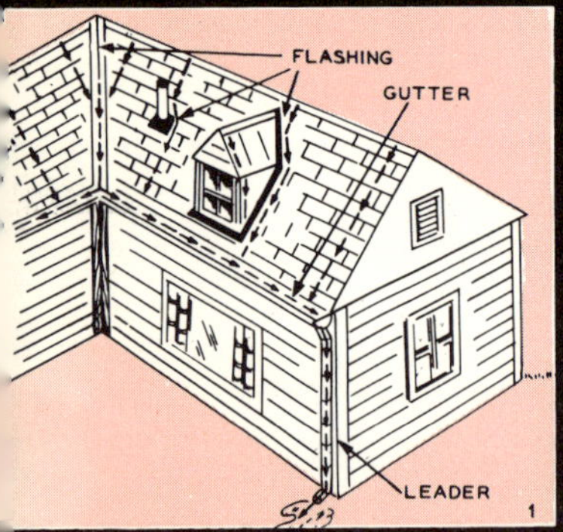

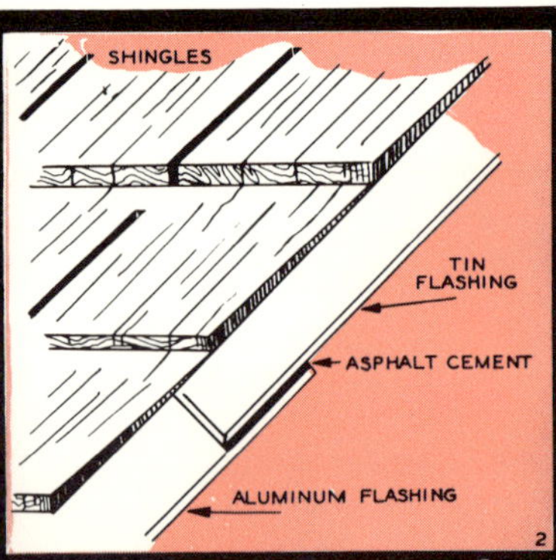

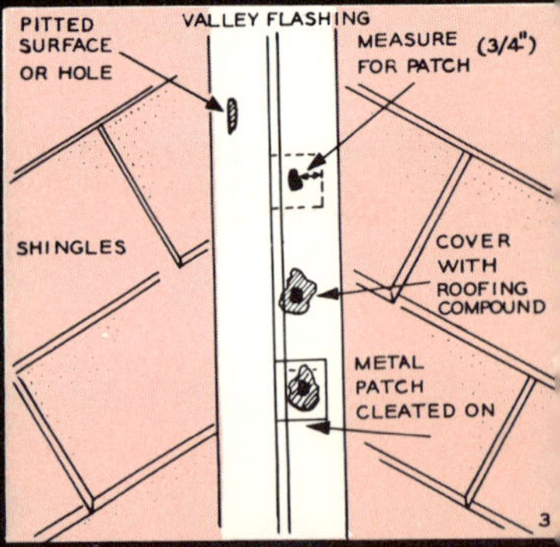

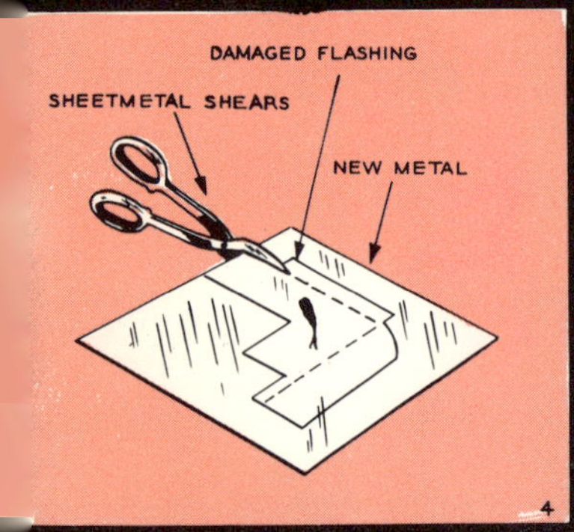

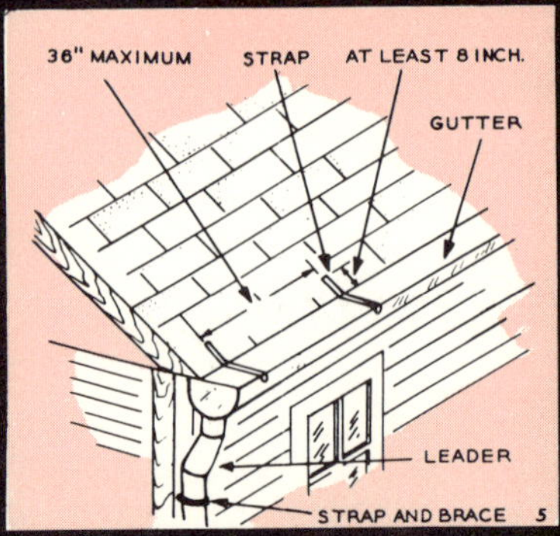

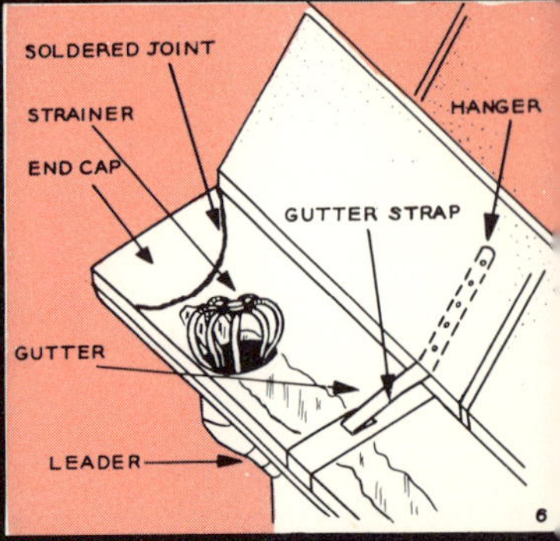

FLASHING

1. Ridge flashing
2. Rake-gable flashing
3. Ridge flashing
4. Cricket flashing
5. Valley flashing

same kind of metal. Remember this also in making a patch on flashing.

If the damaged section is in a valley of the shingled roof, it will pay to try patching unless the old flashing is hopelessly beyond repair. A square of sheet metal, of the same kind of metal as the old, is cut. Crease it diagonally and fold to the angle of the flashing. The square should be large enough so that when folded in this way the tips on each side should fit an inch or two under the shingles at the sides. When in position, the patch will be diamond shaped, except that the tips at the sides will be under the shingles. Before putting the patch in position, coat the area it will cover with roofing cement; press the patch into it.

In proper flashing around a chimney, the edge of each piece of flashing bends into the mortar between the bricks. Each piece of flashing runs at least four inches up the side of the chimney, and each extends at least six inches under the roofing.

A roofer should be hired for major flashing repairs—even for minor ones if there is any uncertainty about your ability to handle yourself on a roof. •

Loose chimney flashing, allowing rain to leak through attic, is renailed and edges are calked.

FLOORS

Take Proper Care of Floors

Correct floor maintenance does more to beautify a home than costly furnishings and elaborate decor.

FLOOR CARE has always posed a problem to mankind. When he first came to appreciate the fact that floors could be beautiful, the problem of durability arose.

Today there is a wide choice of beautiful floors through increased use of colors, materials and design. Despite the increased variety, the durability and ease of maintenance today exceeds all previous standards. But the inherent beauty and durability of floors is dependent upon *correct* floor care procedures. For example, the average person is unable to distinguish by eye the difference between asphalt tile and linoleum tile. Yet, the same maintenance materials used on both could be beneficial to one and harmful to the other.

Following are some professional tips to help you quickly, easily and correctly care for all the floors in your home.

Wood Floors

Care of your wood floor is dependent upon the type of finish on it and the use to which it is put daily. A penetrating wood sealer such as American Pentra-Seal is the preferred finish according to present day trends. Seal offers maximum protection. As an integral part of the wood it locks out damaging dust, dirt and moisture at the same time sealing in the natural beauty of the wood.

Water is the enemy of unsealed wood floors and to many of the finishes used on them. Clean and maintain wood floors with a waterless wax base cleaner. Only in rare cases should floors be subjected to a soap and water scrubbing. Even then you should exercise great care for frequent scrubbings will raise the grain of the wood, spot it and destroy its beauty.

Any liquid that gets on wood floors should be wiped up immediately after the accident. Floors stained by human or animal urine may require replacement. Bleaching with oxalic acid will sometimes remove stains that haven't penetrated the wood too deeply. If this fails the only answer is to replace the stained strips with new wood, as even sanding may not be sufficient. American Pentra-Seal eliminates spotting worries, for wood sealed with it is impervious to liquids.

Wood floors in reasonably good condition, but discolored from dirt and having a slightly oxidized surface, should be gone over with a mild soap or detergent solution and a No. 2 or No. 3 steel wool pad to restore brightness. The scrubbing solution should be used sparingly and dried thoroughly to minimize the

FLOORS

Waxing and buffing with steel wool pads maintains the natural beauty of the wood grain.

danger of warpage and staining. Once the floor is dry, wax for added protection and beauty. If the floor is merely dirty, or has excessive wax buildup, use waterless American Floor Cleaner for an easy one-application cleaning and waxing job.

Sealed floors offer the greatest protection against scratches and mars. A slight sanding, depending upon the depth of the scratch, a few additional drops of seal, light steel wooling, a little paste wax and the floor looks perfect again. But, if you have a surface finish (like shellac or varnish) on your floors and it is scratched, the best action to take is to touch it up with a wax pencil. Another application of the same surface finish will show and cause the damaged area to stand out even more. The only

Water is the enemy of all types of floors. In washing, scrub water must be completely dried with rags, or sucked up by a vacuum which is made for both wet and dry pick-up.

permanent repair treatment for such a floor finish is to remove the entire finish by sanding.

Cork Tile

A newly installed cork floor should not be treated, except for a light sweeping, for four or five days, or until it has firmly gripped the subfloor. Cork is an extremely long wearing, soft-to-walk-on floor if properly cared for. Some cork tile is received from the factory with the surface already sealed. Such tile needs only periodic cleaning and light waxing to maintain its beauty for years. Unsealed cork tile may come from the factory with or without wax on the surface. In either case, scrub as with wood to remove wax and prepare the surface. Then treat it with two coats of Pentra-Seal to fill the air holes in the cork. When the seal has dried, apply a good quality water emulsion or spirit wax. Buffing the wax will increase the gloss and wear resistance.

Cork is subject to indentations, so heavy furniture should rest on cups or casters of sufficient size to bear the weight over the widest possible surface, depending upon general decor. Old or worn cork can be resanded, and the general treatment is similar to that of wood. Water does not injure cork, but may effect the mastic that holds it down.

Linoleum

Using cleaning agents with a high alkaline content will remove the linseed oil. This will cause the linoleum to become brittle, crack, colors to run, wear rapidly, and, it may produce a tendency for linoleum tile to curl. All this can be prevented by following a few simple rules.

Don't wash new installations for four or five days. Keep surface dirt off with a soft-hair brush or sweep-type mop. After the above waiting period, use a safe neutral cleaner to remove imbedded dirt and any oil-like film which may be on the surface. If washing is necessary, use water sparingly. Dry the floor completely and apply two thin coats of wax. Either water emulsion or spirit solvent waxes may be used according to preference. Water emulsion liquid wax should be spread on as thinly as possible, with a short strand mop wrung $2/3$ to $3/4$ dry. Spirit paste wax can be applied either by hand or with a buffing machine. After each coat of either type wax is used, buffing will increase the luster and the life of the protective coating. The waxed floor will remain easy to clean. It may be damp mopped periodically thereafter, and rebuffed to original brilliance.

When the surface has dulled and the wax no longer responds to buffing, it is necessary to remove the dirt by scrubbing. Use a neutral cleaner with a minimum amount of water and scrub by hand or machine. Don't use alkaline soaps or harsh scouring compounds. Use steel wool to remove stubborn accumulations. Remove the water as rapidly as possible, and rewax as above when the floor is completely dry.

Rubber Tile

Floors of this material provide many years of excellent service, if properly maintained. Rubber floors are abrasive resistant and are not easily stained.

FLOORS

SPIRIT OR SOLVENT WAXES

Two types:
1. Liquid
2. Paste

Solvent is usually naptha, carbon tetrachloride and mineral spirits alone or in combination added to wax solids.

Such a base acts as a cleaner, also makes for fast, thorough drying, has high resistance to water and normally is longest wearing wax type finish. Water is not used in its formulation.

Ideal for wood, cork, linoleum but never use a spirit wax on asphalt, vinyl or rubber tile for solvents cause colors to "run," dull appearance in general.

Apply with lamb's wool applicator or soft cloth. Two thin coats, according to label directions, always best.

Lustre can be achieved *only* by buffing, preferably with a machine which can be rented at most hardware, paint or wallpaper stores.

WATER EMULSION WAXES

Two types:
1. Liquid
2. Paste

Carrier is always water and in most cases resins are added to liquid type in combination with wax solids.

Resins make the finish slip resistant and increase wearability. Less water resistant than spirit or solvent type waxes but removal and rewaxing is generally easier.

Can, with care, be used on all types of floor. Especially recommended for asphalt, rubber, vinyl or any floor where ease of application is desirable.

Apply liquid with lamb's wool applicator or short string mop. Water emulsion paste should be machine applied using steel wool. It cleans as it waxes.

Self-polishing waxes are found only in the liquid water emulsion category. Paste water emulsion waxes must be polished for lustre.

Rubber tile is more resilient than linoleum and it is more impervious to indentations caused by furniture or other objects.

In general, rubber tile floors should be cared for like linoleum, but it is important to use only water emulsion waxes. Spirit solvent waxes will injure rubber. Rubber is not as critical with respect to alkaline solutions as is linoleum. However, excessive alkali will cause the rubber to deteriorate and scouring compounds containing abrasive powder will scratch the surface and increase maintenance problems. Neutral soaps or detergents should be used and care is necessary to avoid excessive wetting. Use soft-hair brooms or sweep mops to remove surface dirt. Scrub by hand with scrub brush or with machine using a fine steel wool pad to thoroughly clean the floor before waxing. Rinse the floor thoroughly and be careful to remove excess water as rapidly as possible with either a mop or a wet type vacuum.

Apply water emulsion wax in the same manner as for linoleum and buff or polish for best results. Dry steel wool buffing may be used on rubber floors the same as linoleum.

Asphalt Tile

Asphalt tile is available in standard, grease proof, and acid resisting types. It is important to use grease proof tile in areas such as kitchens. This tile is also resistant to alcohol and alkalis. Therefore alkaline type cleaners can be used for scrubbing without harm.

New floors should not be scrubbed until the tile has had sufficient time to adhere to the mastic in which it is laid.

Equipment, sealer and waxes that will maintain the floors clean, lustrous and durable.

For the first four or five days this floor should be cleaned by light sweeping or damp mopping.

After the initial period, the asphalt tile floor can be scrubbed, but avoid excessive use of water, and dry quickly and thoroughly. (Use warm water for scrubbing. Do not use hot water on asphalt tile.)

Never use a solvent base wax on asphalt tile. The only approved wax is one of the water emulsion type. Apply only to a thoroughly clean and dry floor with a short strand mop. Spread two thin coats evenly. Buffing between coats will increase the luster and serviceability of the wax. Periodic buffing will prolong the periods between scrubbing and rewaxing. With a polishing machine, use a fine steel wool pad to remove excessive dirt and wax.

Plastic Tile

Plastic floors are vinyls, which are basically produced from petroleum by-products or from acids with activating chemical agents or from a wide variety of other chemically treated compounds.

Most vinyls are limited to above-grade installations. Most have lower maintenance cost and are longer wearing than other resilient floor coverings. Vinyl tile is greaseproof, is unaffected by oils and fats, and is highly resistant to alkaline substances, detergents, soaps, and to most solvents. It has high resistance to indentation. A vinyl-asbestos tile is also available which has unusually good resistance to dilute acids.

Vinyl tiles should be scrubbed with a cleaner that leaves no residue. All vinyl or plastic tile is enhanced by the application of the proper wax. In this case use water emulsion types only—never spirit solvent waxes. Buffing with a soft tampico polishing brush increases luster. Light damp mopping, followed by re-buffing restores the original brilliance.

Since vinyls are extremely dense and of less porosity than other resilient floor covering materials, penetration of dirt and foreign materials is practically nil. However, they will get dirty, and waxing will allow for easier cleaning and easier control and prevention of discoloration.

Concrete Floors

Concrete floors present various maintenance problems, depending on age, the manner in which they were mixed and applied, and the type of traffic they receive. The major problem is dusting, a condition in which the surface of the concrete crumbles to a powder. To correct this apply a penetrating seal (comes in various colors) or a rubber base paint. For best results, the concrete should be brushed free of dust, then washed with a solution of muriatic acid and water to neutralize the alkalinity on the floor surface. An alternative would be to cover a concrete floor with asphalt tile or other approved resilient tiling for your location.

Some seals which contain hardening agents should be used only before the concrete has thoroughly cured. Tung oil seals, such as Pentra-Seal, are satisfactory for sealing either new or old concrete floors. Seals with a vegetable base should not be used due to the reaction of alkali inherent in the concrete, which will cause poor bonding. Ordinary paint should never be used on concrete for the same reason. Only materials recommended by a manufacturer for concrete will provide lasting qualities and give maximum protection.

When the concrete floor has been sealed and/or painted, it should be waxed (either spirit or water type) with two coats applied thinly, and adequately buffed

Floor Waxes

The "foreign language" aspect of so many wax labels and advertisements confuses many a householder. You may not know which wax to use, mainly because the differences have never been given to you in plain talk. To better the situation, we have translated the whole area of waxes into an easy-to-read-and-understand chart.

Keep in mind that there are basically four types of waxes for home use. You can choose between a *paste* or a *liquid* wax having either a *solvent* or a *water* base. Those containing solvents are known as spirit waxes and those containing water are known as emulsion waxes.

The self-polishing feature of the liquid water emulsion waxes is due to the physical characteristic of the size of particles of wax in emulsion. When applied to a surface, the water evaporates leaving a thin film of wax. Such a surface reflects light rather than absorbing it. The amount of reflection is the gloss or self-polishing characteristic of the wax. However, any self-polishing wax is enhanced by buffing with a polishing machine.

All waxes in their applications have cleaning properties, but the majority of cleaning waxes are the liquid spirit type. Cleaning is achieved by using the solvent to loosen and suspend the floor dirt. The used solution is squeegeed or blotted with clean cloths or is picked up by the lamb's wool applicator which may have been used for applying. The wax remaining must be buffed, preferably with steel wool, to give the desired luster. •

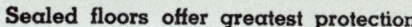
Sealed floors offer greatest protection ..

against floor scratches. A slight sanding . . .

a few additional drops of seal, a little . . .

paste wax, and the floor looks perfect again.

FLOORS

INSTALL BLOCK FLOORING

By David X. Manners

Wood blocks make a handsome covering for any kind of floor and it can be done without nails

WOOD BLOCKS make beautiful and durable floors in any room from the attic to the workshop. They are available in a variety of prefinished woods or can be had unfinished.

FLOORS

WOOD BLOCK FLOORING is readily installed, without nailing, over concrete, plywood, asphalt tile, or any smooth wooden floor. You can get blocks in luxurious prefinished oak, walnut, beech, or mixed hardwoods. Or, if you prefer, you can get them unfinished.

Of particular interest to handymen is the new Dura-Wood block. Made of tough pecan and hickory, and especially designed for industrial use, it's ideal for home workshops. In the workshop, wood is easier and warmer underfoot than concrete, and tools dropped on it are not so readily damaged.

Most popular block size is 9x9-inch in 25/32-inch thickness. Cost ranges from 50 to 65 cents a square foot. Whatever the type chosen, installation is similar.

Surface preparation is important—your finished floor cannot be any smoother than the base on which it is placed. For installations on concrete, first level any high spots, fill in low ones. On high spots, use a carborundum grinder, or hammer and chisel. Fill in low spots with patching mix, following the manufacturer's directions.

If there is any grease on the floor, or remnants of old paint, linoleum paste, or the like, remove it by scrubbing or rough sanding. For scrubbing, use solution of one pound of lye in three gallons of hot water. Take suitable precautions to protect skin, eyes and clothing from accidental spatters. Block flooring can be installed directly over asphalt tile if the tile is in good condition. Rough sand the tile to remove wax and give its surface tooth, then scrub with water and scouring powder. Allow to dry thoroughly.

Though wood blocks can be installed over any concrete floor, above, on, or below grade, installation is not generally recommended over radiant heat slabs. However, successful installations can be made over such slabs if the subfloor surface temperature never exceeds 85 degrees. This regulation can most safely be accomplished by limiting heating system operating temperature to a maximum of 100-120 degrees.

Store blocks in the room where they are to be placed for at least 72 hours prior to installation. Area should be dry, well ventilated, and preferably about 70 degrees. Do not attempt installations at temperatures under 45 degrees.

Blocks may be placed in a square or a diagonal pattern. For halls, corridors, and rooms whose length is more than one and one half times its width, the diagonal pattern is preferred to minimize risk of overexpansion and possible buckling. In other cases, the square pattern is generally more popular.

Concrete floors that are in contact with earth must be dampproofed. This

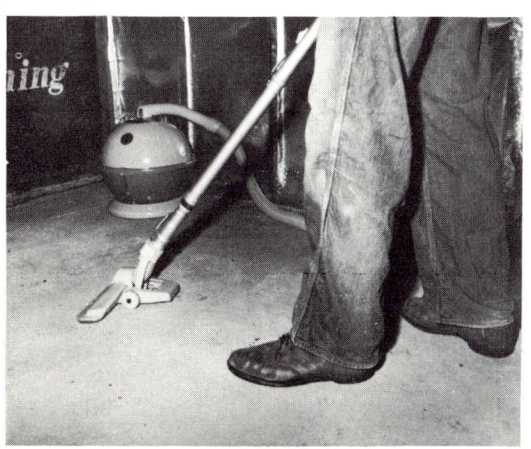

CONCRETE floor must be smooth. Level high spots by grinding; patch low spots. Thoroughly vacuum surface to remove all dirt.

SEAL concrete by applying asphalt primer —approximately 1 gallon to 150 square feet. Allow primer to dry 4 to 8 hours.

FLOORS

is done by first coating the floor with an asphalt primer. In four to eight hours, when primer has dried, apply a coating of hot asphalt, or a mastic such as Bruce's Everbond X. Heating of the mastic may be done over an outside fire. Its purpose is to reduce the semisolid material to liquid. Mastic must not be boiled and care should be taken that no water comes in contact with it.

Spread mastic on floor with a spreader that has 1/4-inch teeth on 3/8-inch centers. When floor has been covered, start at one wall and overlay mastic with a half-width strip of No. 15 asphalt saturated felt. Continue overlay with full-width strips of felt, butting seams, until floor coverage is complete. Apply a second coat of mastic and again overlay with felt, this time starting with a full-width sheet so that seams of first layer are covered. Dampproofing is now complete.

Only one guide line is needed for installing blocks. To establish line for a square pattern, start at the center of the doorjamb of the main entranceway and test-place a row of loose blocks to a point approximately four feet back from this wall. The purpose of this is to make sure that a full-width row of blocks will carry to the middle of the doorway's threshold when installation is complete.

At established four-foot point, snap

HEAT semisolid mastic over outside fire, stirring frequently until entire mixture is liquid. The hotter mastic becomes, the more easily it can be spread, but do not boil.

FLOORS

a chalk line parallel to the entranceway wall. Store tools and materials in this four-foot wide area and spread hot mastic over the remaining main area of the room on the other side of the line. Allow the mastic to dry for several hours, or preferably, overnight. Blocks are difficult to slip into place if an attempt is made to install them before the mastic has set sufficiently.

The secret of aligning the blocks is to place them in a pyramid pattern or sequence. Place the first block at approximately the center of the line, with the grooved side along the line. Lay blocks two and three to the right and to the left of it, aligning the edges of the blocks, rather than the tongues, with the working line. Tap block number four into place to establish the pyramid pattern.

Continue the pyramid pattern of placement, aligning the blocks corner point to corner point. Do not slide the blocks into place or the mastic may pile up into the grooves, making a good fit difficult. Instead, fit tongue and groove together and drop the block into place. Tap gently on the exposed edges to bring to a tight fit. A heavy mason's hammer is effective in driving blocks together, for its large face prevents damaging the blocks' edges. Use mineral spirits to remove any mastic smears

A LARGE CAN makes an excellent container for dipping the heated mastic. Crush its upper edge to form a spout for pouring.

USE trowel to spread a gallon of mastic over each 25 to 35 square feet. Then cover floor with No. 15 asphalt saturated felt.

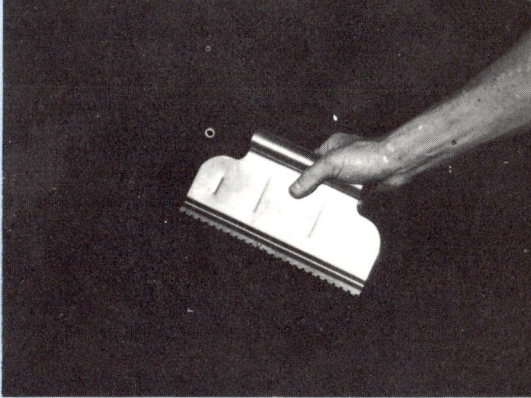

BUTT joints of felt strips. Apply mastic and a second layer of felt. Break joints so seams of first felt layer are covered.

FOR SQUARE pattern, start at center of main door; lay loose blocks to point 4 feet from wall. Draw a chalk guide line.

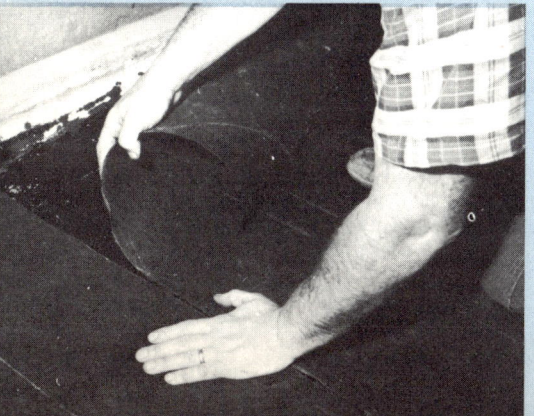

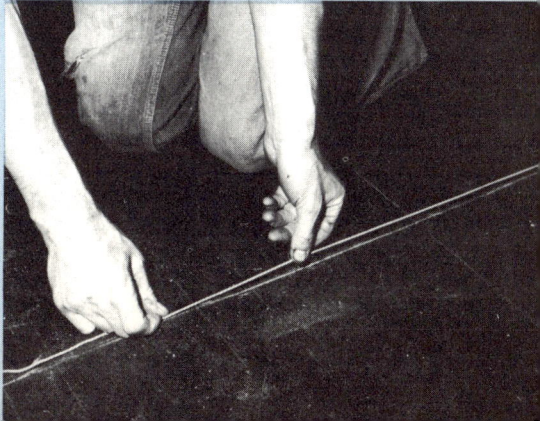

FLOORS

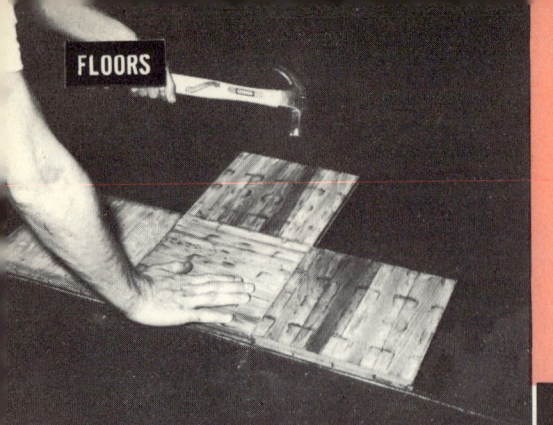

STORE materials in 4-foot wide area; cover remaining area with mastic. Let mastic set several hours, then place blocks in pyramid sequence as shown in photo below. Align blocks corner point to corner point. Drop, don't slide them into place.

you may accidentally get on the block.

If some blocks appear to be undersize, strike them a protected hammer blow on the face. It will help spread the slats and produce a better fit. Do not be worried about small cracks between individual blocks. Blocks will "float" after installation, closing them up.

When you have laid enough blocks in the main area to permit removal of tools and materials from the storage area, cover this remaining area with mastic, then return to work on the main area. Newly spread mastic will then have a chance to dry. When the last full block that you can lay in the main area without trimming has been placed, start installation of blocks in the storage area.

Lay first block in the storage area opposite to the first block that was placed in the main area, and establish a pyramid pattern around it in the same fashion as before. When all full blocks have been placed, start placing rimmed blocks to fill the remaining space to the wall. Blocks may readily be broken by hand into individual slats, or into ½ or ¾ blocks. Cuts across the slats may be made with hand or power saw. If cuts must be made at or near spline position, spline may be pried loose with a screwdriver.

You must allow a minimum of one-inch expansion space at each wall.

 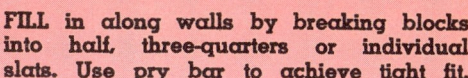

PLACE first block in storage area opposite first block in main area and follow pattern. Hammer the blocks into position.

FILL in along walls by breaking blocks into half, three-quarters or individual slats. Use pry bar to achieve tight fit.

SAW cuts across blocks. Keep blade clear of metal splines. If cut falls next to spline position, remove fastener with screwdriver.

ALLOW at least 1-inch expansion space at every wall. Fill space with cork of same thickness as blocks. Conceal with molding.

Where distance between the walls is over 32 feet, allow an added 1/32 inch for each additional foot. Also allow $\frac{1}{16}$-inch expansion clearance around columns, posts, pipes, hearths, and other obstacles for each foot of distance between it and the nearest wall. To fill any clearance space, spot three-inch strips of cork of a thickness equal to that of blocks at every block joint and fill cork in solidly elsewhere as required. Cork, in tile form, is available at your flooring supply dealer. Laminated wood blocks have great dimensional stability, and no expansion allowance is ever necessary for them.

When all expansion pieces are placed, cover the expansion space with baseboard and/or shoe molding. In attaching molding, nail it to the wall or baseboard, not to the block floor. Allow at least 1/32-inch clearance between underside of molding and the surface of the blocks.

When blocks are to be placed in a diagonal pattern, establish guide line by snapping lines from wall to wall at midpoints in the room. Divide the right angle intersection of these two lines exactly in half with another line. This angle dividing line is the guide line. Installation is made along it just as for the square pattern. Either pattern results in a beautiful block floor. •

FOUNDATION

your FOUNDATION
footings and walls

FOOTINGS

24"x12"	IF THIS SIZE, MEASURE LENGTH OF KEYWAY AND MULTIPLY BY —	.0740
20"x10"	IF THIS SIZE, MEASURE LENGTH OF KEYWAY AND MULTIPLY BY —	.0514
18"x9"	IF THIS SIZE, MEASURE LENGTH OF KEYWAY AND MULTIPLY BY —	.0417

ANSWER WILL BE IN CUBIC YARDS. EXAMPLE: IF YOU HAVE A 24"x12" FOOTING WITH A LINEAL MEASUREMENT OF 128 FEET (CENTER LINE OR KEYWAY) MULTIPLY 128 BY .074 — THE ANSWER IS 9.47 CUBIC YARDS.

WALLS

HEIGHT OF WALL	12" WALL	10" WALL
7'-0"	.2592	.2160
7'-6"	.2777	.2314
7'-8"	.2840	.2366
8'-0"	.2962	.2468

CHOOSE PLANNED WALL THICKNESS AND HEIGHT AND MULTIPLY NUMBER OF LINEAL FEET OF WALL BY THE APPROPRIATE FACTOR. EXAMPLE: FOR A 12" THICK WALL 7'-8" HIGH AND 128' LONG, FACTOR IS .2840 — MULTIPLY BY 128. ANSWER IS 36.35 CU YARDS.

ABOVE: Starting the pour. If your ready-mix concrete is poured from an incline that permits easy flow of the material, you will save a great deal of back-breaking work. Note manner in which corner and sides are braced. Driver on truck controls the rate of flow but you in turn must instruct him at all times. **LEFT:** These two charts will simplify calculating the amount of mix required for the footings and the walls.

FOUNDATION

EVERYONE will agree the foundation is the most important single part of any home. It isn't the most difficult part of a house from the standpoint of planning, but if you are doing the job yourself, you will find no other single construction phase that requires as much physical stamina. If you are pressed for time and energy, investigate the financial feasibility of sub-contracting the complete foundation. If your leanings are in this direction you usually will find a few "foundation specialists" who will quote you a package price on the concrete work.

All foundation footings are concrete, but the walls can be either poured concrete or else built up from either cinder or concrete block. A poured wall produces a better foundation than one built up from block, although block foundations are entirely adequate for most parts of the country The deciding factor in choosing between these two types of construction is not personal preference it can usually be traced to the local building code requirements.

In areas where block is permitted you can always pour a foundation but the opposite is rarely true. If your building code permits block construction you will usually—but not always—find a block foundation more economical than one that is poured concrete. One factor is undisputable; poured concrete foundations are stronger and have a much better chance of being watertight than those made from blocks.

The method most subcontractors use to calculate the cost of a poured foundation (footings and walls) is figured on the number of yards of concrete involved. If you are looking for an "in place" estimate a good rule of thumb is to figure a complete job will cost from two to two and one quarter times the cost of concrete. As an

Diagram labels:
- 4"x6" (OR TWO 2"x6" PLANKS) FOUNDATION PLATE BOLTED IN PLACE.
- S.C.R. BRICK RESTS ON WALL
- VARY THIS DISTANCE IF NECESSARY TO OBTAIN A LEVEL PLATE & FLOOR: SHIM UP TO LEVEL, THEN FILL WITH MORTAR
- 12"
- CEILING HEIGHT OF BASEMENT
- VARY THIS DIMENSION TO OBTAIN DESIRED BASEMENT CEILING HEIGHT. SUGGEST 7'-8" AS THE IDEAL HEIGHT.
- NOTE: WALL CAN BE MADE 10" THICK IF YOU HAVE A FLAT BUILDING SITE. A 10" WALL CUTS CONCRETE COST BY 16%
- BASEMENT FLOOR IS 4" THICK. USE 1:2:3 MIX WITH SMALL AGGREGATE.
- 2"x4" KEY IN FOOTING
- PACK DIRT
- 8" 12" 24" DIG CORNERS SQUARE
- 4" OF GRAVEL OR ASHES OVER FILL DIRT WATER AND TAMP WELL BEFORE POURING FLOOR.
- STAKE
- IMPORTANT: DIG BOTTOM OF FOOTING BY HAND
- 2"x6" PLANK ON BOTH SIDES FOR FORM.

If your excavator left the job with a level floor, setting up your footing forms will be easy. Stake out the outside form first, then add inside form. Width and depth of footing will depend upon code.

The footings taking shape. Work table made from two horses and three 2x10s. A power saw is a must for making the footing and wall forms. Make prior arrangements for temporary electric service.

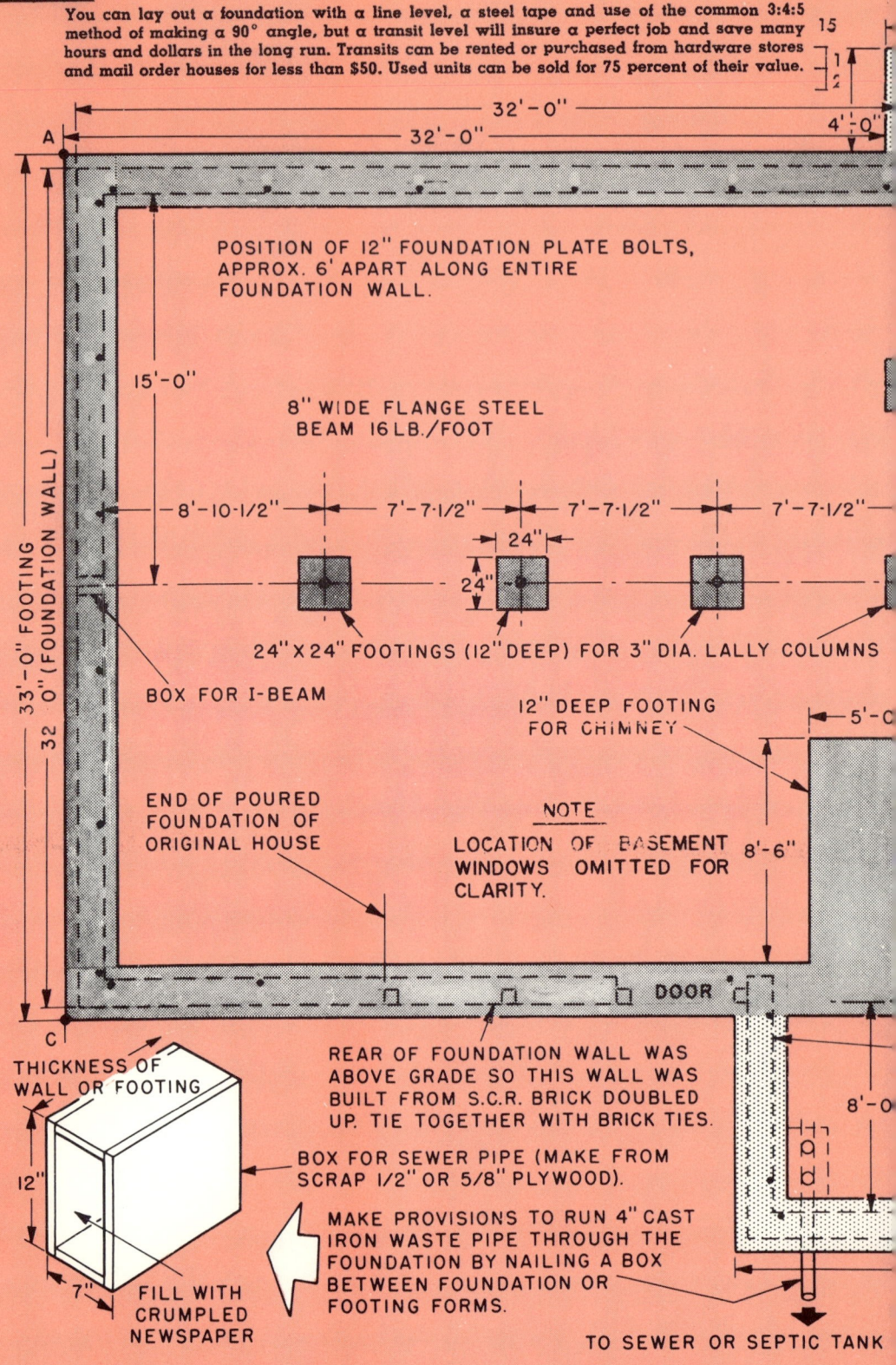

FOUNDATION

You can lay out a foundation with a line level, a steel tape and use of the common 3:4:5 method of making a 90° angle, but a transit level will insure a perfect job and save many hours and dollars in the long run. Transits can be rented or purchased from hardware stores and mail order houses for less than $50. Used units can be sold for 75 percent of their value.

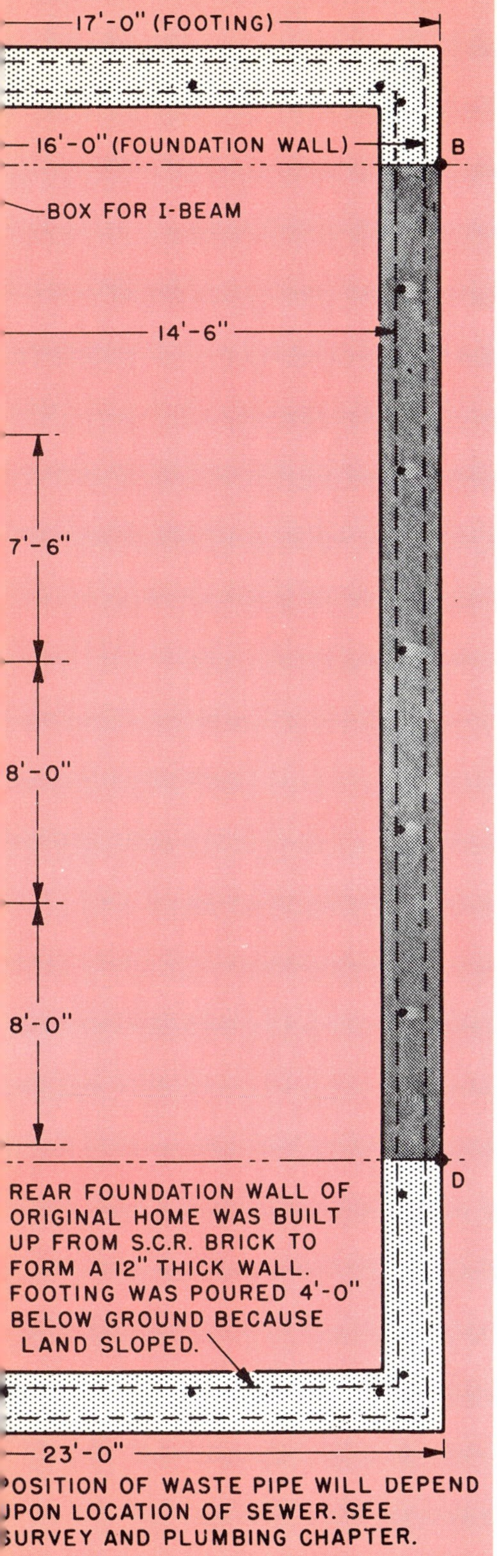

FOUNDATION

example, if concrete sells for 13 dollars per cubic yard, a popular rate in most parts of the country, you should pay about up to 29 dollars per yard for your pour. Thus, if your footing and walls call for a total of 60 yards your "in place" foundation would cost about $1700. Of this about $850 is for materials (concrete and metal accessories used to hold the forms together) so you can see the foundation of this size offers you the opportunity to save nearly $900 if you do it yourself.

If you plan to pour your own foundation, your first step is to stake out the

Ready-mix concrete trucks rarely carry chutes longer than five feet so you will be required to make a simple chute from either sheathing lumber or 2x10s. Here the footings are being poured.

Top quality footings have a keyway formed by setting a 2x4 in the center after the concrete has been poured. The 2x4 is removed the next day with a pick-axe. Don't worry if the corners chip.

1377

FOUNDATION

outside perimeter of your footings. The drawings specify a 12x24-inch footing, which is adequate indeed but your local code and soil may permit a smaller footing —four inches on either side of the wall. Footings measuring 10x20 inches are often used with a 12-inch thick wall so check your building department for the policy in your area.

Once you have your outside perimeter staked out and level, set the 2x6 or 2x8 planks in place, using plenty of stakes and 10-penny nails. After the footing forms are level, excavate by hand to the desired footing depth. Keep the bottom of the footing square and pack the dirt removed, against the sides of the forms. Nail a "cat" —a scrap piece of lumber slightly longer than the width of the footing—at about ten-foot intervals to prevent the pressure exerted by the concrete from pushing the forms out of line. Prepare the footings for the individual lally columns and chimney and you are ready for the pour.

Your local building code will require that your footings be beneath the frost line. In New York this minimum dimension is four feet; in more southerly parts of the country less.

The type of concrete mix permitted in your area will probably be a 1:2:5 mix for the footings and a 1:2:4 mix for the walls. When ordering your ready-mix concrete you will find it most economical to buy in full truckload quantities. The average concrete truck has a five-yard or six-cubic yard capacity and in some communities seven, nine and even 10 yard trucks are available. Order slightly more concrete than your calculations indicate you need because it is better to have a small quantity left over than to run short. Don't waste the extra concrete; have your forms ready for the chimney and lally column footings and plan to pour these with the "extra." Since it is virtually impossible to accurately calculate the amount of concrete you will require down to the nearest cubic foot it is good building practice to have second priority use for left over mix. Concrete costs about 50 cents a cubic foot so why use it as fill? Another tip—and we do mean tip—when buying concrete, make it a point to tip your driver from 50 cents to one dollar a truck load. This is more or less the accepted practice in the trade and will insure the utmost of cooperation from the driver. Remember, he controls the flow of the material and his knowledge and cooperation of how to pour concrete, if applied to your job, can save you hours of back breaking toil. Concrete weighs about 150 pounds per cubic foot—over two tons per yard—and if your driver "just happens" to pour it too rapidly YOU will be shoveling it along to fill the form. If

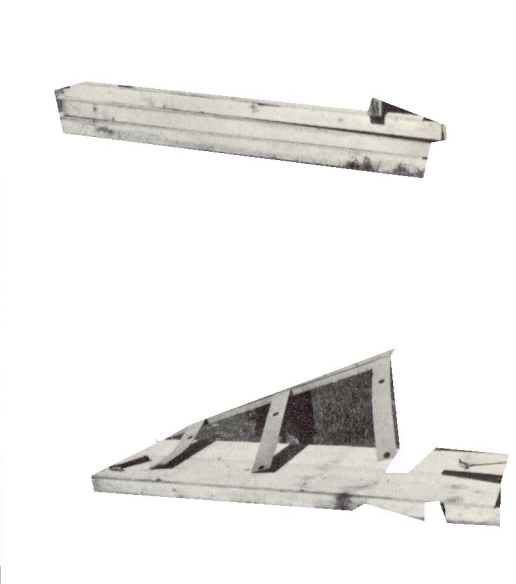

1 Set four pieces of 2x4s 8' long into slots in jig. Author (and charming wife) made all forms.

4 After all four studs are nailed in place, set the jig used to position the holes for the Snap-Tys over each form. Jig is made from 1/8" hardboard.

HOW TO MAKE FORMS

The simple jig illustrated simplifies mass-production of your forms. Sheets of plywood 4x8 and 8' lengths of 2x4s are used, and after forms are stripped, the plywood is used for the sub-flooring.

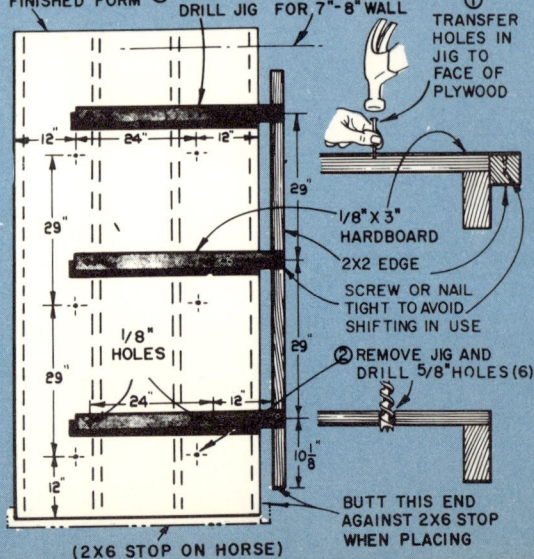

FOUNDATION

2 After all four studs are in place, place a sheet of 4x8 Plyscord on jig against 2x6 back stop.

3 Nail the plywood to each 2x4 stud with four 6-penny nails. Black lines mark inside studs.

5 After each of the six Snap-Ty holes is marked off, drill a ⅝" hole. Regular foundation forms are oiled; for one pour they need not be oiled.

6 Removing the completed form about five minutes after the first 2x4 stud was placed in the jig. All lumber is used again for framing.

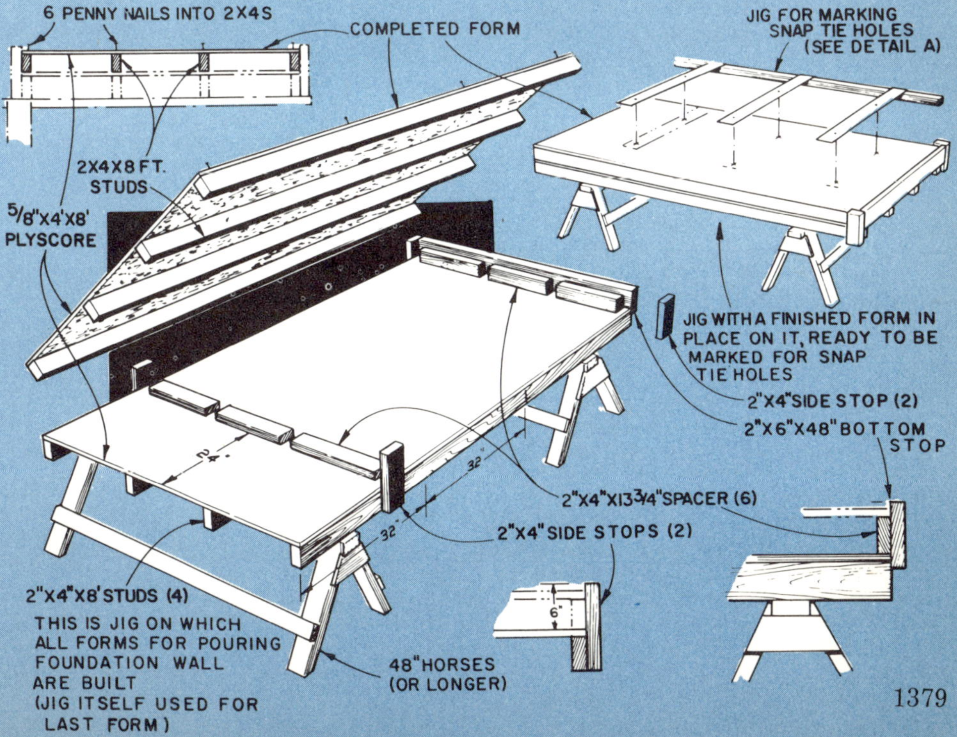

- 6 PENNY NAILS INTO 2X4S
- COMPLETED FORM
- JIG FOR MARKING SNAP TIE HOLES (SEE DETAIL A)
- 2X4X8 FT. STUDS
- ⅝"X4'X8' PLYSCORE
- JIG WITH A FINISHED FORM IN PLACE ON IT, READY TO BE MARKED FOR SNAP TIE HOLES
- 2"X4" SIDE STOP (2)
- 2"X6"X48" BOTTOM STOP
- 2"X4"X13¾" SPACER (6)
- 2"X4" SIDE STOPS (2)
- 2"X4"X8' STUDS (4)
- THIS IS JIG ON WHICH ALL FORMS FOR POURING FOUNDATION WALL ARE BUILT (JIG ITSELF USED FOR LAST FORM)
- 48" HORSES (OR LONGER)

FOUNDATION

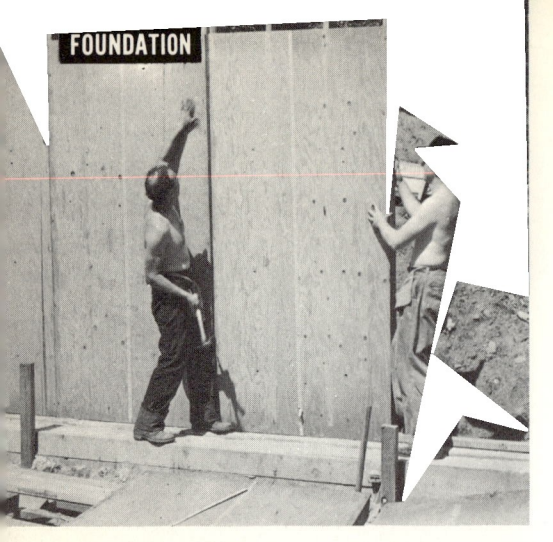

The complete outside perimeter is set in place along the footing. Three 20-penny nails hold each form to adjacent form. Keep joints flush and brace up every fourth form. Keep forms perpendicular.

After outside forms are upright and all inside forms to be used are stacked in the center of the foundation, the Snap-Tys and inside forms are set on the footing.

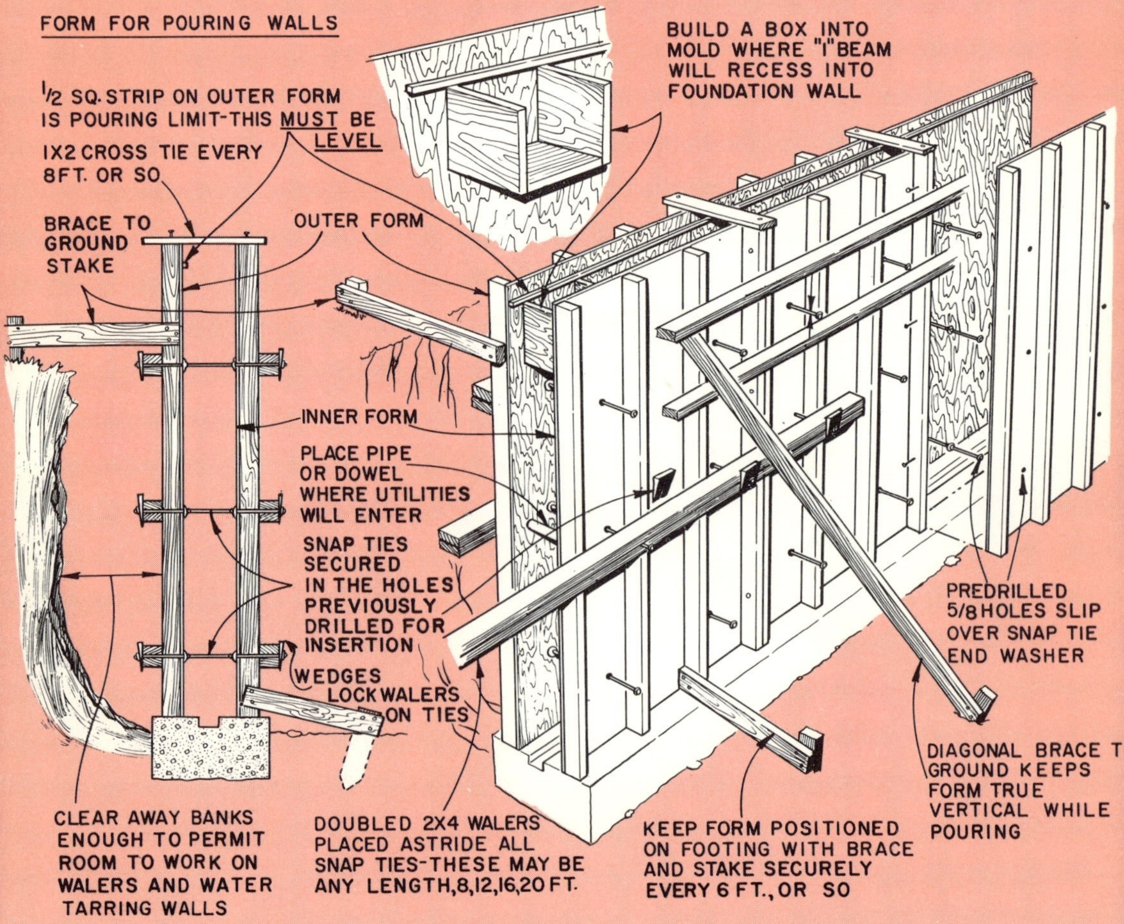

FORM FOR POURING WALLS

- 1/2 SQ. STRIP ON OUTER FORM IS POURING LIMIT - THIS MUST BE LEVEL
- 1X2 CROSS TIE EVERY 8 FT. OR SO
- BRACE TO GROUND STAKE
- OUTER FORM
- BUILD A BOX INTO MOLD WHERE "I" BEAM WILL RECESS INTO FOUNDATION WALL
- INNER FORM
- PLACE PIPE OR DOWEL WHERE UTILITIES WILL ENTER
- SNAP TIES SECURED IN THE HOLES PREVIOUSLY DRILLED FOR INSERTION
- WEDGES LOCK WALERS ON TIES
- PREDRILLED 5/8 HOLES SLIP OVER SNAP TIE END WASHER
- DIAGONAL BRACE T GROUND KEEPS FORM TRUE VERTICAL WHILE POURING
- CLEAR AWAY BANKS ENOUGH TO PERMIT ROOM TO WORK ON WALERS AND WATER TARRING WALLS
- DOUBLED 2X4 WALERS PLACED ASTRIDE ALL SNAP TIES-THESE MAY BE ANY LENGTH, 8,12,16,20 FT.
- KEEP FORM POSITIONED ON FOOTING WITH BRACE AND STAKE SECURELY EVERY 6 FT., OR SO

1380

Where basement windows are located, a form built around the actual window frame is nailed on the outside plywood wall form before the inside form is added.

Inside view of the 12" wall showing the Snap-Tys. Original wall was 12" thick but a 10" wall is adequate for most locations. Labor time for 10" wall is the same as 12" wall, concrete 16 percent less.

your forms don't break, your back probably will—so don't forget to tip!

You will have little difficulty pouring the footings. Do not have the mix too stiff; the consistency of heavy syrup is excellent. Remember, the looser the mix the weaker the concrete.

After the footings are poured and just before the concrete begins to harden, set a row of 2x4s down the center of the footing to form the keyway. You may remove the "cats" to position the 2x4s, but replace them so the concrete does not float the 2x4s above the surface of the footing. Remove the excess concrete to make the surface level but do not trowel the footing. A smooth footing may look pretty, but it does not encourage a good bond between the wall and the footing.

Removal of the 2x4 key and the 2x6 forms should be done the next day. Scrape the excess cement from all lumber used for the forms and stack in a level spot. You will use the 2x6s for the sill plate.

If you plan a poured foundation wall you will need forms, which you can easily make or, perhaps, you may be able to rent them locally. The latter is desirable if, of course, the rental is at the right price. A fair price, for form rental for one week, which is all you normally need, should be less than one hundred dollars.

You will probably conclude that making your own forms will be your best bet, from both the standpoint of having the forms available should rain retard your pouring and to save the rental fee.

You can easily make your own forms without cutting or wasting a single piece of lumber. Use 4x8-foot sheets of Plyscord grade plywood ⅝ inch thick nailed to standard 8-foot lengths of 2x4s for the uprights. With the aid of the simple jig shown on these pages we made our forms in one day! You will be able to permanently use the lumber for the wall partitions and the plywood for the sub-flooring. The one-time use will not harm either material.

The form jig is made directly on a piece of ⅝-inch Plyscord. A single form consists of four 8-foot 2x4s nailed to the 4x8-foot plywood with four 6-penny nails per upright.

The use of 6-penny nails is important because a larger nail will slow down the stripping operation after the walls are poured. The nails do not contribute structurally to the forms; they merely hold the 2x4s against the plywood. Metal ties—in our case we used Snap-Tys—extend through each 4x8 panel and, through a series of "walers" and "wedges," the outward stress caused by the fluid concrete produces a tension on the rods. The walls require bracing on either side, just enough to prevent shifting and to make certain they remain in an absolutely perpendicular position.

You will require six ⅝-inch diameter holes in each form, as indicated on the drawings, to permit the metal Snap-Tys to pass through, and these holes should be drilled at the time the forms are being prefabricated. After all except the eight inside forms for the four corners are made,

1381

FOUNDATION

Horizontal walers will automatically straighten a wall but the inside should be braced with 2x6s as shown to prevent wall from tilting should concrete poured from one position exert undue pressure.

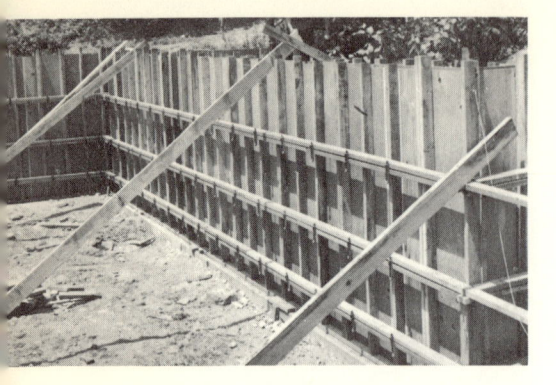

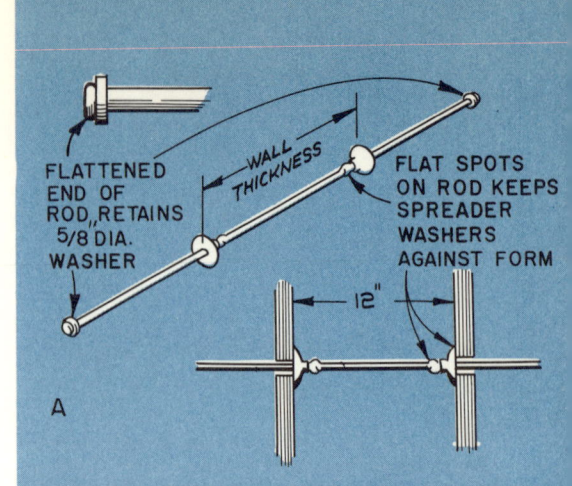

FLATTENED END OF ROD, RETAINS 5/8 DIA. WASHER — **WALL THICKNESS** — **FLAT SPOTS ON ROD KEEPS SPREADER WASHERS AGAINST FORM**

12"

A

Snap-Tys (or similar form ties) cost about 12 cents each. Common sizes are for 8, 10, and 12" walls.

Before pouring is made all wedges should be hammered tight. The possibility of form collapse is always imminent, so do not pour rapidly. Wife, having checked offspring, helped with actual pouring.

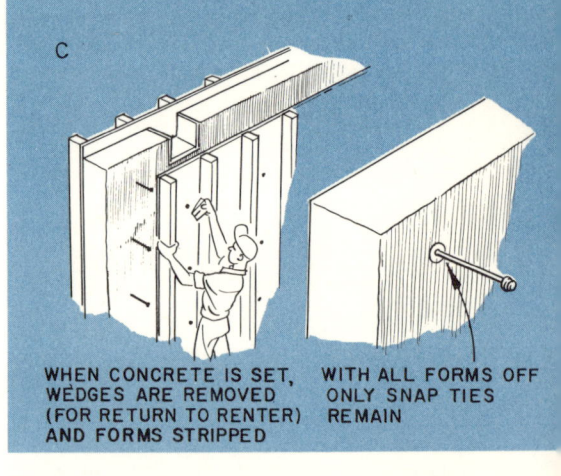

C

WHEN CONCRETE IS SET, WEDGES ARE REMOVED (FOR RETURN TO RENTER) AND FORMS STRIPPED

WITH ALL FORMS OFF ONLY SNAP TIES REMAIN

If necessary set up a wooden chute for each corner and build a scaffold from 2x10s near the top to facilitate tamping the concrete, leveling off the top of the wall and inserting the sill anchor bolts.

Pouring should start with the corners. Allow concrete to flow by itself and tamp it with a 2x4 to prevent honeycombing. Note chute in background. Original pouring required straight 17 hours!

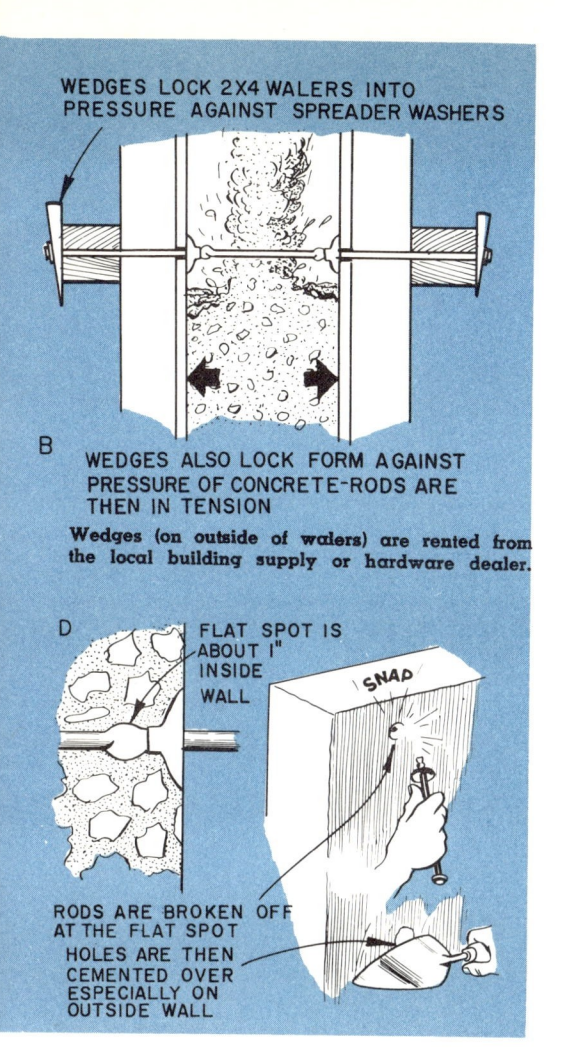

FOUNDATION

WEDGES LOCK 2X4 WALERS INTO PRESSURE AGAINST SPREADER WASHERS

B **WEDGES ALSO LOCK FORM AGAINST PRESSURE OF CONCRETE-RODS ARE THEN IN TENSION**

Wedges (on outside of walers) are rented from the local building supply or hardware dealer.

D **FLAT SPOT IS ABOUT 1" INSIDE WALL**

SNAP

RODS ARE BROKEN OFF AT THE FLAT SPOT HOLES ARE THEN CEMENTED OVER ESPECIALLY ON OUTSIDE WALL

In wall parts where a steel beam must rest, a box is nailed to the form; concrete is poured around box. Inside corner forms require special sizes and must be cut to fit after all others are in place.

sweep the footing clean and proceed to set the outside forms on the footing. Snap a chalk line to indicate the position of the outside walls and start setting the forms from one corner, tacking each form to the next with two 20-penny nails, at the top and bottom. Don't drive the nails home; leave enough of the head so the nails can be easily removed.

Brace every third or fourth form to hold the outside wall in upright. You need not be too concerned over the seemingly crooked line the forms will make; when your outside "walers" are in place the wall will straighten out perfectly. If the top of your basement windows are to be even with the ceiling you can build a box the exact size of the window and, after the forms are stripped, you can slip the windows in from the top. We used this method because our windows were not available at the time of the pour.

A great many complications can be avoided if you build the window into the wall. Many individuals prefer to have the top of a basement window extend below the ceiling and if this is your desire you can easily reinforce the top of the wall over the window section to form a built-in lintel. The use of two or four ½-inch diameter steel reinforcing rods makes a much more economical and superior lintel than setting angle iron on the top of the wall for the sill plate and brick.

To build your windows into the wall make a rugged form for each window and nail it in place on the outside form with 8-penny nails. At this time you should also sight the top of the foundation, using

Inside form view of concrete being poured. The ½" square strip indicates wall height and was nailed in place before the inside forms were erected. Set transit level to check exact height.

FOUNDATION

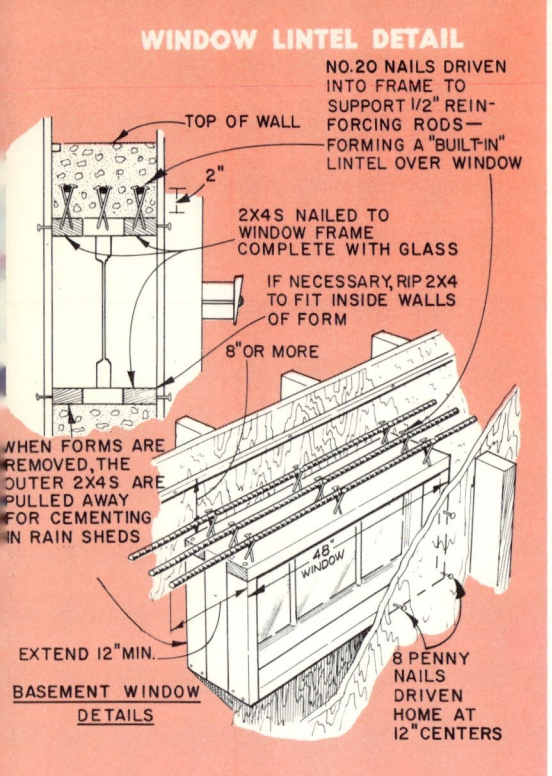

WINDOW LINTEL DETAIL

- TOP OF WALL
- NO. 20 NAILS DRIVEN INTO FRAME TO SUPPORT 1/2" REINFORCING RODS—FORMING A "BUILT-IN" LINTEL OVER WINDOW
- 2"
- 2X4S NAILED TO WINDOW FRAME COMPLETE WITH GLASS
- IF NECESSARY, RIP 2X4 TO FIT INSIDE WALLS OF FORM
- 8" OR MORE
- WHEN FORMS ARE REMOVED, THE OUTER 2X4S ARE PULLED AWAY FOR CEMENTING IN RAIN SHEDS
- 48" WINDOW
- EXTEND 12" MIN.
- 8 PENNY NAILS DRIVEN HOME AT 12" CENTERS

BASEMENT WINDOW DETAILS

Foundation form before complete interior bracing was added. Note the three walers, iron wedges.

a transit, and nail a scrap piece of ½-inch square wood around the complete perimeter of the outside form. This will represent the top of the wall and actually is a double check to correct any unevenness you may have had in your floorings.

Before you set the inside form in place you should mark off the exact position of any sewer, water, electric or telephone lines, if, of course, your elevations are such that you did not make provisions for these service entrances at or below the footing level. Nail a 7x12-inch box where the 4-inch cast iron sewer line passes through the wall. An iron pipe or paper mailing tube about 2 inches in diameter should be built into the wall for your future water or other service lines.

Sweep out the keyway again and set the inside forms in place. The inside corners will require forms less than the standard 4-foot width which should be made after all other forms are up. Now add the inside walers, brace the corners carefully as shown in the photographs and then check every form with a level to make certain it is absolutely perpendicular. If you find part of the wall leaning out or in, nudge the form into position with a sledge hammer or, if it is stubborn, use your automobile jack to straighten it out. After the inside form is in place, mount the box or boxes to accommodate your steel beam and, where necessary, drill ½-inch holes in the outside forms for ½-inch steel reinforcing rods you may insert to hold a future garage, patio, or porch footing next to the foundation. This is important because you just cannot pour another footing on

Detail showing wedges on side of foundation and walers. If concrete leaks through a joint or hole, leakage will stop when aggregate is forced against crack. Dry up leaks with a shovel of dirt.

FOUNDATION

your backfilled area and not expect substantial settling.

Before you order your concrete draw a yellow line about one foot from each corner and at six-foot intervals thereafter, along the top outside waler. This will remind you where to insert the 12-inch long foundation bolts in the top of the wall. The simple jig shown will insure accurate placement of the anchor bolts. Careful placement of the bolts will in turn simplify and save a great deal of time when setting the sill plate in place.

Set your chute up to pour the corners of the foundation first. Start your pour early in the morning and unload one truck every hour for the first four loads. The bottom two feet of your foundation walls should start to set before you continue to fill the form. Tamp the concrete with a long 2x4 as it is being poured to prevent the aggregate from setting against the forms and forming a honeycomb. Always pour from the corners and bring up the level of all four sides a little at a time in an effort to equalize the tremendous stress. After the top of the wall has started to harden, with the aid of the simple jig shown, set the sill anchor bolts in place. The job is done!

Allow the concrete to set for about two days before removing the walers. After another 24-hour period you can safely pull out the 20-penny nails holding the forms together; then strip the forms from the wall and pull the 2x4s from the plywood. Scrape all wood clean, remove the nails from the plywood and stack the sheets on the inside of the foundation. Now you can snap off the protruding metal ties and fill the holes with a 1:2 mixture of portland cement and sand.

If you anticipate a water problem you may find it desirable to route water that may collect along the base away from the walls. This can be done effectively by laying agricultural drain tile along the outside of the footing, setting the one-foot lengths with about a ½-inch crack between them and covering the crack with a strip of 15-pound roofing felt. A six to 12-inch layer of 1 to 2-inch gravel over the drain tile will prevent mud from clogging up the cracks. All water seeping to the footing depth will eventually find its way into the foundation drains. Lead the drains around the corners so the water seeps away from the walls.

You may not require such elaborate precautions to keep your basement dry but if your local conditions are such that your neighbors are having water problems you will be wise to prevent a similar problem from developing.

Next, waterproof the exterior of the walls and the top of the footing with an asphalt base foundation waterproofing

BELOW: Poured concrete wall showing stripped plywood forms. Note anchor bolts along top, reinforcing rods. Also stack plywood sheets on inside of foundation, waterproof walls, then backfill.

After foundation is poured and the walers removed, separate 2x4 studs from forms with a gentle tap from a 25-pound sledge hammer. After 2x4s are pulled off, stack them carefully to prevent warpage.

FOUNDATION

Waterproofing the wall after the Snap-Tys were broken off and the voids plastered. Asphalt waterproofing compound troweled on proved more effective than liquid type brushed on. Apply two coats.

Waterproofed wall, showing water service entrance and poured-in reinforcement rods for front door entrance platform. Allow waterproofing to dry at least two days before backfilling foundation.

compound. Two types of waterproofing are generally available, a fairly fluid asphalt mixture that can be brushed on and a mastic type that must be troweled on. We tried both and found the latter preferable. Apply an extra heavy coating at the base of the wall where it meets the footing and also cover the top of the footing.

After your foundation is waterproofed you can arrange for the backfilling, a tedious chore that will require no more than a few hours. You may find it necessary to brace up sections of the wall from within, but the careful dozer operator can safely back-fill a foundation without pushing a wall in. The latter can happen, and all reputable excavators carry insurance to cover such occurrences.

BLOCK FOUNDATIONS

Concrete and cinder blocks are widely used for foundations in many parts of the country where basements are prevalent. They are adequate for most homes, but cannot be considered anywhere equal to poured concrete; block construction is invariably weaker and therefore requires less strain to crack and leak. Poured concrete also cracks, but it can be repaired much easier than a cracked block wall.

As mentioned earlier, your local building code will specify if block can be used in your area. You will find that localities approving block construction will always approve a poured concrete job, but the opposite is rarely true.

Jig to insure correct placement of foundation anchor bolts. Note that edge rests on ½-inch strip.

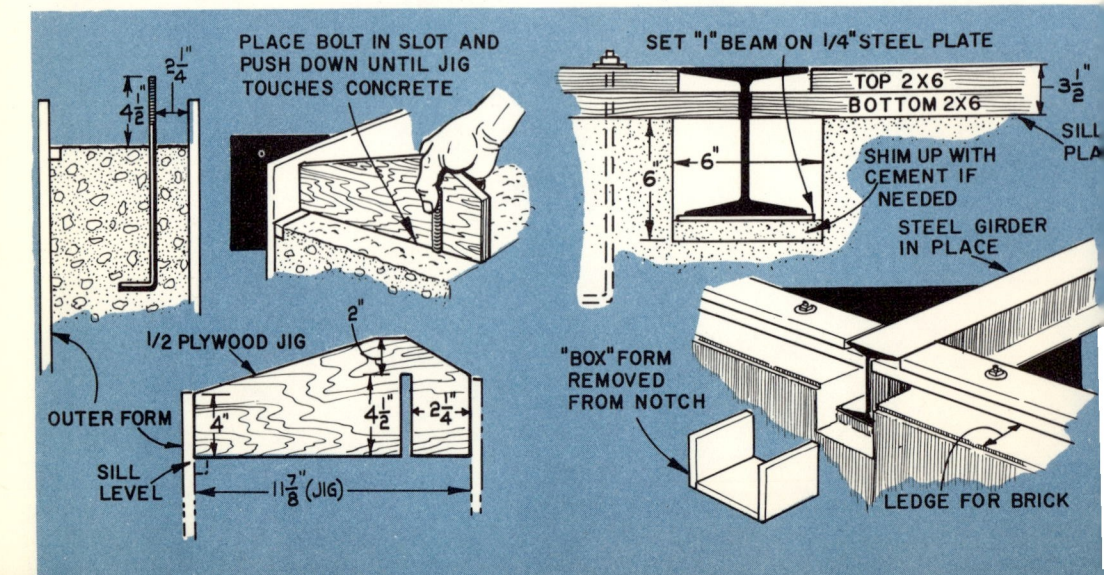

Box detail for steel "I" beam. Depth of box is varied to accommodate the size of beam. Shim up.

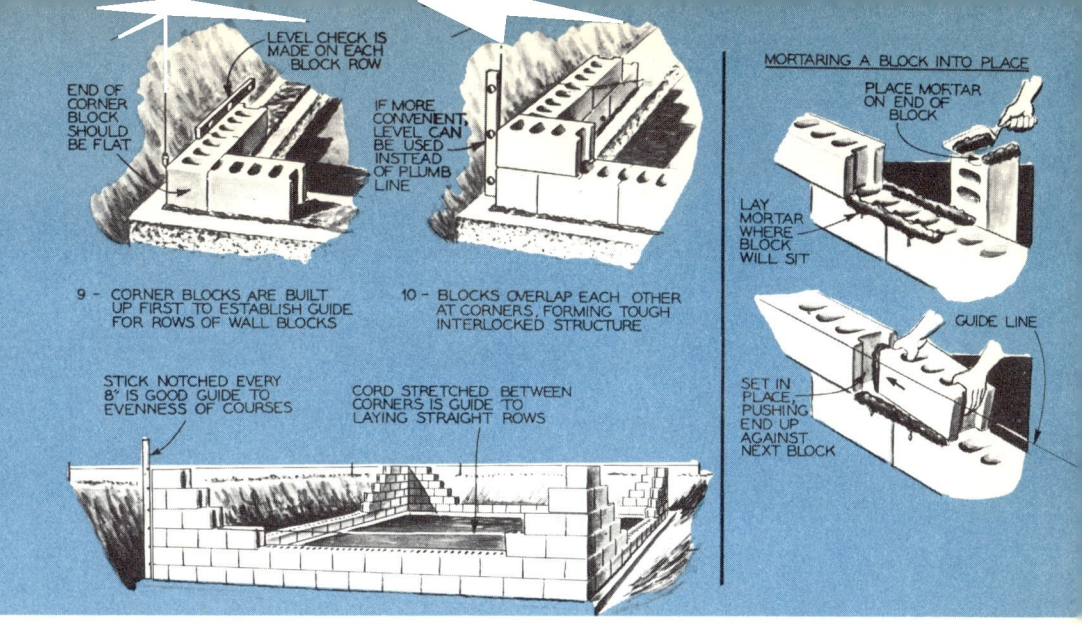

9 — CORNER BLOCKS ARE BUILT UP FIRST TO ESTABLISH GUIDE FOR ROWS OF WALL BLOCKS

END OF CORNER BLOCK SHOULD BE FLAT

LEVEL CHECK IS MADE ON EACH BLOCK ROW

10 — BLOCKS OVERLAP EACH OTHER AT CORNERS, FORMING TOUGH INTERLOCKED STRUCTURE

IF MORE CONVENIENT, LEVEL CAN BE USED INSTEAD OF PLUMB LINE

MORTARING A BLOCK INTO PLACE

PLACE MORTAR ON END OF BLOCK

LAY MORTAR WHERE BLOCK WILL SIT

GUIDE LINE

SET IN PLACE, PUSHING END UP AGAINST NEXT BLOCK

STICK NOTCHED EVERY 8" IS GOOD GUIDE TO EVENNESS OF COURSES

CORD STRETCHED BETWEEN CORNERS IS GUIDE TO LAYING STRAIGHT ROWS

The footing for a cinder or cement block wall is the same as required by a poured concrete wall. Anchor bolts for the sill plate extend into the top two courses, the upper one of which is solid. The exterior of all block walls must be cement plastered and the area thoroughly waterproofed with asphalt. Backfilling block foundations always require interior bracing because they are much weaker than poured walls.

In prior years block foundations were more economical than those of poured concrete, but this is not necessarily the case today because a block foundation requires many more man hours than one that is poured. Since the wage scale of masons has been steadily increasing, during which period concrete form manufacturers have been developing new labor-saving forms and techniques of pouring, the poured concrete foundation is now being used in more and more areas that only a few years ago had used block exclusively.

However, if for other reasons block construction is still the most economical method in your area and you either cannot contract or do not wish to pour your own walls, here are a few points on how block is priced and quoted:

Masons will often quote a foundation job on a "per block" basis, the rate being determined by the size of the block. An 8-inch block which sells for about 20-26 cents will cost anywhere from 35 to 40 cents for labor. Naturally 10 and 12-inch blocks will cost more, with a 50 to 65 cents per block (12-inch size) labor charge common in areas where masons are in demand.

Unless you have had some good experience laying blocks for other than an ordinary simple retaining wall or outdoor grill, we do not recommend that you attempt to learn on your house foundation. We have seen owner-builders who have never even built a doghouse make their foundation forms (we never built a doghouse either), but these same individuals would not dare consider laying their own block! •

Garage footing will not settle if tied into foundation wall with steel reinforcing. Set rods in form.

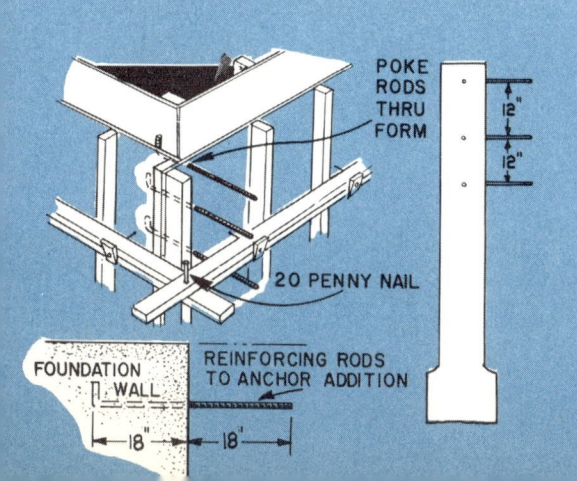

POKE RODS THRU FORM

20 PENNY NAIL

REINFORCING RODS TO ANCHOR ADDITION

FOUNDATION WALL

If your code permits block construction you must sill plate width, depending upon the wall thickness.

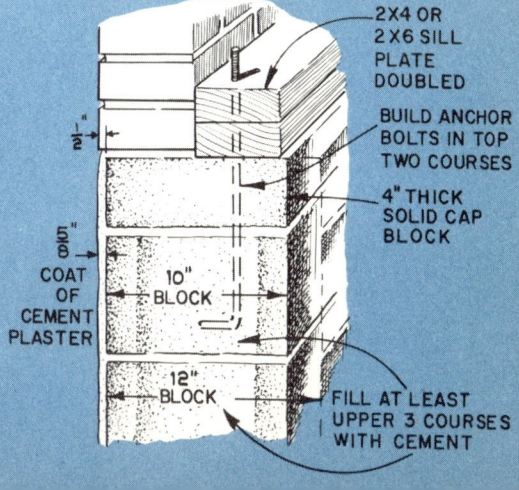

2X4 OR 2X6 SILL PLATE DOUBLED

BUILD ANCHOR BOLTS IN TOP TWO COURSES

4" THICK SOLID CAP BLOCK

10" BLOCK

COAT OF CEMENT PLASTER

12" BLOCK

FILL AT LEAST UPPER 3 COURSES WITH CEMENT

FOYER

ADD A FOYER

Rooms with exterior doors can be sheltered from cold winds and rain with this simple structure.

By David A. Howard

DO winter winds whistle through your house when the door is opened? Are water and mud tracked in by the children in rainy weather? The way to solve the problem is to add a foyer. This will serve as a fine windbreak as well as a depository for wet clothes and other items that mess up your floors.

The foyer shown was added to the exterior of a kitchen. No great skill was required to do the job and one man did it alone. First the cement slab was poured in one piece in a form made of three 10-inch boards. To provide for a footing, the outside edges within the form were dug deeper than the center area. The original small slab was removed and broken up, then scattered with other stones in the dug-out area before the cement was poured.

After pouring, the slab was leveled off and floated with a longer board, using the side forms as support. While the cement was still wet, stove bolts were set in, heads down and four inches in from the edge, to receive the floor plate.

CEMENT SLAB is given a 2-inch outward pitch; while it is still wet, stove bolts are set head down around the perimeter. When the cement has cured, the plate is simply bolted down. Erection of framing then proceeds quite rapidly.

The slab floor of the foyer shown is 106 inches wide and 54 inches deep. The framed area was set two inches in so that the outside measurements are 102x52 inches. The addition of red cedar clapboards to match the outside finish of the house brought the outside measurements closer to the edge of the slab. Finish the lower section of your foyer in the same material as the house for uniformity. If shorter material is used, such as shingles, this section must first be covered with sheathing. Use ship-lap, shelving or plywood for this purpose.

Frame the structure as shown in the illustrations. The floor or shoe plate is put down first, using the stove bolts. Washers keep the nuts from biting into the wood and all framing is painted with aluminum paint to protect it against the elements.

Construct the frame of pine stock. For the plate and corner posts up to the railing section, 4x4s are used. Studs set between the posts for extra supports are 2x4s and the framing above the railing is constructed of 3x3 pine. The 2x6 rail is beveled at the outside top edge as a drip line and for a decorative finish.

The top back plate is nailed against the wall of house. Allow space above it for the corrugations of the plastic roof. To insure a good hold against house, locate the house studs and screw into

FOYER

TEMPORARY BRACE supports the uprights while the roof framing is being nailed up.

ENTRANCE is framed with 1x6-inch lumber for the installation of an aluminum door.

CLAPBOARDS are nailed directly to framing. Siding and shingles also may be used.

CORRUGATED PANELING is easily cut with hand saw; it comes in a variety of colors.

BONDING MATERIAL prepared for use with Corrulux is applied where panels overlap.

CALKING is used around the edges of the panels to provide for weathertight joints.

them through the plate with long wood screws.

Note that the railing boards are cut at 45° angles to make finished corners. Paint the inside angles cuts before nailing the boards in place for protection against rot. The railing is face nailed to the posts and studs.

Uprights on the top section are toe-nailed into the railing, those against house are nailed to the wall. Roof members are toenailed to the top rear header plate, face nailed through the front top plate. Corrugated rubber insulation strip, made to conform to the corrugations on the plastic roof, is nailed to the top header plates.

When the framing is complete, siding is installed on the areas below the railing board and on the short filler space next to the wall of the house. Corrulux may now be cut and put in place.

Carefully measure areas and transfer measurements to the sheet of Corrulux being worked on. Use an ordinary hand saw to cut the plastic. Then raise the piece into place and check it for a close fit. Make necessary adjustments until the piece fits perfectly, then hold it in place while holes are drilled for wood screws. Use brass roundhead screws and Neoprene washers.

The outside corners of the structure, after the Corrulux has been screwed into place, are covered with 1½"x1½" right-angle aluminum fastened with aluminum screws. Calk the edges after the metal is in place to insure weather-tight joints.

The size of the enclosed foyer shown was dictated by the space between the windows on the side of the house. You may wish to change the size to suit your situation. The methods will be the same, the over-all size different. Check with your local dealer as to the standard sizes of the plastic material and make your plan accordingly.

To finish interior of the foyer, insulate the bottom section by installing short batts between the studs. Cover the unfinished short walls with pine paneling, plywood or other material. The floor may be painted with cement paint or tiled. To complete the job, an aluminum storm and screen door was installed. •

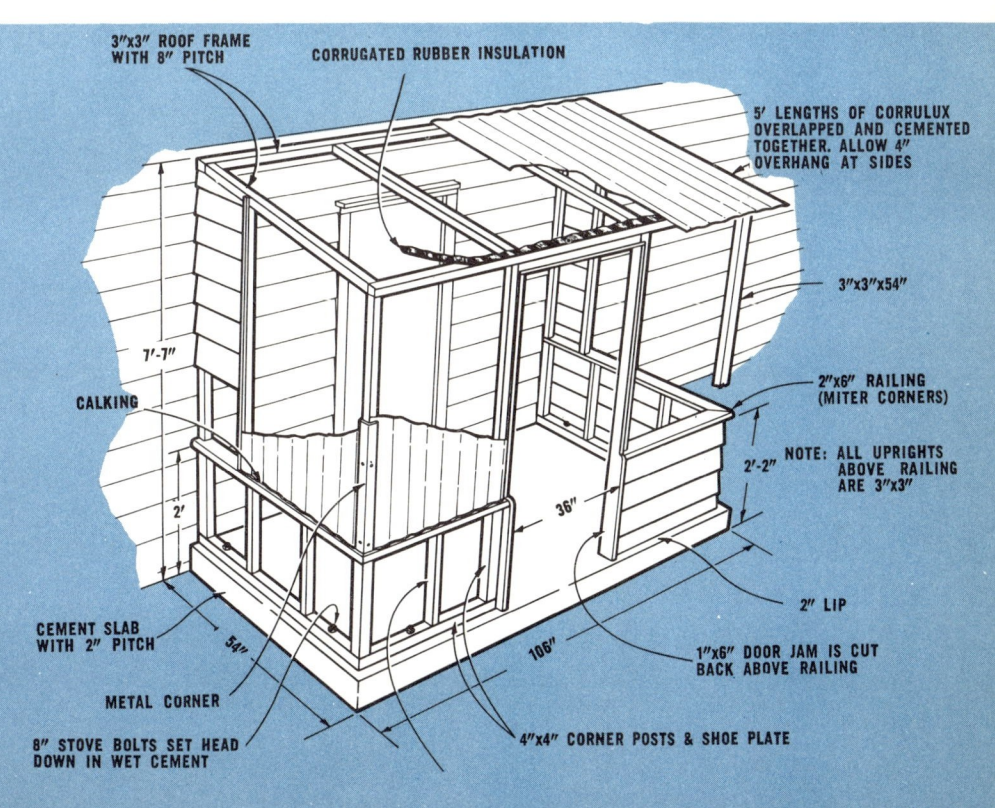

FRAMING

Framing the House

Know the basic elements of sound wood-frame construction

The frame of the house is not a tremendously complex job, but care should be taken to make it solid.

FRAMING

THE entire house frame is anchored to the foundation by means of the sill which is bolted to the foundation wall. Actually there are different types of sills. Most often a 2x6 or a 2x8 is sufficient, but sectional building codes may require a 4-inch stock. Greater nailing surface for sheathing provided by the extra thick sill assures rigidity in sections of the country that may have frequent high winds.

All of the sill designs shown here will do a good job but the box sill construction is popular with most builders. Again, codes must be considered. In the West, where

Support long wood blocks with sawhorses. Use a jig to precut all the studs to the desired size.

Floor plates are nailed directly over the subfloor, tied with nails to every joist underneath.

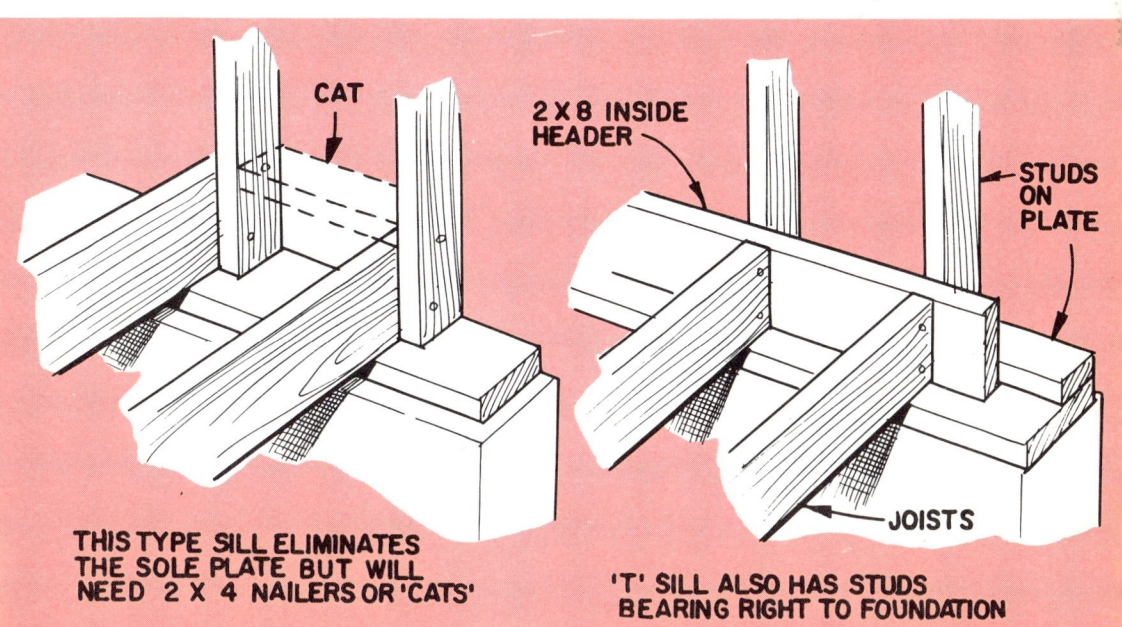

THIS TYPE SILL ELIMINATES THE SOLE PLATE BUT WILL NEED 2 X 4 NAILERS OR 'CATS'

'T' SILL ALSO HAS STUDS BEARING RIGHT TO FOUNDATION

1393

Close-up of wall shows details of stud and filler stud placement supporting window frame above.

Correctly and solidly assembled partition posts provide good nailing surface for wall coverings.

many houses are built over crawl spaces, and climate does not reach extremes, the tie to the foundation is even more simple. Beams span the foundation walls, supported between with underpinnings on concrete piers. A 2x4 subfloor is nailed directly to the beams and floor plates are nailed to this.

Where sheathing is used, the outside edge of the sill should be set in from the edge of the foundation a distance equal to the thickness of the sheathing material. This is so the sheathing will be flush with the outside foundation wall surface.

If beams are not used, then floor joists are laid down over girders which span across the walls. Headers (called header joists and end joists) are placed first. These come flush to the edge of the sill, are butt-nailed together where they meet at the corners and are toenailed to the sill. Floor joists are spaced 16 inches on centers and should be as level as possible. Any high point should be placed top-side. Joists not long enough to make the complete span should be overlapped by at least the thickness of the girder they cross, and the lap should be made at the girder. Nail the joists together at this point and also toenail them to the girder.

Where openings are necessary, such as you might need for a stairwell or for a

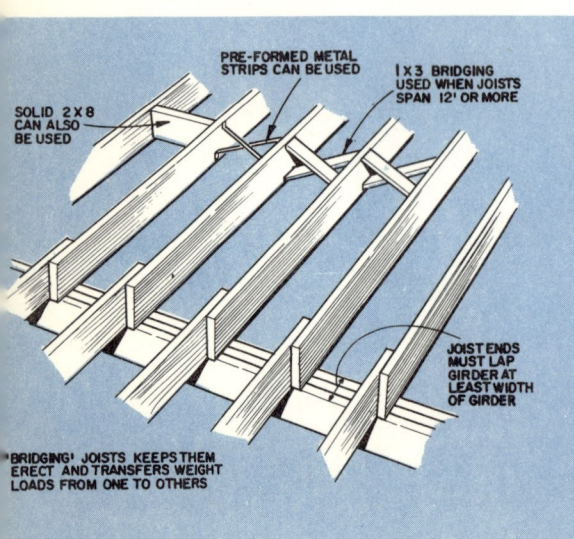

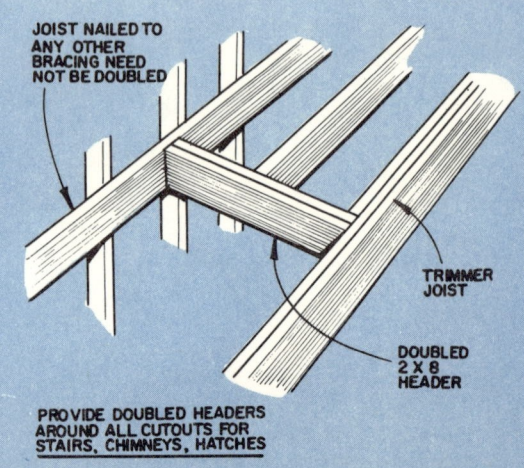

"BRIDGING" JOISTS KEEPS THEM ERECT AND TRANSFERS WEIGHT LOADS FROM ONE TO OTHERS

SOLID 2 X 8 CAN ALSO BE USED

PRE-FORMED METAL STRIPS CAN BE USED

1 X 3 BRIDGING USED WHEN JOISTS SPAN 12' OR MORE

JOIST ENDS MUST LAP GIRDER AT LEAST WIDTH OF GIRDER

JOIST NAILED TO ANY OTHER BRACING NEED NOT BE DOUBLED

TRIMMER JOIST

DOUBLED 2 X 8 HEADER

PROVIDE DOUBLED HEADERS AROUND ALL CUTOUTS FOR STAIRS, CHIMNEYS, HATCHES

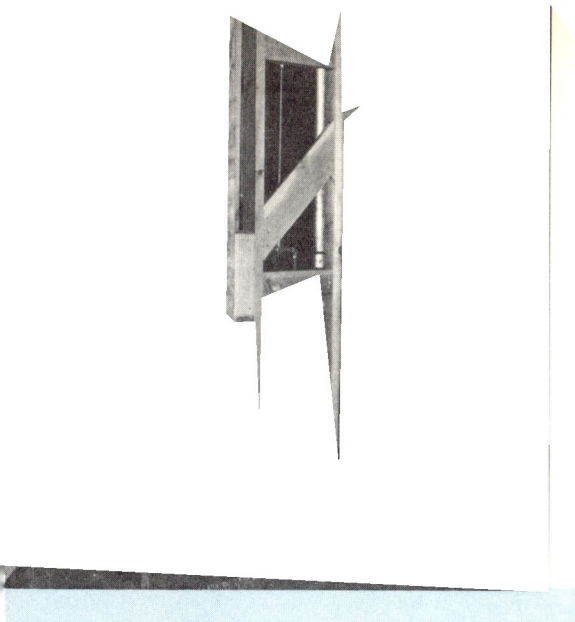

Use up odd length pieces, such as 2x4's, to make interior or exterior wall braces that are rigid.

As soon as the frame is up, put rough plumbing in; notch frame so that pipes will fit in place.

chimney you must compensate for the strength lost by the cutting of the joists. This is done by installing double headers of the same material across the cut ends. Where a double header butts against the wall studding or rests on a sill, it isn't necessary to reinforce at the end. But if the other side of the opening is somewhere between foundation walls, then the joist the double header butts against must also be doubled. In construction language the doubled joist is called a "trimmer."

Joists are stiffened by "bridging" about every eight feet. This can be done with rough 1x3's you can buy or cut from scrap material. Actually, if you have a lot of short lengths of 2x4's that you'd only end up discarding, those pieces would make excellent bridging. Bridging may seem like extra, unnecessary work, but do not neglect it. Good bridging leads to sounder, stronger floors. The best method is to cut one piece and fit it to the job. Then use this as a pattern to cut the rest. If your joists spacings are accurate, you'll have no trouble turning out pieces for bridging on such a production line basis.

Many builders nail only the top of the bridging in place first, then come back and nail the bottom after the subfloor is put down. This is good practice since it will enable you to pull joists into line when

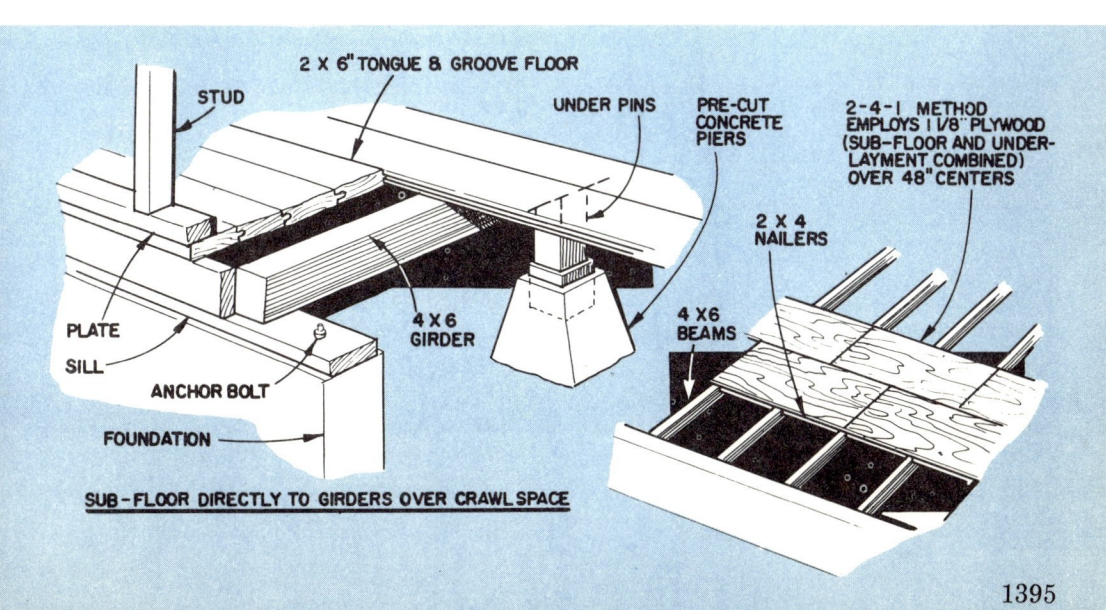

SUB-FLOOR DIRECTLY TO GIRDERS OVER CRAWL SPACE

2 X 6" TONGUE & GROOVE FLOOR
STUD
UNDER PINS
PRE-CUT CONCRETE PIERS
2-4-1 METHOD EMPLOYS 1 1/8" PLYWOOD (SUB-FLOOR AND UNDERLAYMENT COMBINED) OVER 48" CENTERS
2 X 4 NAILERS
PLATE
SILL
4 X 6 GIRDER
4 X 6 BEAMS
ANCHOR BOLT
FOUNDATION

FRAMING

FINISH FLOOR CAN BE LAID IN EITHER DIRECTION

1 X 6 TONGUE & GROOVE SUB FLOORING LAYS ON DIAGONAL

BUTT OVER JOIST ONLY

5/8" PLYWOOD IS ALSO FLOORING – COVERS FAST

2 X 4 PLATE

TWO NO. 8'S PER BOARD

HEADER BOXES IN ALL JOISTS – KEEPS THEM VERTICAL

SILL LAYS IN APP. 3/4" FOR SHEATHING TO FIT

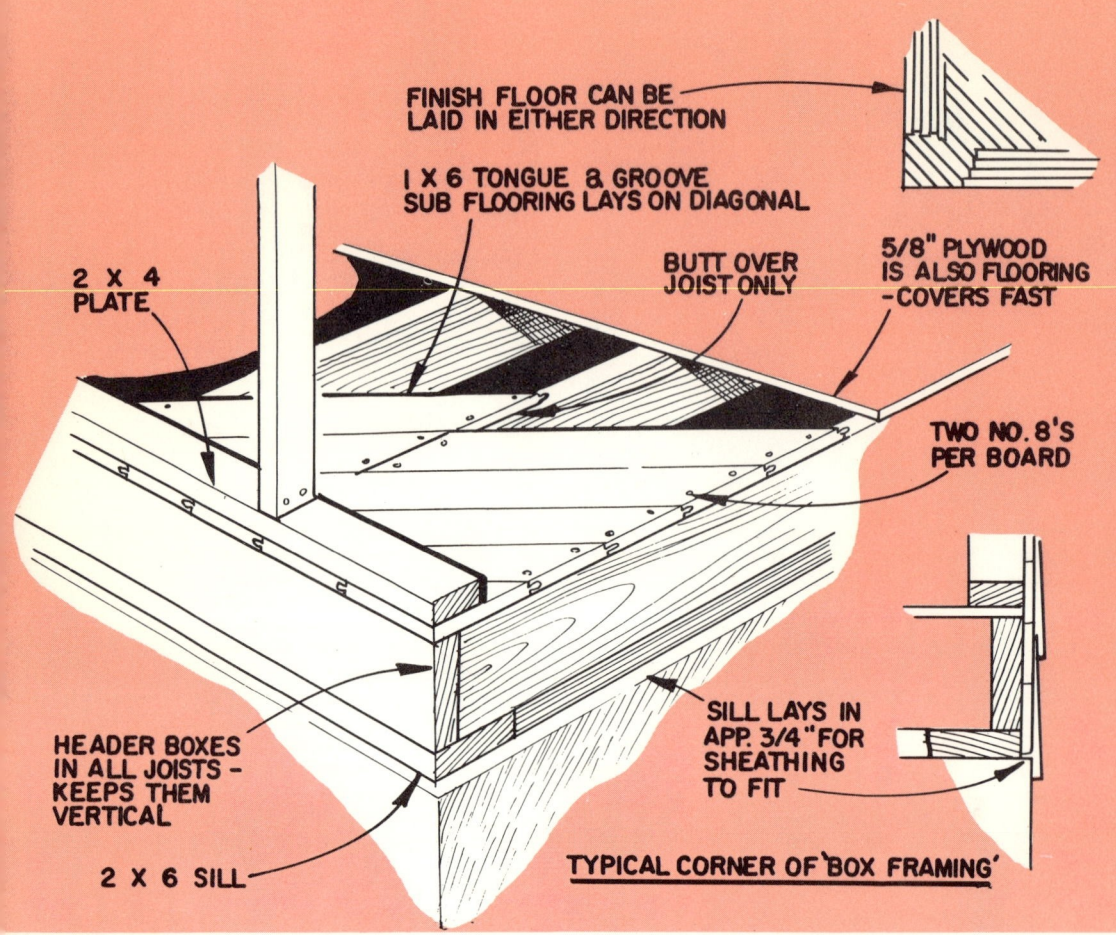

2 X 6 SILL

TYPICAL CORNER OF 'BOX FRAMING'

nailing down the subfloor, if correction is necessary. Metal bridging is available. This will cost a little extra but it is easy to install and saves considerable time.

Subflooring is easy because it involves only cutting and nailing. Subflooring can be the material you used to make concrete forms, or it can be 1x6's bought for the purpose. Plywood makes a good subfloor and a new extra-thick type, which is end-matched, has recently been introduced. Finished floor is placed directly over the plywood.

Diagonally placed subflooring (if you are using boards) provides great rigidity and permits running the finish in any direction. Try to place boards to minimize cutting. This will save labor and add strength. Where a joint must be made be sure it falls over a joist. Don't try to cut each piece individually at the edges of the structure. Instead, let them project slightly, and when the job is finished snap a chalk line and cut along it with a portable saw.

Wall framing starts with the installation of the floor plates. These are 2x4's which outline the house and also the inside rooms and partitions. To these plates are toe-nailed the vertical studs. To the top of the studs are nailed the doubled ceiling plates. You could proceed in this fashion, but the best method is to construct the whole frame, using the subfloor like a big platform to work on.

This also eliminates a great deal of toe-nailing which is necessary if studs are installed after the plate is nailed to the floor. Nails are driven up through the bottom of the floor plate into the ends of the studs.

All studs should be precut to exact length. Building supply houses can supply studs already cut as needed. If you cut your own, set up a jig that will assure length uniformity.

Corner posts and partition posts should be preassembled and attached to plates as a unit. Be careful with stud spacing. Little

FRAMING

If you plan to have a deck extension, cantilever floor joists so there are joists for deck floor.

Cut floor plate for door and make openings large enough for door, jambs, and leeway for squaring

Diagonally end-cut ceiling joists to match pitch of roof rafters and span them across top plates.

inaccuracies here won't mean anything as far as house strength is concerned, but you'll run into trouble later when attaching inside and outside wall coverings if you can't depend on the stud placement. In order for studs to be perfectly vertical, place floor plates and top plate down in correct position but against each other (like a double plate). Then stud markings can be carried across both of them. If you wish to avoid marking, make up a stud spacer, which is no more than a length of 2x4 cut to provide proper spacing between studs. This is used to space studs as they are nailed in place. Start from a corner, and space the first stud from the center of the nailing surface provided by the corner post. Any joints in plates should fall over a stud. When plates are doubled, don't allow two joints to fall in the same place.

When you are done, you've got a wall frame of the house assembled and, with the help of a strong-armed friend, you raise

FRAMING

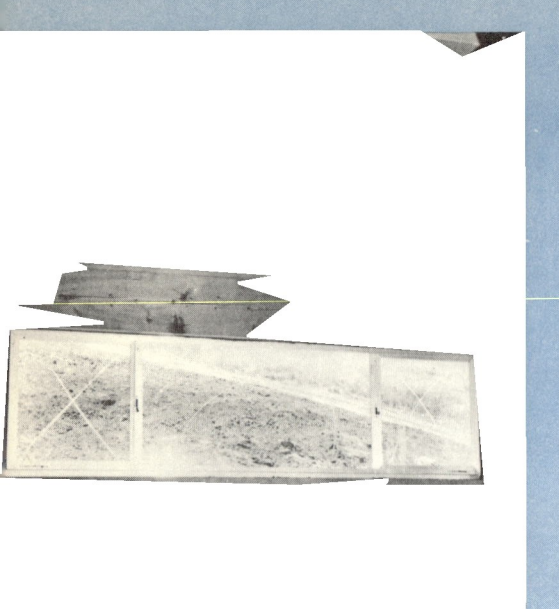

Size of header which is needed to carry overhead weight is determined by the length of the opening.

While the framework is still opened, the job of installing the electrical wiring is unhampered.

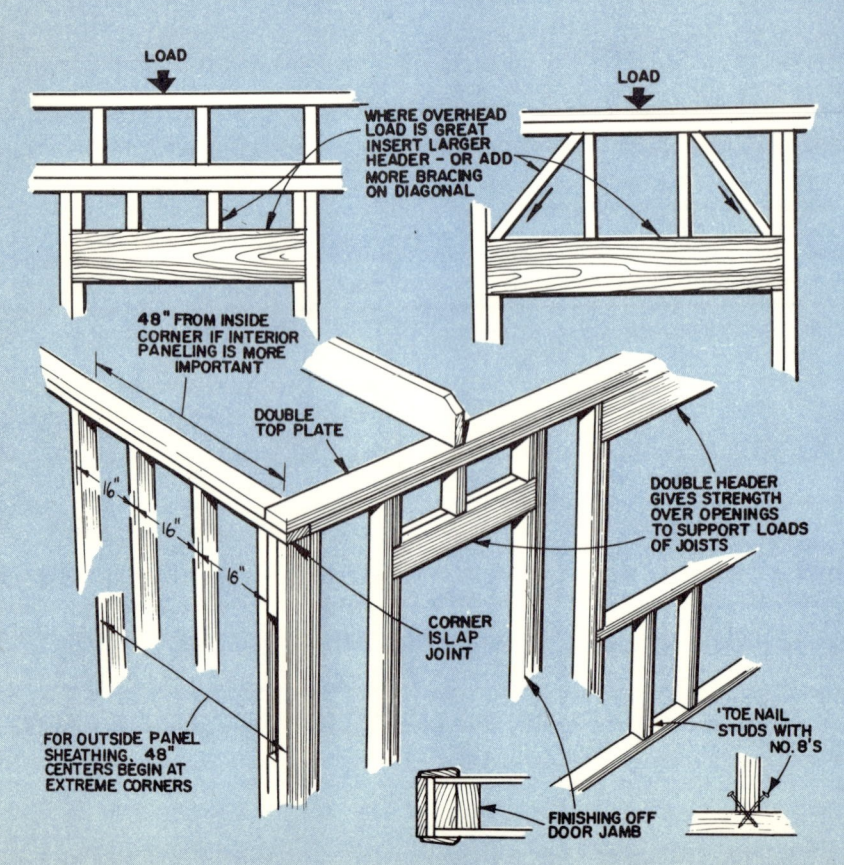

LOAD

WHERE OVERHEAD LOAD IS GREAT INSERT LARGER HEADER – OR ADD MORE BRACING ON DIAGONAL

LOAD

48" FROM INSIDE CORNER IF INTERIOR PANELING IS MORE IMPORTANT

DOUBLE TOP PLATE

DOUBLE HEADER GIVES STRENGTH OVER OPENINGS TO SUPPORT LOADS OF JOISTS

16"
16"
16"

CORNER IS LAP JOINT

FOR OUTSIDE PANEL SHEATHING, 48" CENTERS BEGIN AT EXTREME CORNERS

TOE NAIL STUDS WITH NO. 8'S

FINISHING OFF DOOR JAMB

1398

FRAMING

For the effect, use a wrought iron grille as an outside support in place of the usual wood post.

When the frame is completely put in place, then the next step is the installation of the gutters.

GROUPING CORNER STUDS TO FORM POSTS

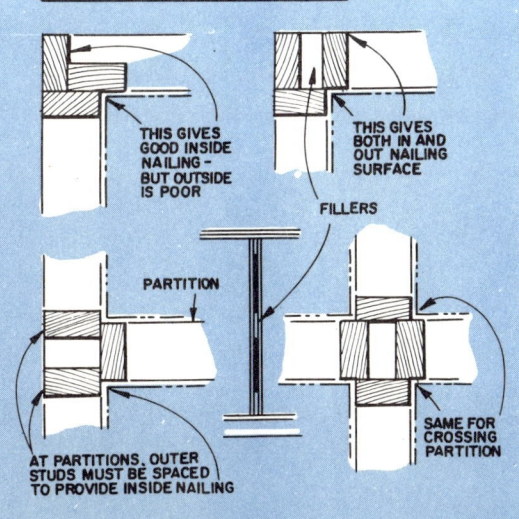

THIS GIVES GOOD INSIDE NAILING - BUT OUTSIDE IS POOR

THIS GIVES BOTH IN AND OUT NAILING SURFACE

FILLERS

PARTITION

SAME FOR CROSSING PARTITION

AT PARTITIONS, OUTER STUDS MUST BE SPACED TO PROVIDE INSIDE NAILING

it to a vertical position. Use diagonal braces to hold the wall in place while you plumb it, then nail the floor plate down. It's a good idea to provide sufficient temporary bracing to keep the wall plumb until construction has reached a point where the wall can't move anymore.

Follow this same procedure with all four walls and when the sections are up, double the top plate by adding a second 2x4 over the first one. At corners, place the second plate so it forms a lap joint with the plate under it.

Adequate permanent bracing can be provided by running 1x4 stock down a corner post, across four or five studs and into the floor plate. Each of the frame members the diagonal brace crosses is notched so the brace is flush with exterior edges of those pieces. Be careful with the notches. The tighter the fit of the brace into the recess, the stronger the job. •

1399

Furniture Refinishing

You can add that professional finishing touch to your furniture in your own home. Only inexpensive paint materials are needed.

IF you discover a deep scratch or dent in the polished surface of a prized piece of furniture, do not feel discouraged. You can make repairs that will render the damage completely invisible.

The only satisfactory way to remove deep scratches and dents is to fill them with melted stick shellac. This method is used by professional furniture finishers. With a little practice you can become expert.

Stick shellac in a great variety of colors and shades of colors can be purchased at a well stocked paint store. It is essential to use shellac which matches the color of the damaged surface. Stick shellac is similar in appearance and behavior to the sealing wax used to seal letters. In fact, sealing wax is shellac mixed with chalk, clay, etc., and a coloring material, whereas stick shellac is pure shellac mixed with a small amount of coloring material.

The tools and materials needed are a stick of shellac of a shade which matches the finish on the furniture piece undergoing repairs, a single-edge razor blade, an alcohol lamp, and a flexible putty knife or spatula. An electric soldering iron is useful but not essential.

Clean out the scratch or dent with the point of a penknife blade, removing all crushed or loose wood fibers, varnish, etc. Undercut the edges slightly and if necessary enlarge the marred spot enough so that it is not difficult to force in the molten shellac. Hold the stick shellac and the hot soldering iron over the spot. Apply the iron to one end of the stick and allow enough molten shellac to drip into the crack or dent to slightly overfill it. It is important for the iron to be only hot enough to melt the shellac. If too hot, the shellac will be discolored. Shellac melts far below the temperature required to melt solder and the iron will be hot enough to melt shellac long before it will melt solder.

Push the molten shellac into the injured spot and smooth it with the blade of a flexible putty knife or small metal spatula which has been warmed in the flame of the alcohol lamp. Be careful not to let the hot metal touch the surrounding varnished surface. Allow the shellac to harden for two or three hours before using the razor blade to scrape it down practically even with the rest of the surface.

The final smoothing is done with fine flint paper followed by rubbing with pumice or rottenstone. Pumice will produce a slightly dulled finish, rottenstone produces a high polish. Wrap a piece of felt around a small block of wood and use it as a rubbing pad. An old hat is a good source of felt. Dip the pad into a mixture of pumice and water, or rottenstone and water, of the consistency of cream. Rub the repaired spot with the pad. Wipe the surface clean after rubbing for a few seconds and examine the spot to ascertain what has been accomplished. Too much rubbing will soon cut through the surrounding varnish. If this occurs, clean off all traces of pumice or rottenstone and give the area a coat of rubbing varnish applied with a fine brush. When the varnish has dried for 48 hours, rub it with rottenstone or pumice, whichever is required, to match the finish on the rest of the surface.

Deep scratches and dents in furniture surfaces can be filled with melted stick shellac without using a soldering iron. Heat the blade of a putty knife in the flame of an alcohol lamp and use the hot blade to melt enough shellac off the end of the stick to fill the scratch or dent. There is considerable risk of overheating the knife blade and spoiling its temper. The novice is advised to use a "dime store" putty knife. It will not be a great loss if you spoil it.

The Removal of Stains Caused by Alcohol, Water, Perfumes, Hot Plates, etc.

Surfaces finished with varnish made from natural resins are easily marred by strong soaps, alcoholic beverages, etc. Fortunately, these marks do not usually penetrate far into the finish and can be removed by a fine abrasive. A paste made of whiting and water rubbed on the stains will often remove them. Apply the paste to a small pad of clean soft cloth and rub the spots with it. Rub gently with a circular motion. Bon Ami can be substituted for whiting.

If whiting or Bon Ami do not produce results, try finely powdered pumice mixed with enough linseed oil to form a thin paste. Apply the pumice with a small pad of felt or soft clean cloth and use the same gentle, circular rubbing motion recommended for whiting. Pumice is a much coarser and faster-cutting abrasive than whiting. Wipe off the pumice and oil frequently with a cloth dampened with turpentine so that you can check your progress. Do not rub with pumice any longer than is necessary to remove the stains because pumice cuts varnish quickly.

White shellac is an excellent sealer for new wood. Use a thin coat and brush it on quickly.

Remove old finish down to raw wood. Use three coats of shellac to provide a durable finish.

FURNITURE

First step to good varnishing results: On raw wood, brush on filler across grain only. Thin filler with turpentine to a cream consistency.

Wipe off filler coat when surface turns dull, rubbing cloth across grain. Liquid fills pores and levels surface for finish. Let it dry 24 hours.

If it is necessary to rub through the varnish to eliminate the stains, or if it is done accidentally, the surface must be revarnished.

Tables, bar tops, vanity tables, etc., upon which perfumes or alcoholic beverages may be spilled, should be finished or refinished with a varnish containing phenolic resin. The finish afforded by this type of synthetic resin is quite resistant to alcohol, mild alkalis, etc., and not easily marred.

Metal Kitchen Cabinets

To renew the old finish or change the color of metal kitchen cabinets, apply a coat of enamel undercoater and finish with a coat of enamel of the color desired. The preparatory work necessary will depend upon the condition of the old surface. If it is badly chipped and cracked, try to remove the old finish with paint and varnish remover. If the old finish is a baked enamel, the remover will not be effective. All traces of paint and varnish remover should be wiped off with a cloth moistened with mineral spirits before applying the undercoater. When the undercoater has dried for 36 to 48 hours, rub it lightly with No. 00 flint paper to remove all brush marks and rough spots.

Removal of an Old Finish and Preparation for Refinishing

A first class new finish on wood furniture cannot be secured when the old finish is in bad condition without taking off the old finish and starting from bare wood. This is true also if the type of finish is to be changed, for example, from enamel to varnish or vice versa; the best results are obtained only when the old coatings are removed.

Scraping and sanding without the assistance of chemical paint and varnish removers are practical methods for taking off some finishes, especially from flat surfaces, but they involve considerable physical effort. The use of a chemical remover is messy but saves time and labor. The solvent type removers are preferable to alkaline removers (applied hot) because the latter raise the grain of wood and roughen surfaces, whereas solvent removers do not.

If you use a solvent paint and varnish remover, remember the following safety measures:
1. Wear rubber gloves.
2. Keep varnish remover away from fire.
3. Work only where there is good ventilation.

It is necessary to wipe off all traces of remover from a surface undergoing refinishing before applying stain, filler, shellac or varnish. Solvent type removers contain chemicals which evaporate very rapidly. They often contain also a small amount of wax which does not evaporate. Wax is included because it rises to the surface and prevents rapid evaporation of the solvents when the remover is applied. It gives the solvents time to soften the old coatings before evaporating. If the wax which remains behind is not completely removed it will prevent the adherence and drying of the new finish.

That portion of a furniture refinishing job which requires varnish remover and sandpaper should be done outdoors if possible. When sanding is done indoors, a fine dust settles on everything, making extra housework.

Varnish remover should be applied lib-

1402

Pour small amount of varnish into cup, brush with grain. Don't dip brush into stock can as this puts air into a varnish and thickens it.

HOW TO MAKE FURNITURE STAINS

All formulas include 2 pints linseed oil, 1½ pints turpentine and ½ pint japan drier, unless otherwise noted.	
LIGHT OAK:	½ lb. raw sienna, ⅛ lb. yellow ochre.
DARK OAK:	½ lb. raw sienna, ⅛ lb. burnt turkey umber.
MISSION OAK:	1 lb. black, ½ oz. rose pink.
ANTIQUE OAK:	½ lb. raw sienna, ½ lb. burnt turkey umber, 1 oz. lampblack.
EBONY:	¾ lb. black, ½ oz. Prussian blue.
WALNUT:	½ lb. burnt turkey umber, ½ lb. Vandyke brown.
GOLDEN OAK:	½ lb. raw sienna, ¼ lb. burnt turkey umber.
MAHOGANY BROWN:	½ lb. burnt sienna, ⅛ lb. rose pink, ⅛ lb. Vandyke brown.
CHERRY:	¾ lb. burnt sienna.
ROSEWOOD:	½ lb. burnt sienna, ¼ lb. rose pink.

erally with a medium-sized brush. Pour a small quantity into a tin can in which you can dip the brush. Do not pour out more than you can use in the next few minutes because a solvent remover loses its strength rapidly when exposed to the atmosphere. It is most effective if allowed to flow off the brush with little or no brushing. Allow it to remain undisturbed for 10 or 15 minutes. Then scrape off as much of the softened paint or varnish as possible with a putty knife or painter's broad knife. Scrape with the grain and use care not to gouge or scratch the surface. Put the strippings of old paint or varnish on a newspaper for later disposal in the trash can. Keep the putty knife clean by wiping it frequently. The most common mistake is to start scraping too soon. Solvent removers usually penetrate through a varnish finish to the wood underneath, unless the varnish is very thick. When there are several layers of old paint, the remover may penetrate and soften only one layer at a time. It will then be necessary to apply fresh remover to each underlying layer after the one above has been scraped off. The softened finish on molding, beading and carving can be scrubbed off with a small, stiff scrubbing brush. You can buy such brushes at a dime store for 10 to 20 cents each. Fine steel wool is effective on spots which cannot be reached with a putty knife.

When the old finish is all off, the entire surface should be thoroughly cleaned with gasoline, mineral spirits or turpentine to rid it of all traces of the remover. Gasoline

Staining requires opening of wood's pores by sanding. Electric vibrator sander speeds job. Sanding produces a fine dust so work outside.

Work with grain in applying stain. Excess can be wiped off with clean rag after a few minutes. Stain may be applied with either brush or rag.

is most effective but is a fire hazard and must be used with great caution. A spark of static electricity or a careless "kibitzer" standing by with a cigarette can start a conflagration. Mineral spirits is not as dangerous as gasoline and is a better solvent of wax than turpentine.

Any furniture surface which is to be given a polished finish, regardless of whether the finish is to be varnish, wax, rubbed oil or enamel, must be "smooth as a baby's skin" before the new finish is applied. This necessitates sanding. If a really fine finish is the goal, it is hardly possible to spend too much time in preparing a smooth surface to build the finish upon. A cabinet scraper and fine steel wool will help in spots which are hard to reach with sandpaper. It may be necessary to shape a block of wood to fit some of the difficult places. Fasten a piece of sandpaper to the block with rubber cement. This will take time and patience but is well spent if you like to take pride in your finished work.

Only the fine grades of sandpaper should be used. Start with No. 0 flint paper or its equivalent and rub only with the grain. Remember that small across-the-grain scratches which are invisible on the bare wood will show as dark lines in a transparent finish, especially on a veneered surface. The final sanding should be with Nos. 00, 000 and 0000 in succession.

A surface from which an old finish has been removed and which has been well sanded is, in effect, new woodwork and is refinished in the same manner as new woodwork.

Natural Finishes

Shellac, varnish and wax darken woods slightly but provide a "natural" finish which displays the characteristic grain of the wood. If the wood is an open grain variety,

Varnish removers are toxic or inflammable. Be safe. Work outdoors in removing old finishes and you'll minimize threat of fire or headache.

it should be filled with transparent paste filler. After the filler has dried for 24 hours, it is sealed with a thin coat of white shellac. The shellac will dry in two or three hours so that it can be lightly sanded with No. 000 flint paper. After sanding the surface wipe it with a cloth moistened with turpentine to rid it of all dust. You can build either a wax or a varnish finish upon this shellac base, using three coats.

Staining

Do not expect to produce a first class finish by using a varnish stain (stain and varnish combined). Staining and varnishing are separate operations in the produc-

SOME POPULAR EFFECTS

ANTIQUE TAWNY BROWN:	Light oak stain glazed with light grey paint.
PICKLED PINE:	Bleach if desired. Stain any color from olive green to driftwood grey, then glaze with white tinted with raw umber and black. Do not wipe too smoothly.
WHITE LIMEY:	(for knotty pine) Glaze with flat white, tinted slightly. Use extra-thin and merely wipe the knots alone. Clean off the glaze.
DUSTY ANTIQUE:	Add about 1½ oz. of rottonstone to one quart of glaze mixture. Rottonstone used as a polishing agent will make a glossy varnish or paint take on a dull sheen.
WORN GOLD EFFECT:	Stain some dark color. Glaze with gold paint. To add age, dry and follow with a pale cream glaze to which rottonstone has been added.
STREAKED GOLD EFFECT:	Works best on wood like yellow pine that has grain in raised streaks. Glaze with gold paint. Dry and follow with some dark contrasting color. Wipe so as to leave the dark pigment in the valleys and the gold showing through on the high spots. This finish can be protected by a wash coat of shellac and then clear wax paste.
ANTIQUEING:	This is done by staining, then glazing, but instead of wiping the glaze off evenly, it is wiped thinnest at the usual wear areas.

tion of a fine finish of which you can be proud.

Two types of stains are available to the amateur—penetrating stains and oil stains. Penetrating stains can be used on either hard or soft new wood and on either hard or soft previously finished woods. They require some skill in handling when applied to soft, porous woods because they penetrate quickly and deeply. The author overcomes this difficulty to some extent by wearing rubber gloves and applying stain with a soft cloth in place of the usual brush.

Oil stains are more suitable for soft woods than penetrating stains. Oil stains will not prove quite satisfactory, however, on previously finished surfaces from which the old finish has been removed unless the surface has been sanded sufficiently to expose the pores of the wood.

Oil stain is applied with either a rag or a brush and wiped with a clean rag a few minutes later to remove any excess which has not soaked into the wood. Considerable variation in shade of color and in either hiding or accentuating the grain is possible by varying the amount of stain applied and the extent to which it is wiped afterward.

Filling

Filling has been explained in connection with floors and interior woodwork. It is required on all new open grain woods (these include mahogany, walnut, oak and chestnut) and on all wood of these varieties from which an old finish has been completely removed. Transparent filler is used for natural finishes. Filler of the same color as the stain is used when wood is stained. Heavy paste filler should be thinned with turpentine or gasoline until it has the consistency of thick cream. Filler is brushed on after staining and allowed to stand until it loses its gloss. Then it is wiped off across grain with a coarse cloth in such a way as to fill the pores and level the surface for the finishing coats to follow. It is highly important that all filler be removed from the surface; any that remains will discolor it and obscure the grain. Filler should dry for 24 hours before the next operation.

Shellacking

White shellac is applied over stain and filler to keep the stain from bleeding through the finishing coats which follow. The ordinary "5 lb. cut" is thinned with an equal amount of denatured alcohol for this purpose.

Varnishing

Furniture varnish is a hard varnish "short" of oil and it is the only varnish suitable to use on furniture which is not exposed to the weather. Furniture should be varnished only in a room where no dust or insects will settle on it while the varnish is hardening. The first coat should be applied after the surface has been sealed with shellac and lightly sanded. The surface and the brush used should be free from dust. Dust can be eliminated from the surface by wiping with a tack rag. To make a tack rag put on rubber gloves, soak a piece of cloth about two feet square in varnish and wring it out, then hang the rag up. It is ready to use when it is sticky but not wet.

The first coat should dry for 48 hours and then be sanded very lightly with No. 000 flint paper. After all dust has been wiped off with a tack rag the second coat may be put on. This should also be allowed to dry for 48 hours and be lightly sanded with No. 000 flint paper.

The third and last coat can be flat-drying varnish if a dull finish is desired, or rubbing varnish if a polish is wanted. •

Inexpensive spray gun of the electric vibrator type is faster than brush. Don't try to spray heavy liquids with it. Clean well after using.

Spray gun is fine on wicker furniture, but use it outdoors. Indoor spraying may be unpleasant or toxic. Do not spray furniture on windy day.

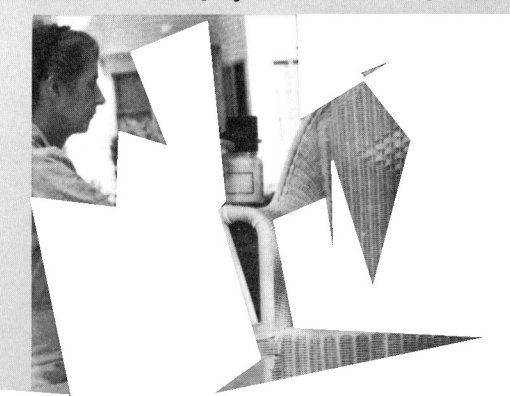

GAMES

GAME BOARD STEP STOOL

By David X. Manners

Inlaid tile top makes this neatly designed and durable table a colorful addition to your playroom.

CHILDREN love this versatile stepstool. Besides using it for climbing, yours will find it perfect as a worktable. They'll scramble to use it for watching TV, and as they watch they can eat their lunch or supper off its wipe-clean vinyl-surfaced top. It's handy as a checker or chessboard too.

Though it's fun furniture for children, it is also a very practical and attractive piece for the living or family room. There it can serve as an end table, coffee or snack table, or as an unusual plant stand.

The stepstool can be cut from a single 3x4-foot ¾-inch plywood panel with a minimum of waste, as shown in the sketch. For natural finishing, any hardwood plywood can be used. For an enameled finish, Old Craftsman pine plywood was selected because of the ease with which it can be worked and finished and the smoothness of its cut edges. In addition to the plywood, 6½ feet of ½x1-inch molding and two 14-inch lengths of 1¼-inch dowel are needed.

After laying out and cutting the six plywood pieces to size, divide the 15x32-inch side sections into a grid of 5-inch

GAMES

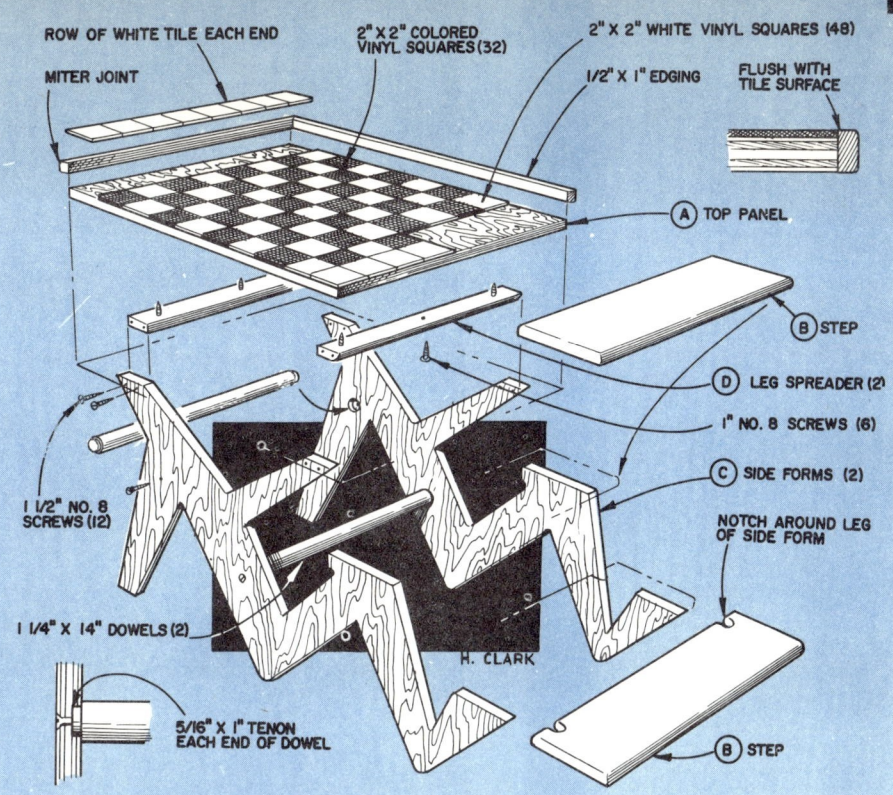

Labels (exploded diagram):
- ROW OF WHITE TILE EACH END
- MITER JOINT
- 2" X 2" COLORED VINYL SQUARES (32)
- 2" X 2" WHITE VINYL SQUARES (48)
- 1/2" X 1" EDGING
- FLUSH WITH TILE SURFACE
- (A) TOP PANEL
- (B) STEP
- (D) LEG SPREADER (2)
- 1" NO. 8 SCREWS (6)
- (C) SIDE FORMS (2)
- NOTCH AROUND LEG OF SIDE FORM
- 1 1/2" NO. 8 SCREWS (12)
- 1 1/4" X 14" DOWELS (2)
- 5/16" X 1" TENON EACH END OF DOWEL
- H. CLARK
- (B) STEP

DRAWINGS SHOW details of construction. Sides and top are made of 3/4-inch plywood. Top is covered with 2x2-inch scraps of vinyl tile. Adhere tile to table top with mastic cement. Other tiles including ceramic, of course, may be used. If ceramic tiles are used, fill in space between tiles with a thin mixture of grout.

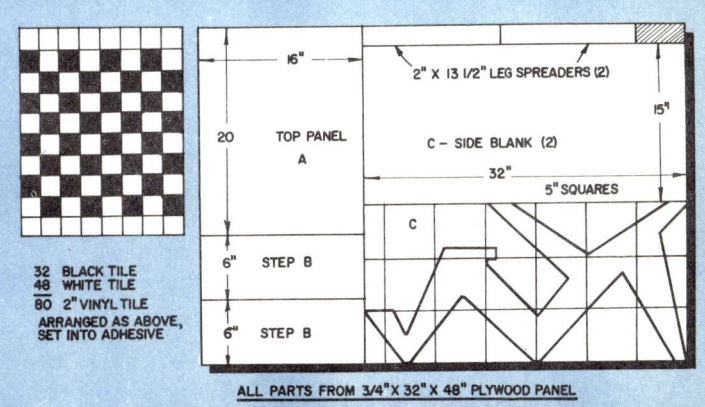

32 BLACK TILE
48 WHITE TILE
80 2" VINYL TILE
ARRANGED AS ABOVE, SET INTO ADHESIVE

- 16"
- 20 — TOP PANEL A
- 6" STEP B
- 6" STEP B
- 2" X 13 1/2" LEG SPREADERS (2)
- C — SIDE BLANK (2)
- 32"
- 15"
- 5" SQUARES

ALL PARTS FROM 3/4" X 32" X 48" PLYWOOD PANEL

1407

LAY OUT PARTS either on paper pattern or directly on the plywood before cutting.

INTRICATE SIDES may be cut on band saw, though keyhole and handsaw may be used.

PORTABLE ROUTER is used here to round edges. These may also be filed and sanded.

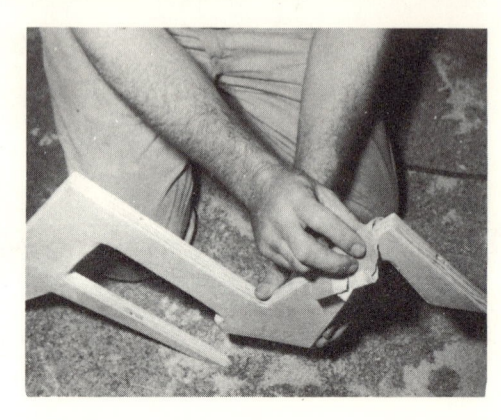

USE FINE SANDPAPER for a smooth finish. Do not round off any of the top flat areas.

CUT TWO 1¼-inch dowels 14 inches long. Trim ends to one-inch diameter as shown.

TRIMMED ENDS fit into 5/16-inch holes on inside of sides. Use glue and screws.

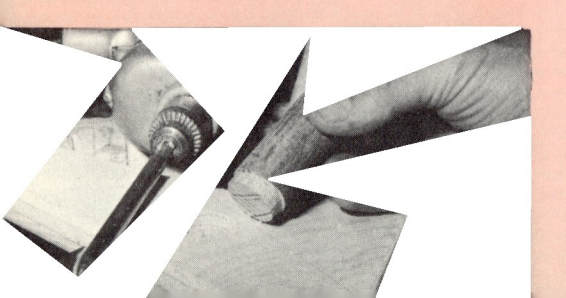

squares. Start blocking out the squares from the right-hand side, so that the final tier of narrower 2-inch squares will be at the left. Using the squares as a guide, copy the pattern onto the boards for cutting.

If need be, you can do all cuts except one with an ordinary handsaw; that last cut can be handled with a keyhole saw. But, of course, the whole job is a natural one for a bandsaw, and the trusty Delta makes quick work of it.

All exposed edges require rounding over. For the amateur, a portable router with a rounding-over bit does it like nothing else can. The professional craftsman or skilled operator, of course, can achieve a comparable result with only hand tools. Edges of the two steps are rounded over, but the 16x20 top section is left as is.

For a well-braced fit, dowel ends are trimmed down to a 1-inch diameter for $\frac{5}{16}$-inch recessing in holes drilled in the stool sides. The simple way to do the

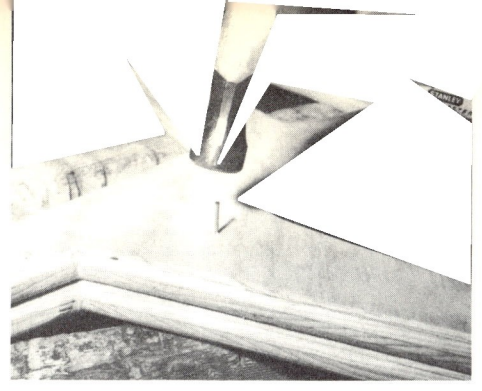

PILOT HOLES for dowels and screws to hold them are marked with nail, then drilled.

SPREADERS for underside of top are pre-drilled, countersunk for flathead screws.

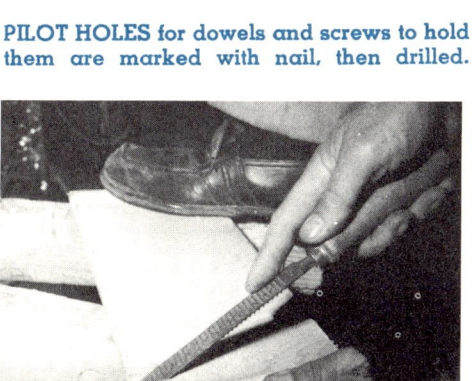

BOTTOM STEP is notched as shown to fit against sides. Bevel slot with rasp as shown.

TOP EDGING is tacked in place with finishing nails and glue; height flush with tile.

trimming on a radial saw is to raise the blade to 1-inch height above the table. Revolve the dowel as passes are made with the blade. On a table saw, adjust blade height to ¼ inch above the table, and revolve the dowel as it is passed over the blade.

At the center of the holes drilled in the stool sides for the dowels, continue a ⅛-inch pilot hole all the way through the stock. After drilling dowel holes in one side, place both sides together with the holes facing in, and tap a nail through the pilot holes to mark their location on the opposite side. Assemble sides and dowels with glue, and with screws through pilot holes.

Spreader pieces are needed to brace the attachment of legs to stool top. For added screw-holding power, you may prefer to cut these pieces of solid 1x2 stock instead of using plywood for the purpose. Cut a bevel along the rear edge of the back spreader so it will conform to the slant of the rear legs.

After centering the spreaders along the front and back edges of the underside of the top, attach with glue and countersunk woodscrews. Position top on sides and attach legs to spreader ends with screws. Steps are attached with glue and countersunk 4-penny finishing nails. So that the bottom step will fit snugly against legs, provide slanting slots in its underside. These are quickly cut with a rasp.

Finish off the edges of the top with ½x1-inch molding strip nailed so its upper edge is ⅛ inch higher than the top. This will make it flush with the vinyl tile you'll use as surfacing. Miter the molding at the corners, round over its outside edges.

Give the stool a final going over with very fine grit paper, dust, and then apply alkyd enamel undercoat according to manufacturer's directions. Follow with alkyd enamel finish. Paint the molding around the top, but not the top itself. Vinyl tiles in mastic go on top. •

GAMES

Table soccer is skill and luck; object is for teams to rotate and slide dowel, hit ball to left goal.

1410

Components of game are made from two 2x4-inch panels of fir plywood. Mark and cut as shown.

Table Soccer

When the weather has ruled out badminton or croquet and the family's tired of table tennis, this brand new indoor "soccer" game will entertain the entire household.

Table soccer is an imaginative combination of simplicity and fun. It is an open plywood box which can rest on a tabletop anywhere in the house. Two, four or six persons can play the game. Wooden rods extend across the box through holes in the sides, with enough rod sticking out to form a handle on each side. Each rod has small wooden paddles fastened to it. Players attempt to manipulate the rods so that the paddles will bat a Ping-pong ball toward their goal, a hole at each end of the box.

Construction

Carefully lay out all the parts on the two fir plywood 2x4 Handy Panels as shown on the cutting diagram.

Next, cut plywood bottom, sides and ends to size. Drill ½-inch holes in upper

GAMES

To assemble game, first nail sides to ends; cut holes in side larger than dowel for free movement.

CUTTING DIAGRAMS

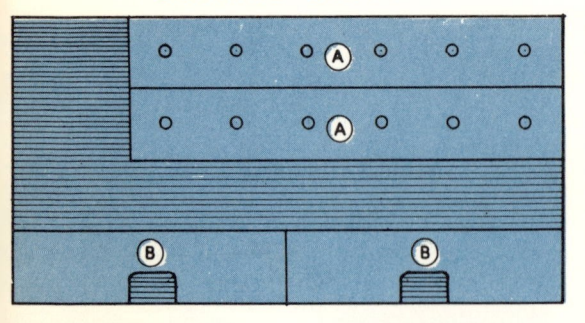

corners where goals have been marked out and make cutouts with a keyhole saw. Drill six 7/8-inch holes in the sides, spaced as shown and centered 3¼ inches above the bottom edges.

The playing rods are made from ¾-inch diameter hardwood dowels. Select these carefully at your lumber dealer's to insure getting the six straightest rods available. Cut paddles to size from ¼-inch plywood. Drill and countersink one screw hole on the center line of each paddle ⅜ inch from one end. Mark center lines for paddles as shown along each dowel on the left side as the dowel is held in the right hand. Provide a shoulder for each paddle on all the dowels by making ⅜-inch deep cuts one half inch to each side of center lines. Remove material between cuts with a wood chisel.

Drill screw holes in dowels to prevent splitting. Using glue, attach each paddle as shown with one ⅝-inch No. 6 flat head screw. Hold the paddle firmly as the screw is turned down. Slide a rubber washer over the ends of each rod and push it over to touch the nearest paddle.

1412

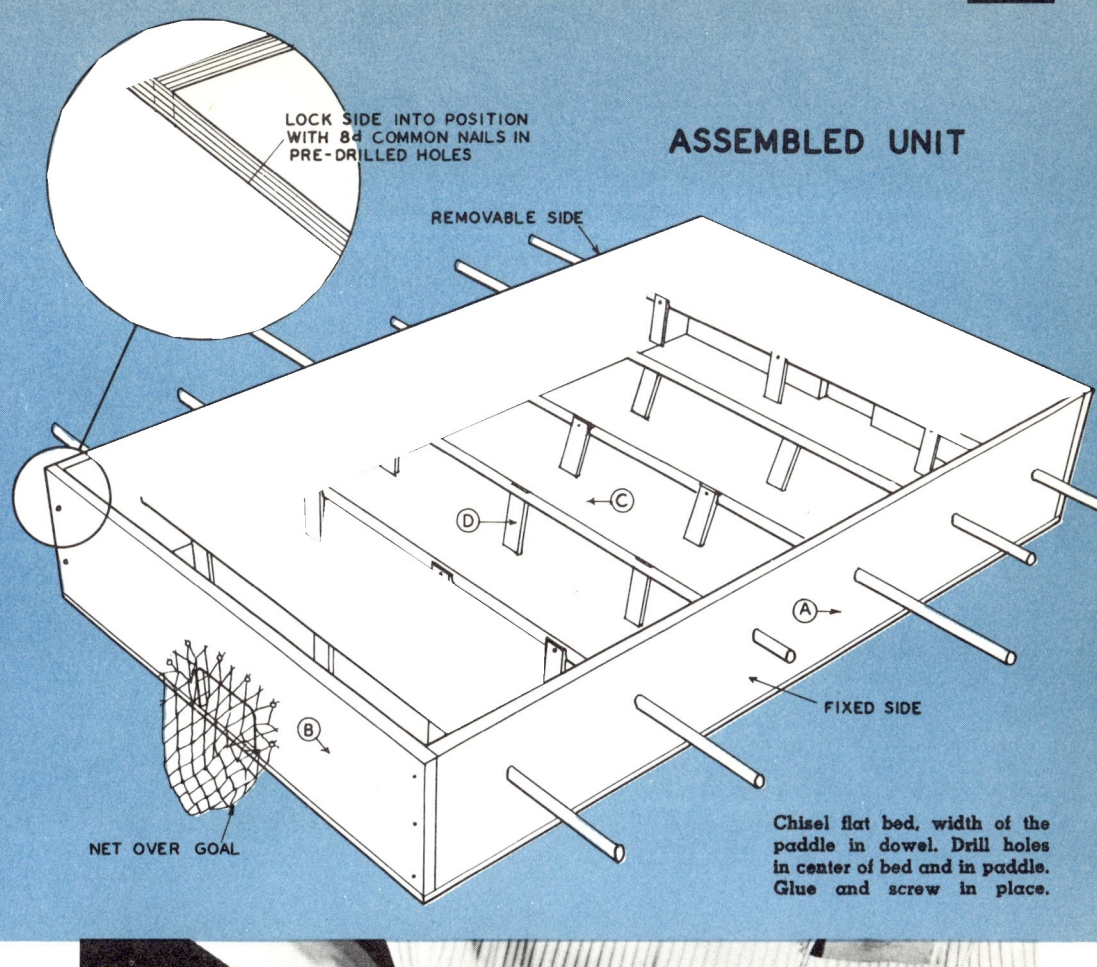

GAMES

ASSEMBLED UNIT

LOCK SIDE INTO POSITION WITH 8d COMMON NAILS IN PRE-DRILLED HOLES

REMOVABLE SIDE

FIXED SIDE

NET OVER GOAL

Chisel flat bed, width of the paddle in dowel. Drill holes in center of bed and in paddle. Glue and screw in place.

SIDE VIEW

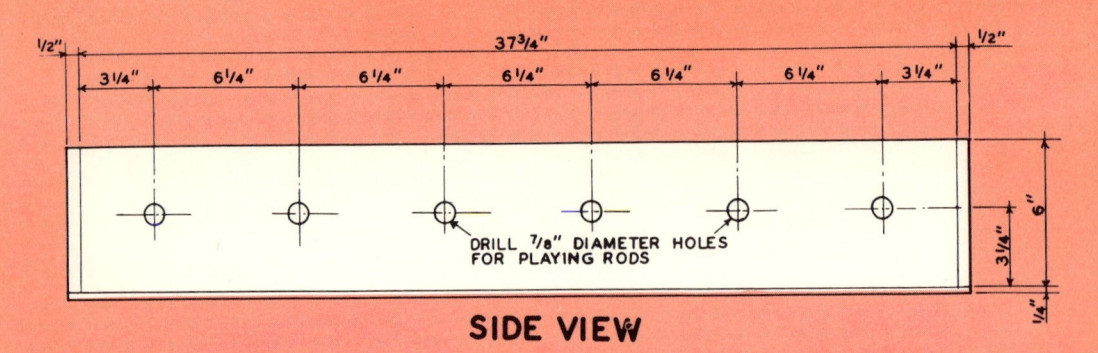

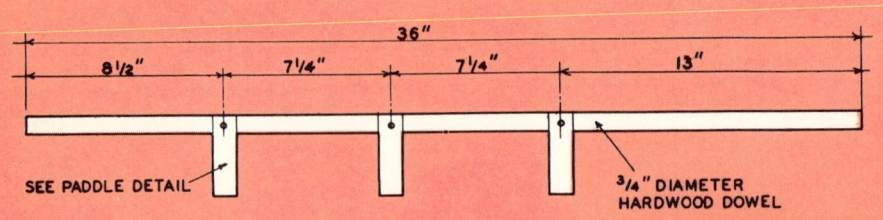

DRILL 7/8" DIAMETER HOLES FOR PLAYING RODS

PLAYING ROD

SEE PADDLE DETAIL

3/4" DIAMETER HARDWOOD DOWEL

On the floor of the playing box drill and countersink screw holes one quarter inch in from the edges where the ends and the fixed side will be fastened. Assemble with glue and 1-inch No. 4 flat head wood screws. Use glue and three 6-penny finishing nails at each corner to fasten the ends to the fixed side.

Place the removable side in position and drill two holes in each corner for 8-penny common nails, to hold the side firmly when the game is in use.

Sand all edges and ease corners with 1-0 paper on a soft block. Painting is unnecessary unless the table tennis ball picks up static electricity from the unfinished wood. This can be overcome by painting the ball or playing box. Use a primer and two coats of semigloss enamel. Paint the last 6 inches of the long end of the rods a distinctive color so players can quickly tell their own rods from their opponent's.

Assemble the game by sliding rods through the holes of the fixed side with ends alternating. Lock removable side into position with 8-penny common nails in predrilled holes. Now choose your partners, toss in the ball and start the game. •

Use fish net for goals; insert dowels in holes; hold in place with two nails in predrilled holes.

1414

GAMES

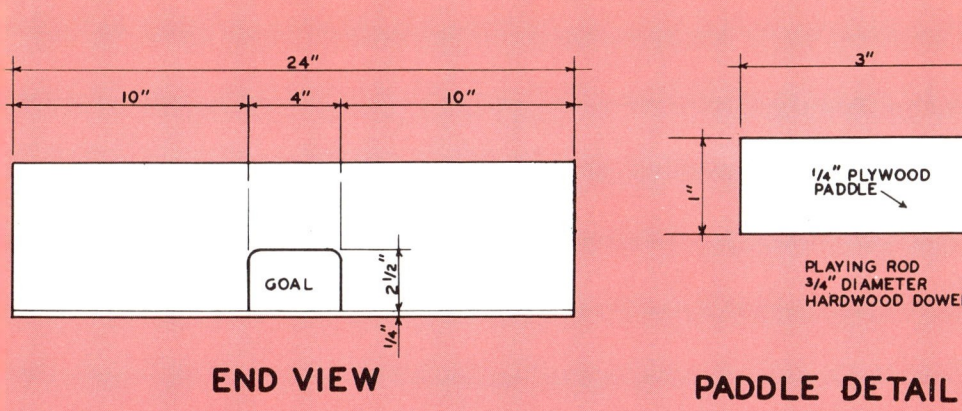

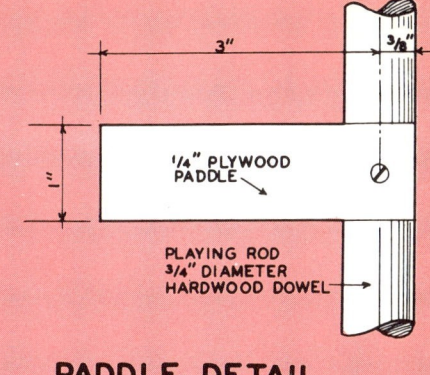

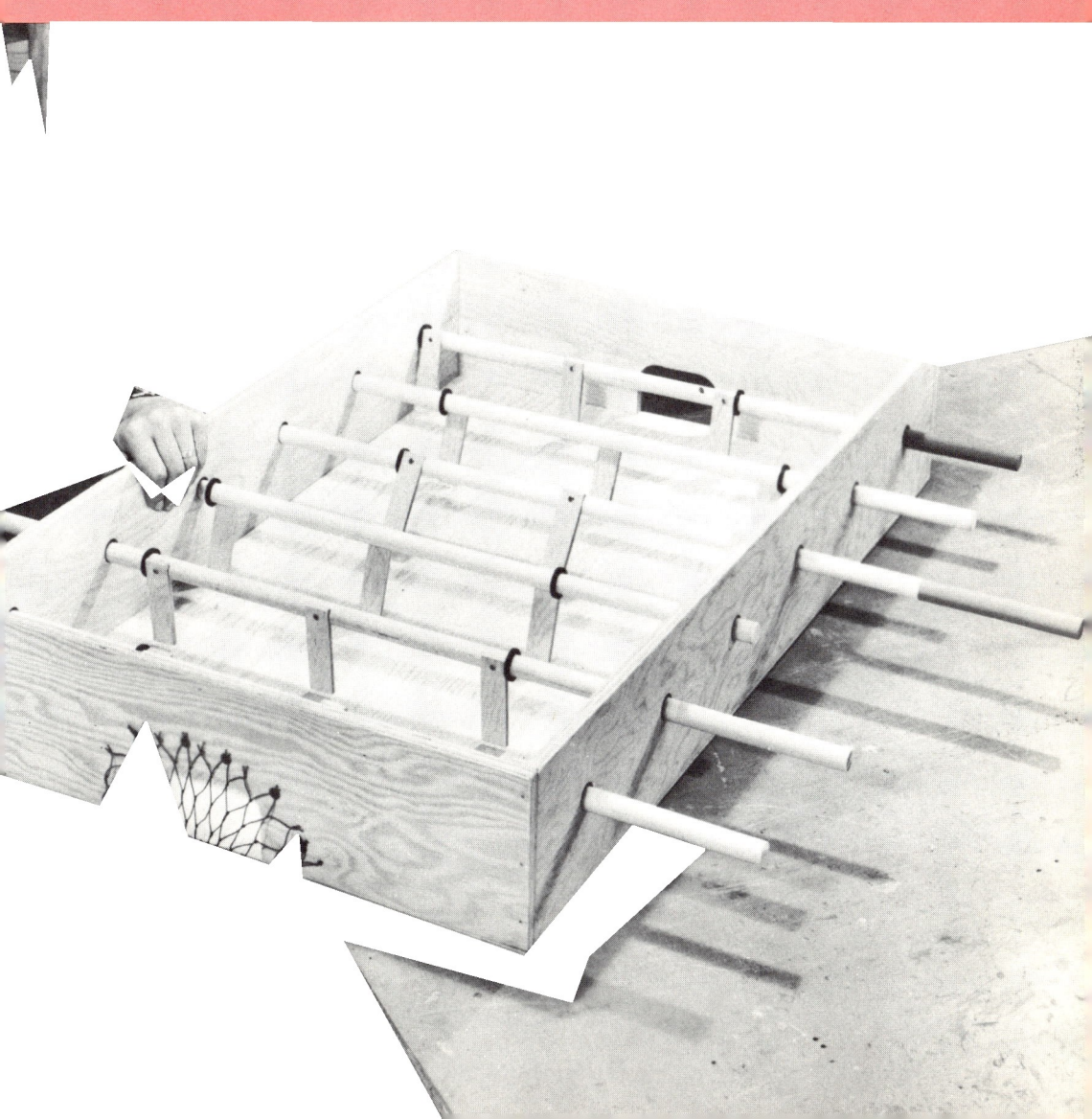

END VIEW

24"
10" — 4" — 10"
GOAL
2½"
¼"

PADDLE DETAIL

3"
3/8"
1"
¼" PLYWOOD PADDLE
PLAYING ROD
¾" DIAMETER HARDWOOD DOWEL

GARAGES

How to Build a Garage

You can add a spacious garage and breezeway to your present home.

IT TOOK exactly 32 hours to frame and sheathe this garage; two men can do the job in a weekend. If three work at it, they can take time out for a midday siesta.

The secret of the speedy construction is accurate squaring, plumbing and leveling to within $\frac{1}{16}$ in. at every stage of the operation. This enables all studs and rafters to be cut in one job lot and walls to be built on the floor—eliminating time-consuming ladder work.

Though the construction shown is for a garage and breezeway, exactly the same technique can be used in framing any addition to your house. Finishing details, such as siding and roofing, can be done as you please to suit your own situation. However, for appearance's sake, make the roof pitch conform to that of your house and line up all windows at the same level.

Garage size is a generous 14x24 ft., big enough to allow a workbench at one end; breezeway size is 6x9. Three cubic yards of concrete went into the foundation footings, 16 in. wide and 8 in. thick, poured directly into the ground just below the frost line. The slab required 4 cubic yards of concrete—a 1:2:4 mix. Cost of the entire construction was $160 for slab and cinder block foundation and $500 for lumber and other materials. Get a building permit before you start construction and be sure you comply with all local ordinances.

Pour the 4-in. concrete slab on a 6-in. bed of packed-down coarse gravel. It is advisable to cover the gravel with roofing paper before pouring, lapping it 4 in. at the edges. This seals out vapor, which can bring rust and deterioration to your car and tools, as well as to the garage structure itself. Many slabs are

GARAGES

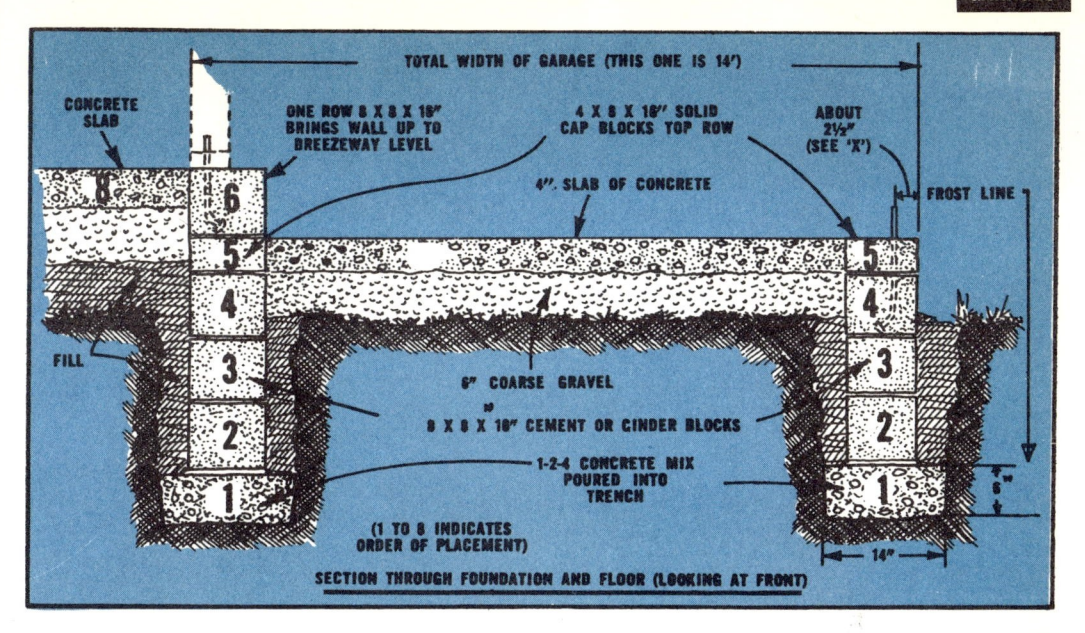

SECTION THROUGH FOUNDATION AND FLOOR (LOOKING AT FRONT)

Labels: CONCRETE SLAB; ONE ROW 8 X 8 X 16" BRINGS WALL UP TO BREEZEWAY LEVEL; TOTAL WIDTH OF GARAGE (THIS ONE IS 14'); 4 X 8 X 16" SOLID CAP BLOCKS TOP ROW; ABOUT 2½" (SEE 'X'); FROST LINE; 4" SLAB OF CONCRETE; FILL; 6" COARSE GRAVEL; 8 X 8 X 16" CEMENT OR CINDER BLOCKS; 1-2-4 CONCRETE MIX POURED INTO TRENCH; (1 TO 8 INDICATES ORDER OF PLACEMENT); 14"

The 4-in. thick concrete garage slab measures 14x24 ft.; breezeway area is 9x6 ft.

Nuts are turned down over anchor bolts in a hole drilled into the 2x4 bottom sole.

poured without reinforcement but if you are on filled ground, or you don't want to see your slab made unsightly by cracks, use a 6x6 wire mesh to strengthen it. Pull the mesh up to midpoint in the slab after pouring over it.

For drainage it is advisable to slope the slab slightly toward the entrance. Level off the concrete with a straight 2x4. Best finish is obtained with a wood float but wait until the concrete has set fairly stiff before going to work on it.

Insert three ½x10-in. anchor bolts along each side of the slab and two at the ends, placed to receive the 2x4 sole or shoe—the bottom member of the wall frame. Bolts hold the garage structure to the slab and keep the walls from getting shoved out of line by accidental bumps from the car. Select your straightest 2x4's for sole members. Brush liberally with Penta wood preservative after drilling holes for insertion of anchor bolts.

It is important that the sole be level. Check the level of each side as well as across from side to side. Wood shingles, being rot-resistant, are especially good

1417

Select straight pieces for studs. Corner studs are omitted in the above operation.

Corner posts consist of a "sandwich" made from two 2x4's, with spreaders in between.

for shimming up low places on the sole until it is all dead level.

Select straight 2x4's for the plate—the top member of each wall frame. Lay them alongside the sole members and simultaneously mark on both plate and sole the position of the 2x4 studs. Studs are spaced 16 in. from the center of one stud to the center of the next. Studs on facing walls should be located exactly opposite each other. All door and window openings are framed with doubled 2x4's set on edge. These "headers" are supported on each side by jack studs. All openings thus have both a jack and regular stud on each side.

For the outside wall, two 8-ft. 4-in. studs are cut from each 18-ft. length of 2x4. Because of grade conditions in the construction shown, the foundation wall near the house had to be higher and studs for this wall were 7-ft. 8-in., cut from 8-footers. Reserve the straightest studs for use as jacks and corner posts. Skip corner studs but attach the top plate to all others at marked positions. Angle an 8-penny nail through the side of the plate into each stud, then toenail two 16-pennies into it. It doesn't matter which of the side walls you frame first. Double the top plate of each side wall frame with a second 2x4, 3⅝ in. shorter at each end. The top plates on the end walls are 3⅝ in. longer at each end, permitting a lap joint where walls intersect.

Construct corner posts by spiking together two 2x4's, inserting as spreader blocks between them the pieces left over from cutting up the 18-foot 2x4's; corner posts thus have a thickness of three 2x4's. Place a corner post at each end of the first wall to be raised. Nail each post into position, plumbing it on two adjacent faces. Attach a brace to hold it.

Raise the first assembled wall and nail the extended ends of the top plate to corner posts. Sight along top plate to make sure there are no sags or high places. Shim up where necessary with shingles under the sole. If any studs are high, trim them down. When fit is perfect, toenail studs to the sole with 8-penny nails, placing one nail on each short face of the stud and two on each long face.

Frame the wall for the second side and raise it into place like the first wall. Do not attempt to plumb walls perfectly at this stage. Frame and raise the end wall, then the front. Make a header across the door opening of two 2x6s spiked together. The size of the door opening should conform to recommendations of the door manufacturer.

Use sheathing boards as diagonal braces to hold the walls firmly fixed after you plumb them into perfect alignment. To keep the walls from going out of plumb when the roof is put on, place braces from sidewall to sidewall across the garage. Cross the braces to form an X and nail them where they meet; three pairs of braces will do the trick.

Rafters are placed on 16-in. centers on the outside of stud positions. At every third rafter, attach a 2x4 collar beam directly over the studs. Collar beams should extend over the outside edge of the plate, equal to the distance the roof

GARAGES

When all walls are in place, use sheathing boards to brace each corner, as shown.

Attach a 2x4 collar beam at every third rafter. Follow drawing for correct dimension.

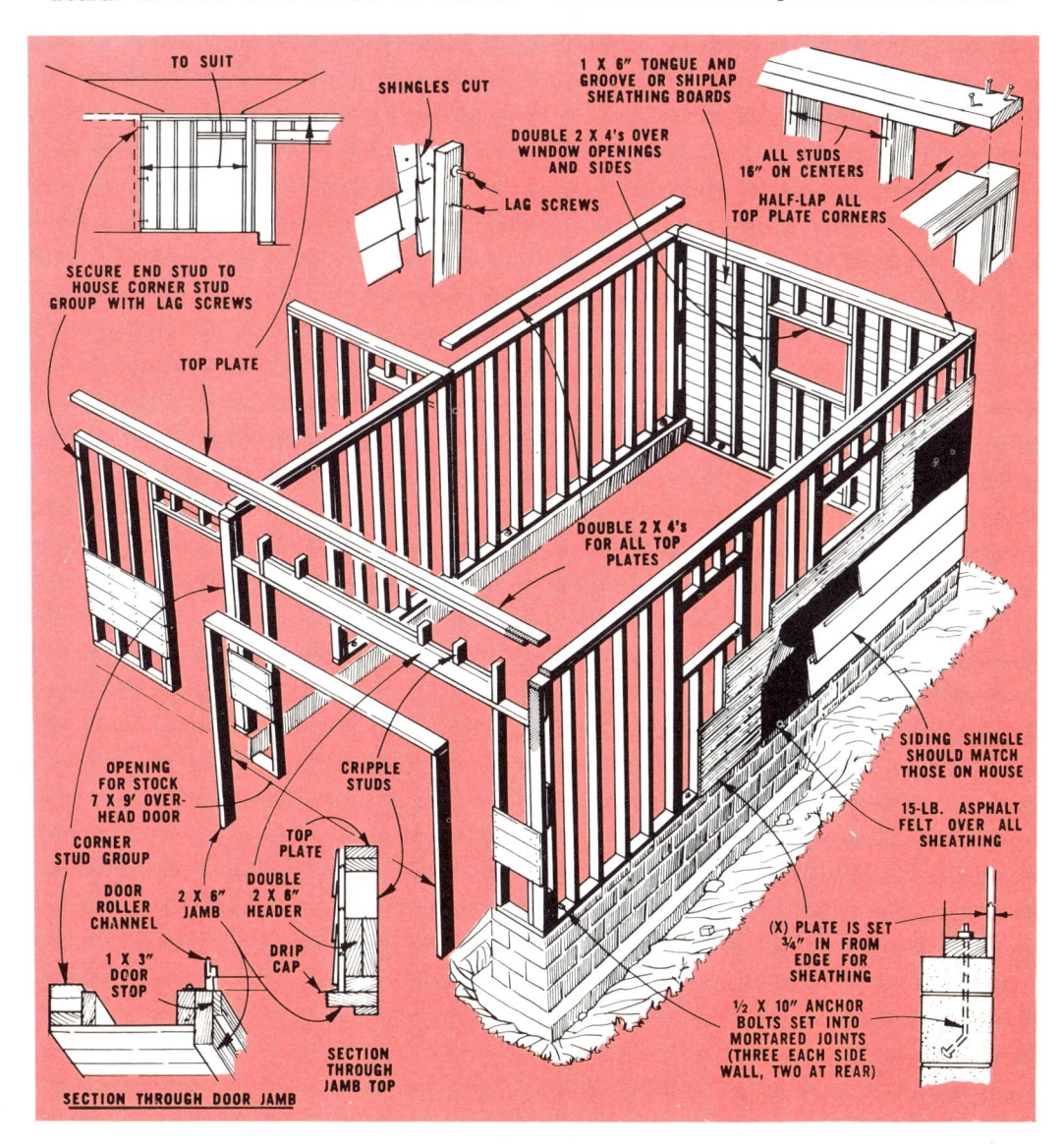

- TO SUIT
- SHINGLES CUT
- 1 X 6" TONGUE AND GROOVE OR SHIPLAP SHEATHING BOARDS
- DOUBLE 2 X 4's OVER WINDOW OPENINGS AND SIDES
- LAG SCREWS
- ALL STUDS 16" ON CENTERS
- HALF-LAP ALL TOP PLATE CORNERS
- SECURE END STUD TO HOUSE CORNER STUD GROUP WITH LAG SCREWS
- TOP PLATE
- DOUBLE 2 X 4's FOR ALL TOP PLATES
- SIDING SHINGLE SHOULD MATCH THOSE ON HOUSE
- 15-LB. ASPHALT FELT OVER ALL SHEATHING
- OPENING FOR STOCK 7 X 9' OVERHEAD DOOR
- CRIPPLE STUDS
- CORNER STUD GROUP
- TOP PLATE
- DOOR ROLLER CHANNEL
- 2 X 6" JAMB
- DOUBLE 2 X 8" HEADER
- DRIP CAP
- 1 X 3" DOOR STOP
- (X) PLATE IS SET ¾" IN FROM EDGE FOR SHEATHING
- ½ X 10" ANCHOR BOLTS SET INTO MORTARED JOINTS (THREE EACH SIDE WALL, TWO AT REAR)
- SECTION THROUGH DOOR JAMB
- SECTION THROUGH JAMB TOP

1419

Temporarily, tack ridge boards to wall and mark off studs for proper rafter placement.

The ridge board, two 12-ft. lengths of 1x6, is raised and rafters are attached, as shown.

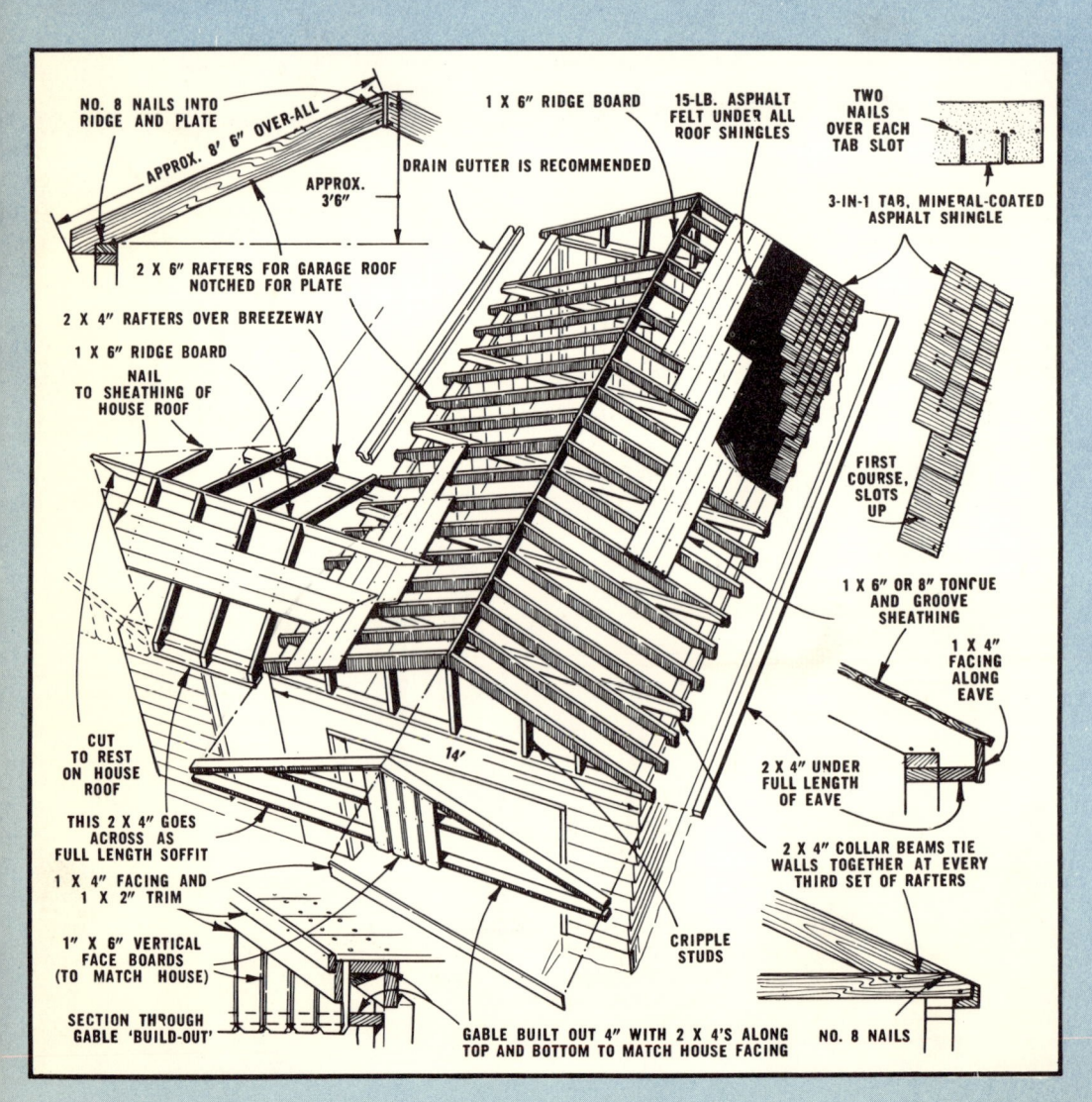

NO. 8 NAILS INTO RIDGE AND PLATE
APPROX. 8' 6" OVER-ALL
APPROX. 3' 6"
1 X 6" RIDGE BOARD
DRAIN GUTTER IS RECOMMENDED
15-LB. ASPHALT FELT UNDER ALL ROOF SHINGLES
TWO NAILS OVER EACH TAB SLOT
3-IN-1 TAB, MINERAL-COATED ASPHALT SHINGLE
2 X 6" RAFTERS FOR GARAGE ROOF NOTCHED FOR PLATE
2 X 4" RAFTERS OVER BREEZEWAY
1 X 6" RIDGE BOARD NAIL TO SHEATHING OF HOUSE ROOF
FIRST COURSE, SLOTS UP
1 X 6" OR 8" TONGUE AND GROOVE SHEATHING
1 X 4" FACING ALONG EAVE
CUT TO REST ON HOUSE ROOF
2 X 4" UNDER FULL LENGTH OF EAVE
THIS 2 X 4" GOES ACROSS AS FULL LENGTH SOFFIT
2 X 4" COLLAR BEAMS TIE WALLS TOGETHER AT EVERY THIRD SET OF RAFTERS
1 X 4" FACING AND 1 X 2" TRIM
1" X 6" VERTICAL FACE BOARDS (TO MATCH HOUSE)
CRIPPLE STUDS
SECTION THROUGH GABLE 'BUILD-OUT'
GABLE BUILT OUT 4" WITH 2 X 4'S ALONG TOP AND BOTTOM TO MATCH HOUSE FACING
NO. 8 NAILS

1420

After all rafters are in place, install the tongue-and-groove sheathing to the walls.

The roof over the breezeway is miniature version of garage roof, attaches to house.

will overhang the side walls. In this case it's the width of a 2x4.

Refer to the construction drawings on the preceding pages.

Mark and cut the 38 rafters needed for the roof. Provide a ridge board by tacking two lengths of sheathing to the side wall and marking stud positions on it. Rafters will be nailed to the outside of these positions. A plumb-cut rafter end is nailed to each end of the ridge board section. Where ridge boards meet at middle of the roof, attach a 14-in. "scab" as reinforcement for the joint.

After intermediate rafters are placed and nailed, tongue-and-groove sheathing is applied to the walls and the roof. Allow sheathing boards to extend beyond the ends of the side walls as support for a scaffold. The roof over the breezeway is a miniature version of the roof over the garage and is erected in the same way.

A 2x4 nailed to the upper edge of the front and rear rafters provides for the overhang.

Joints where roofs intersect should be covered with copper or aluminum flashing; cover the roof with felt before application of shingles. Follow roofing manufacturer's instructions for details.

Apply trim and exterior finish to the garage to conform to your house. Window and garage door installation varies according to the type selected. Here, again, follow recommendations of the manufacturer. Frequently, the door manufacturer installs his product as part of the deal, employing factory-trained experts. •—*David X. Manners*

Vertical 1x6 in. face boards decorate the front of the gable, should match your house.

View of nearly finished garage shows wall treatment. Doors, etc., can now be installed.

GARAGES

Two-car garage wing under construction. Carport may be substituted without interfering with overall design. Windows are optional. Inside wall is cement plastered after ceiling is in place.

add a GARAGE and FAMILY ROOM

The garage and family room wing is built on a concrete slab. Size can be varied to suit.

BUILDING the garage wing, which you can extend to include a family room, as we did, calls for the same construction method used in the basement foundation footings. There are a few construction problems that differ because the garage floor is a solid slab of concrete and the techniques described can serve as a basis should you plan your home on a slab.

Your garage wing should be tied into the foundation of your home, but because the footings of each are at different levels it normally would be difficult to excavate for the two footing elevations at the same time. This can be done by stepping the garage footings down until they meet with the basement footings.

Pour your footings and then prepare the garage floor area by packing about six inches of gravel or ashes on the settled earth. You can either pour the floor at this time or else wait until after the brick work is done. Whatever you do, make certain the screeds for the floor slope slightly to permit hosing out the floor.

If you plan a family room in the rear of

SLOPE FLOOR 6" TO PERMIT HOSING OUT.
GARAGE FLOOR HAS A WOOD FLOAT SURFACE
6" CONCRETE 1:2:3 FLOOR
6" GRAVEL PACKED OVER SETTLED EARTH
GARAGE FLOOR—SIDE VIEW

ROOF PLATE

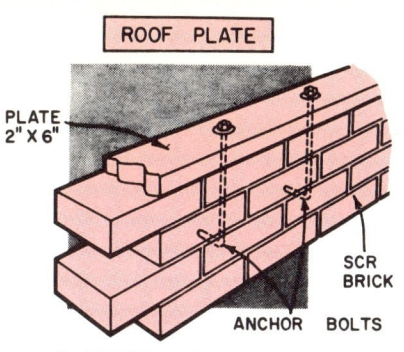

PLATE 2" X 6"

SCR BRICK

ANCHOR BOLTS

IF WINDOWS ARE TO BE USED IN GARAGE USE REGULAR BUILT-UP LINTEL. IF WALLS DO NOT HAVE WINDOWS USE ROOF PLATE SHOWN.

Heating and cooling family room is through floor registers. Sonoairduct is buried around the edge.

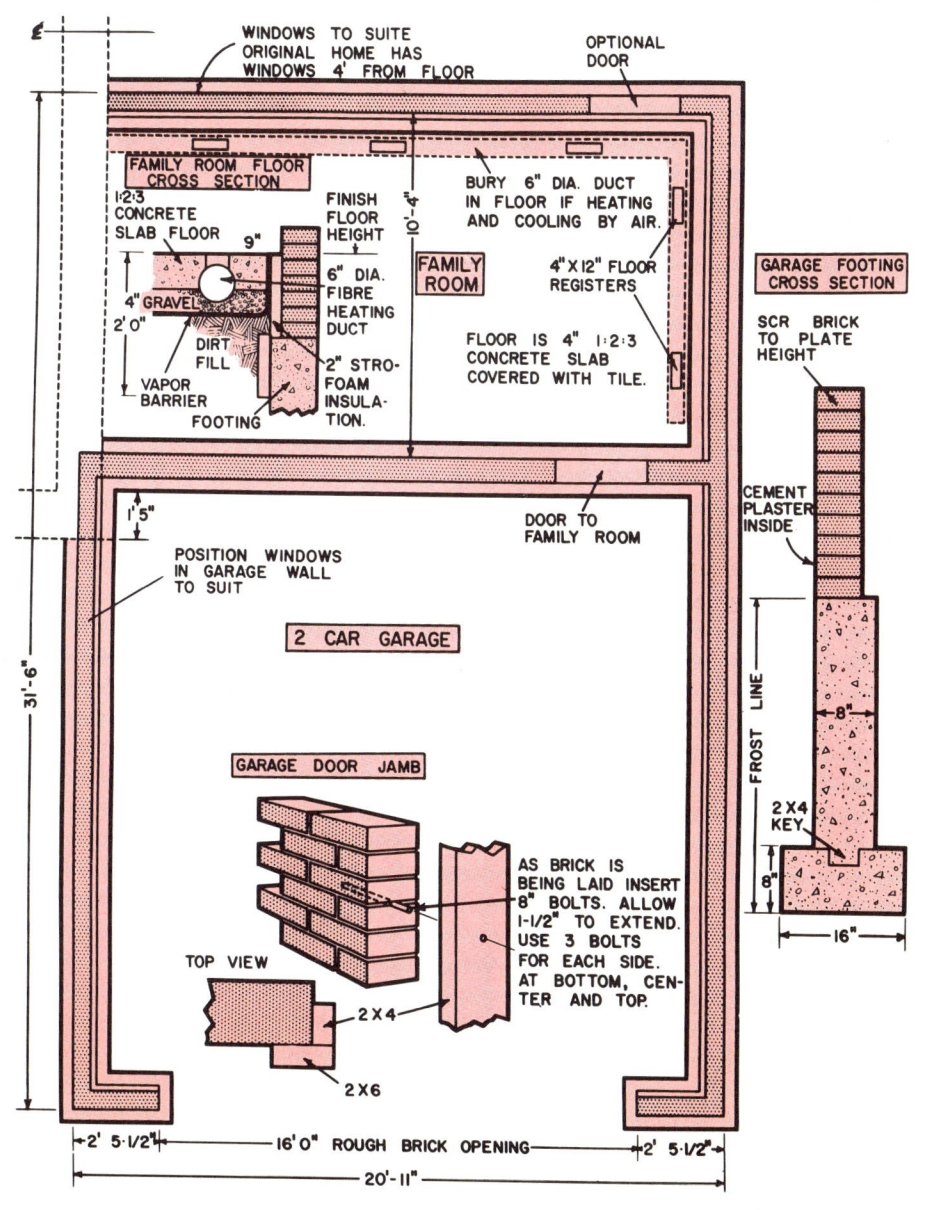

WINDOWS TO SUITE ORIGINAL HOME HAS WINDOWS 4' FROM FLOOR

OPTIONAL DOOR

FAMILY ROOM FLOOR CROSS SECTION

1:2:3 CONCRETE SLAB FLOOR

FINISH FLOOR HEIGHT

9"

4" GRAVEL

2' 0"

DIRT FILL

VAPOR BARRIER

FOOTING

6" DIA. FIBRE HEATING DUCT

2" STROFOAM INSULATION.

BURY 6" DIA. DUCT IN FLOOR IF HEATING AND COOLING BY AIR.

FAMILY ROOM

4" X 12" FLOOR REGISTERS

FLOOR IS 4" 1:2:3 CONCRETE SLAB COVERED WITH TILE.

10'-4"

GARAGE FOOTING CROSS SECTION

SCR BRICK TO PLATE HEIGHT

CEMENT PLASTER INSIDE

FROST LINE

2 X 4 KEY

8"

8"

16"

DOOR TO FAMILY ROOM

1' 5"

POSITION WINDOWS IN GARAGE WALL TO SUIT

2 CAR GARAGE

31'-6"

GARAGE DOOR JAMB

TOP VIEW

2 X 4

2 X 6

AS BRICK IS BEING LAID INSERT 8" BOLTS. ALLOW 1-1/2" TO EXTEND. USE 3 BOLTS FOR EACH SIDE. AT BOTTOM, CENTER AND TOP.

2' 5-1/2" — 16'0" ROUGH BRICK OPENING — 2' 5-1/2"

20'-11"

GARAGES

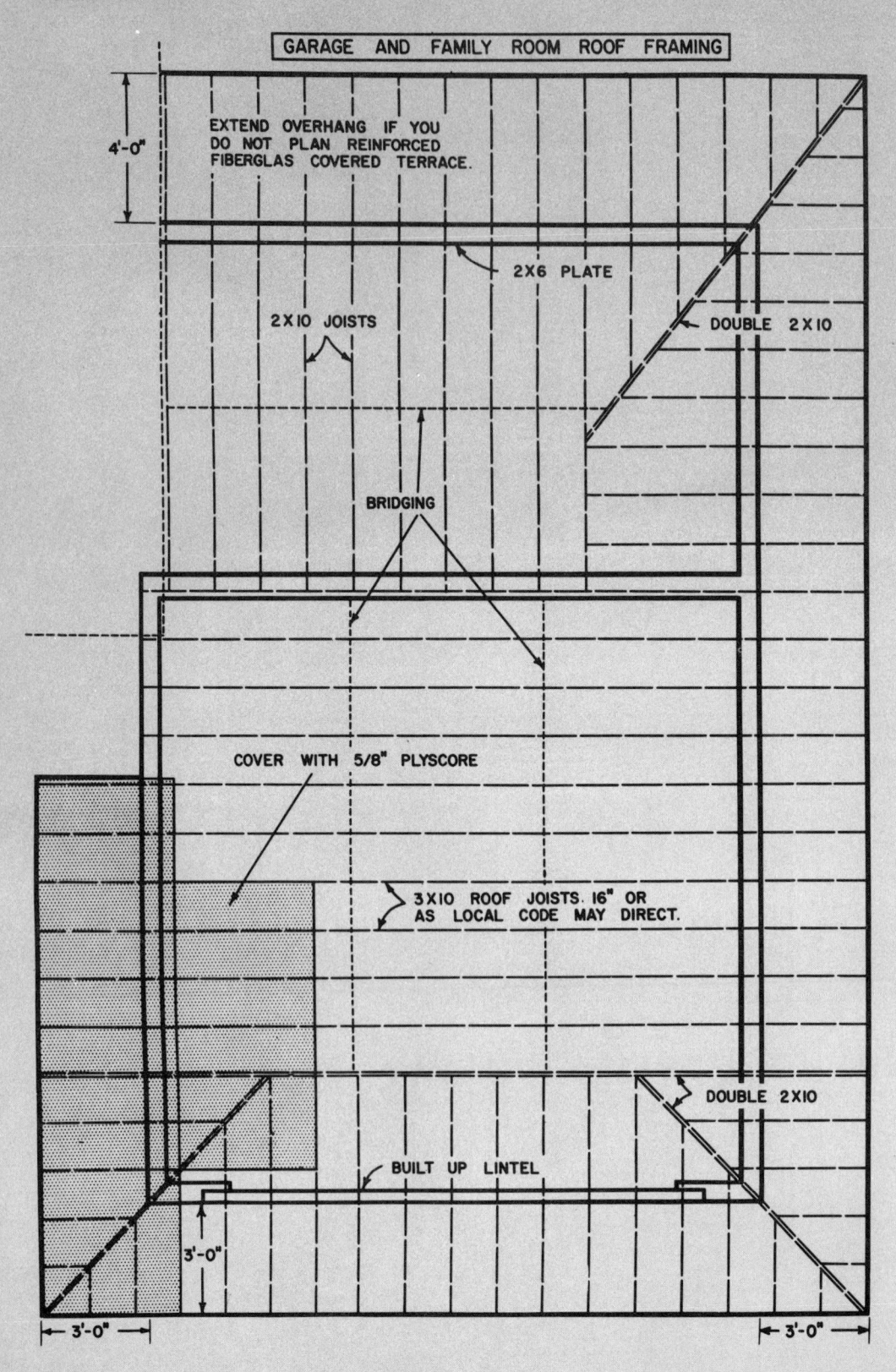

GARAGE AND FAMILY ROOM ROOF FRAMING

- 4'-0"
- EXTEND OVERHANG IF YOU DO NOT PLAN REINFORCED FIBERGLAS COVERED TERRACE.
- 2X6 PLATE
- 2X10 JOISTS
- DOUBLE 2X10
- BRIDGING
- COVER WITH 5/8" PLYSCORE
- 3X10 ROOF JOISTS. 16" OR AS LOCAL CODE MAY DIRECT.
- DOUBLE 2X10
- BUILT UP LINTEL
- 3'-0"
- 3'-0"
- 3'-0"

GARAGES

the garage, as indicated on the drawing, you will require a special floor treatment for this area. Even if you apply a wooden floor directly over the concrete you should lay a vapor barrier on the earth before your 4 inch gravel or ashes cushion is added. It is also advisable to place a 2 inch thick slab of rigid non-decaying type insulation around the outside edge.

After the insulation is in place bury the round ducts on the outside wall, if you are using a warm air heating system. If a hot water system is used your heating contractor will probably suggest burying coils directly in the slab. Finish the floor with a steel trowel so you will have a perfectly smooth surface when you lay your floor covering.

You can best divide the garage area from the family room with an 8-inch cinder block wall which, when furred out, should also be insulated. Your brickwork, which will be done at the same time as that of the home proper, should present no special problems for your masons. Just make certain the garage door opening fits the size and door you intend to use. Doors come in a multitude of sizes, types of construction and material. Some brands are sold only through franchised dealers who most always sell you an "in place" door while other brands of doors are obtainable through your local lumber dealer.

The lintel above the door is very important because if you have the slightest dip, water will collect in the low spot and spill over the facia if you have a built-in gutter. •

We made forms for footings because our frost line was 4 feet. Check frost line depth before building.

Concrete truck was backed into garage area to pour family room floor, then poured garage floor.

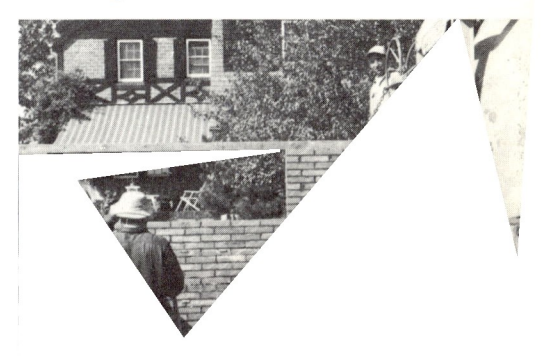

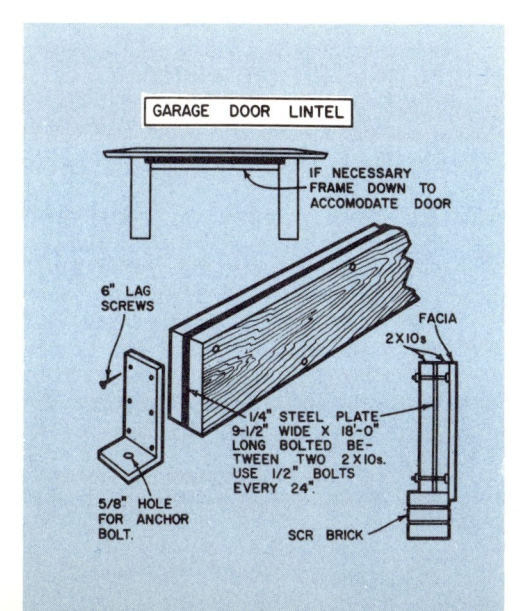

Wood floating the garage floor. Cinder block wall dividing family room from garage was built later.

GARAGES

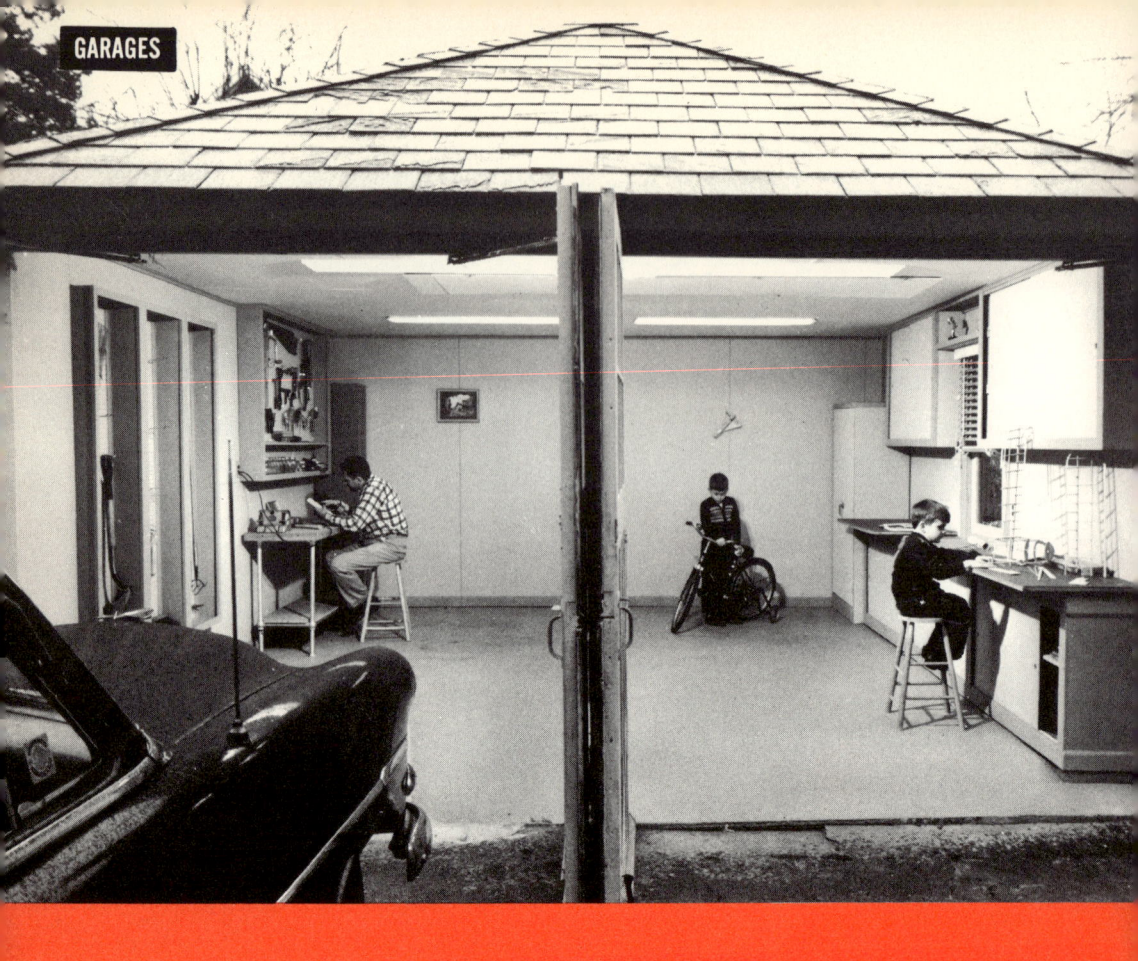

USE YOUR GARAGE

You can get more out of your garage by remodeling it to include work, hobby, game and storage space.

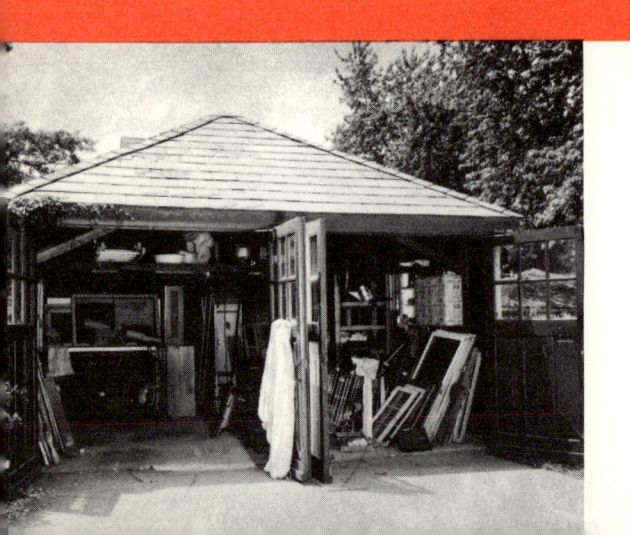

By R. J. Capotosto

IS your garage an eyesore—chock-full of haphazardly stored items—with barely enough room for the car? Then the "before" and "after" photographs on this page should inspire you to do something about it. With careful planning and a little elbow grease

BEFORE its transformation, garage was cluttered eyesore shown at left.

GARAGES

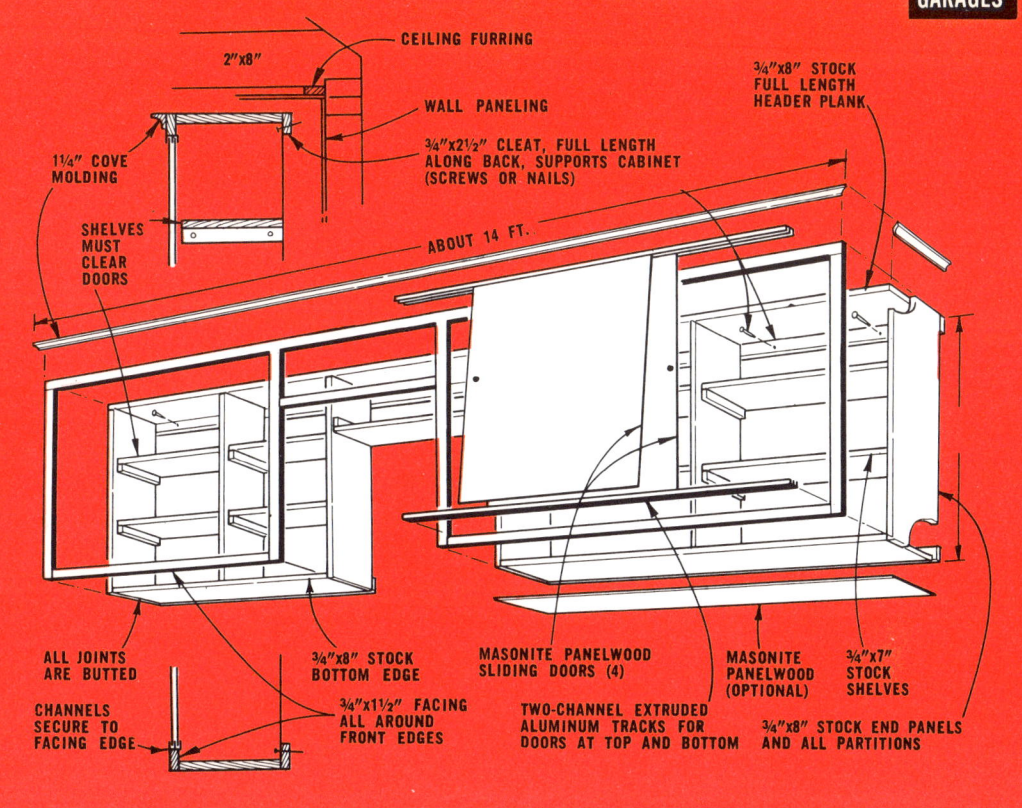

Diagram labels:
- 2"x8"
- CEILING FURRING
- WALL PANELING
- ¾"x8" STOCK FULL LENGTH HEADER PLANK
- ¾"x2½" CLEAT, FULL LENGTH ALONG BACK, SUPPORTS CABINET (SCREWS OR NAILS)
- 1¼" COVE MOLDING
- SHELVES MUST CLEAR DOORS
- ABOUT 14 FT.
- ALL JOINTS ARE BUTTED
- CHANNELS SECURE TO FACING EDGE
- ¾"x8" STOCK BOTTOM EDGE
- ¾"x1½" FACING ALL AROUND FRONT EDGES
- MASONITE PANELWOOD SLIDING DOORS (4)
- TWO-CHANNEL EXTRUDED ALUMINUM TRACKS FOR DOORS AT TOP AND BOTTOM
- MASONITE PANELWOOD (OPTIONAL)
- ¾"x7" STOCK SHELVES
- ¾"x8" STOCK END PANELS AND ALL PARTITIONS

you can utilize a great deal of space for orderly storage and also provide extra room for family activities.

The garage shown was remodeled almost entirely with Masonite Panelwood, from the ceiling to the walls and cabinets. Running 14 feet along the right wall are deep base cabinets with sliding doors; these hold frequently-used household articles, garden supplies and children's playthings and the tops serve as work, hobby or game areas. On the wall above are two shallower cabinets for storing seldom-used items. At the far end, fitted snugly into the corner, is a steel cabinet for sports and hobby equipment. The rear wall is left bare and is useful as a screen for showing movies to the neighborhood children.

The left wall of the garage is set off with a recessed peg board garden tool rack. Above a sturdy workbench is another peg board rack for workshop and car maintenance tools. A steel closet fitted with shelves to accommodate auto lubricants, paints and other miscellaneous products is neatly tucked in the corner of this wall.

Four fluorescent light fixtures are re-

AREA beneath hip roof was enclosed to form an attic for orderly storage.

CARDBOARD TEMPLATE assures accurate cut on joists.

JOISTS are secured to each rafter with half-inch bolts.

ROUGH FLOORING, nailed to joists, is sufficient in attic.

cessed in the Panelwood ceiling, affording ample illumination. They're economical, too, because all of them (eight 40-watt tubes) consume only 320 watts. Above the ceiling is a storage attic. Even though there is only 5½ feet of headroom at the center, it is remarkable how much stuff can be stored in such a seemingly small area. Access to the attic is by means of a magnesium ladder which is retractable and hidden from view by a hinged ceiling panel. With adequate wiring installed, the place leaves nothing to be desired.

You too can convert a drab garage into a cheery hobby, work and playroom in which there's still space for the buggy. The cost is relatively low and the increased value of your property is high.

Study the plans carefully, for although the dimensions of your garage will vary, the basic idea can be modified to suit. Elaborate drawings are not necessary; make simple outline sketches of the floor plan and elevations, indicating all dimensions. Then stop. Before progressing any further, consider the size of your car. Add at least one foot to the length and width and let this guide you in allocating cabinet and work space.

The following detailed account of this job, done by a non-professional in spare time, will guide you in your remodeling project:

Masonite Panelwood was chosen for

WIRING is done just before ceiling panels are installed.

BX CABLE is carried along the joist to fluorescent fixture.

FOUR SWITCHES control all lights and electrical outlets.

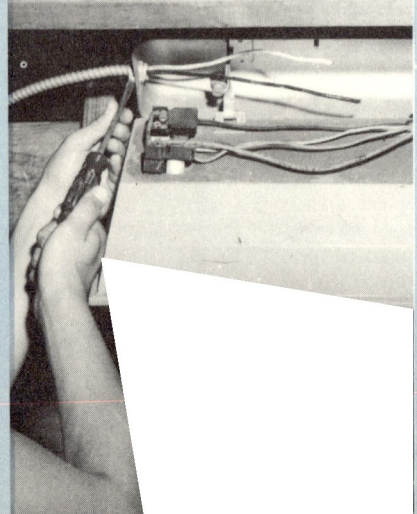

GARAGES

surfacing the walls and ceiling as well as for cabinets and table tops because of its durability and ease of fabrication. The cost was slightly higher than other materials, but its advantages more than justified the expenditure. Panelwood will take a beating and dampness or water will hardly affect it, though this doesn't mean that it is suitable for outdoor use. To effect a saving on material cost, second-hand lumber was purchased for use in framing.

Work began with the attic floor. First 2x8-in. joists, cut to fit the angle of the rafters and notched slightly at the bottom to rest on the plate, were fastened to the rafters with half-inch bolts. To span an 18-ft. length and eliminate the need for support columns in the center of the garage, braces (2x4's) were bolted between the rafters and the joists four feet from each side. This still left a ten-foot square unobstructed storage area in the center of the attic. One joist was offset from the 16-in. on center spacing in

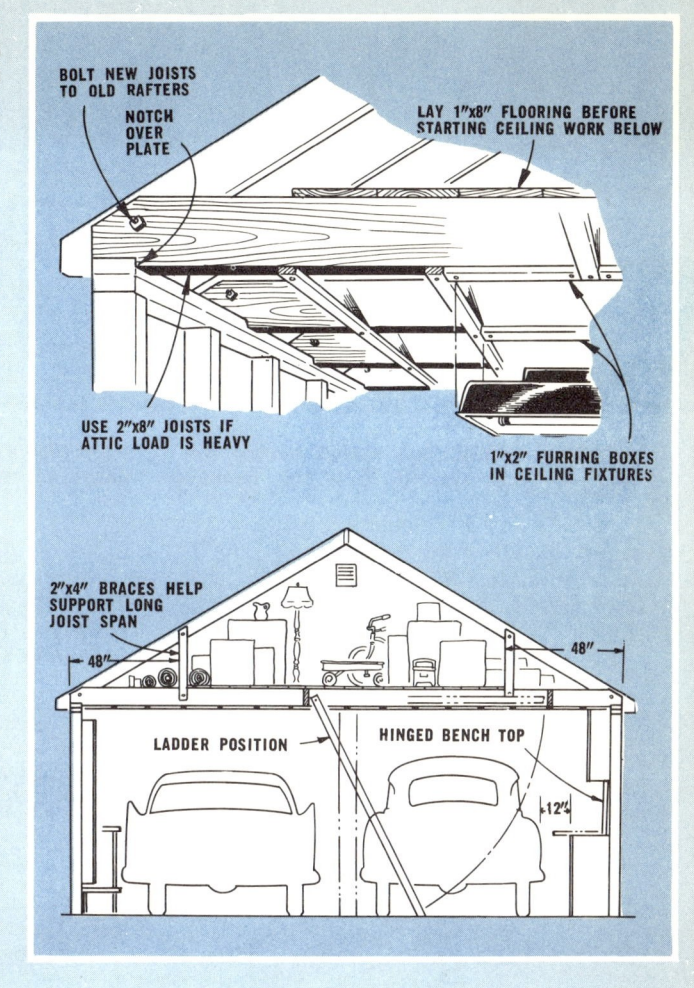

FRAMEWORK of the lower cabinet is shown completed; lap joints are used throughout.

SHELVING will be fitted into wall cabinet framework; no backing panels are used.

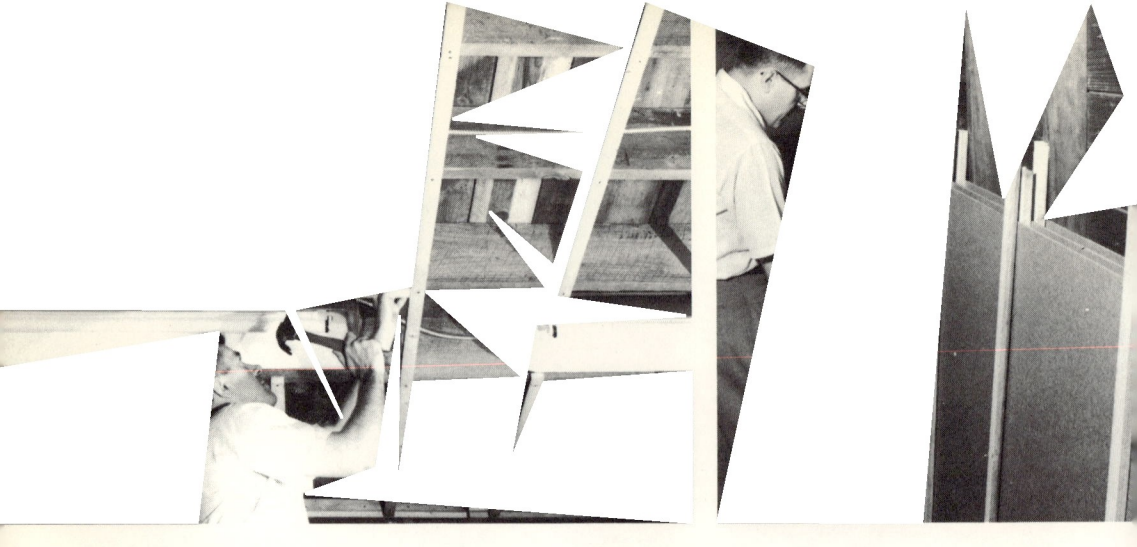

FURRING STRIPS are nailed across bottoms of joists, spaced 16 in. on centers.

PANELWOOD is stacked in garage for 24 hours so that it may adjust to humidity.

order to allow a 2x10-ft. opening to accommodate a ladder. The rough attic floor, consisting of ¾x8-in. pine, was then nailed in.

Electric wiring was next. The existing wiring was old and insufficient so it was ripped out up to the junction box. Then No. 12 BX cable was connected from the junction box to four Pass & Seymour Despard switches, one to con-

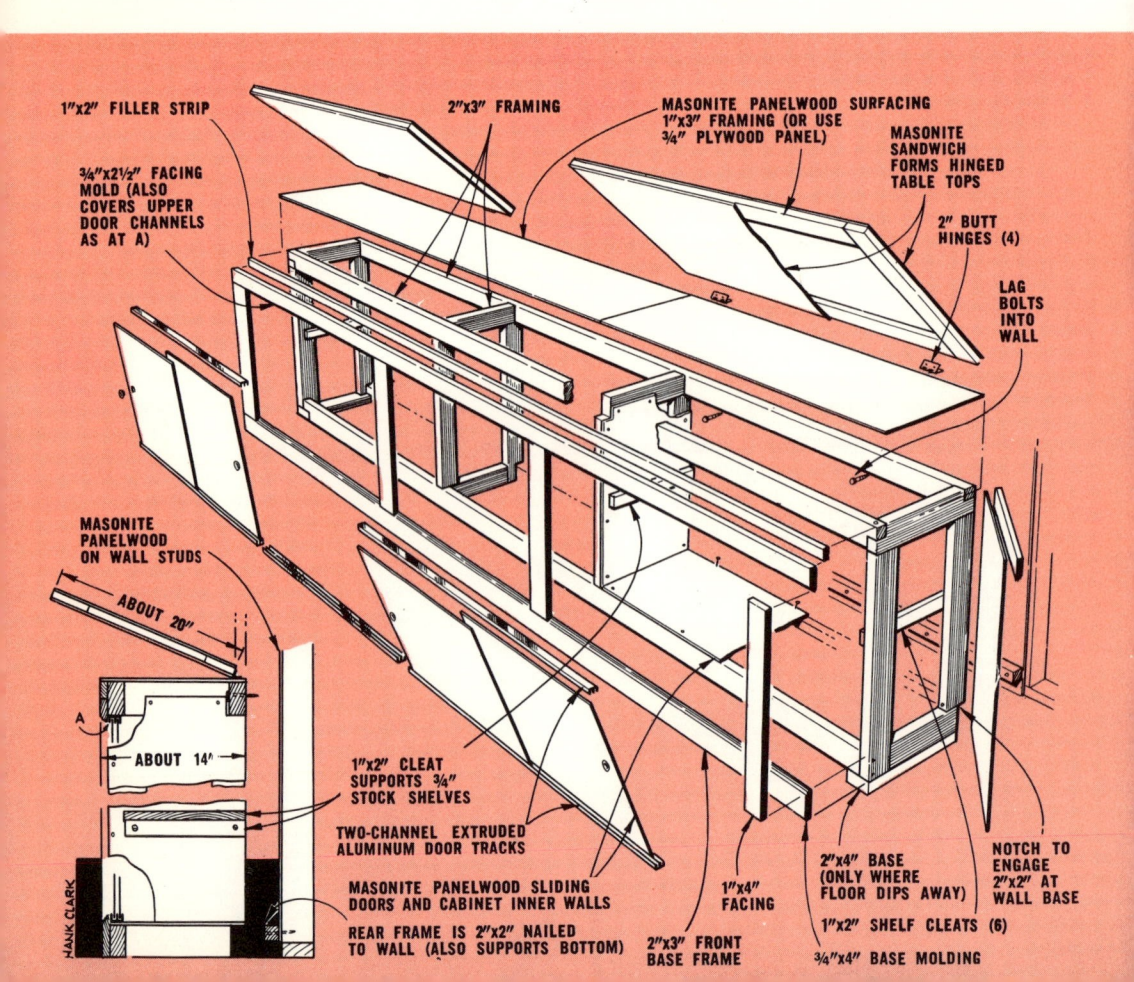

SAWED EDGE of a panel is sanded. Panelwood works easily with woodworking tools.

BRACES hold ceiling panel in place until measurements for a lamp cutout are taken.

trol the attic light, two for the fluorescent fixtures and one for the outlets. The reason for switching the outlets is to prevent the possibility of accident to the small fry when they are left unattended. The double 40-watt fluorescent fixtures were arranged so that left or right bank could be used independently. Where possible, the BX cable was run in the space between the plate and the

ABOVE, pattern of opening for lamp is traced onto the panel with carbon paper under drawing. Below, section is sawed out when the ceiling panels have been put up.

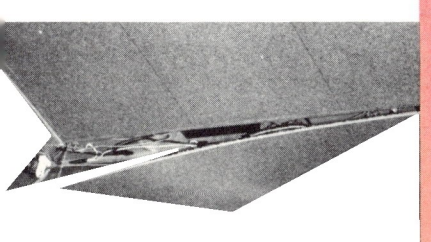

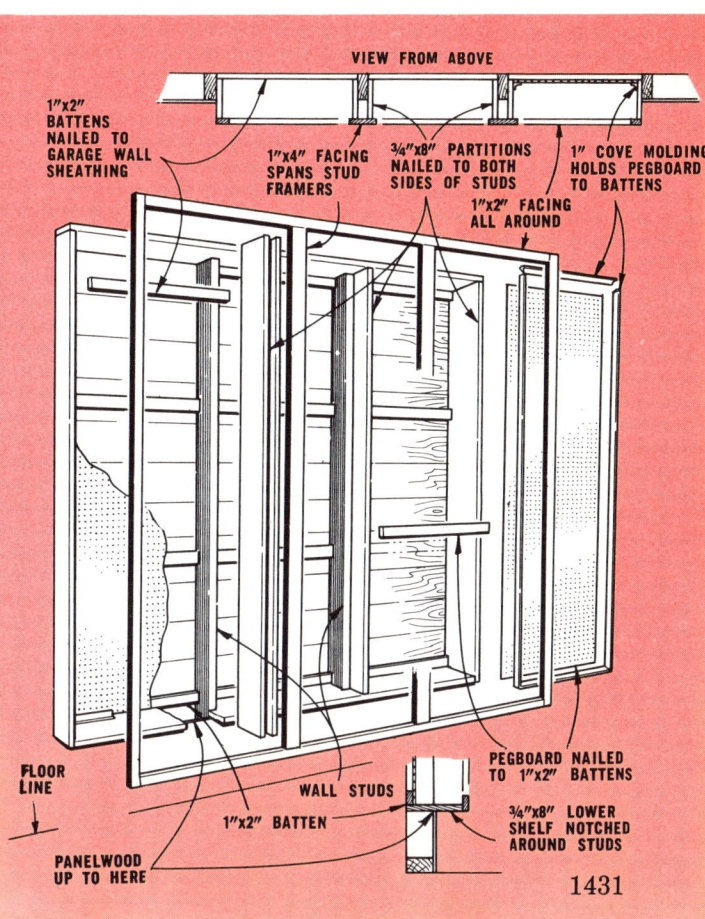

VIEW FROM ABOVE

1"x2" BATTENS NAILED TO GARAGE WALL SHEATHING

1"x4" FACING SPANS STUD FRAMERS

3/4"x8" PARTITIONS NAILED TO BOTH SIDES OF STUDS

1" COVE MOLDING HOLDS PEGBOARD TO BATTENS

1"x2" FACING ALL AROUND

FLOOR LINE

WALL STUDS

1"x2" BATTEN

PANELWOOD UP TO HERE

PEGBOARD NAILED TO 1"x2" BATTENS

3/4"x8" LOWER SHELF NOTCHED AROUND STUDS

1431

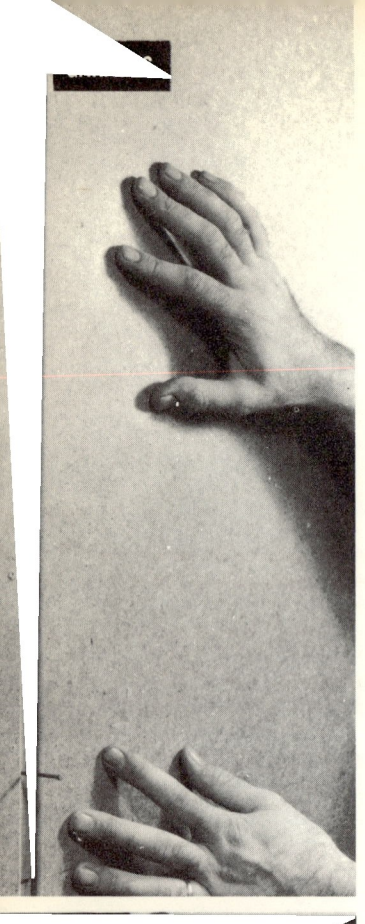

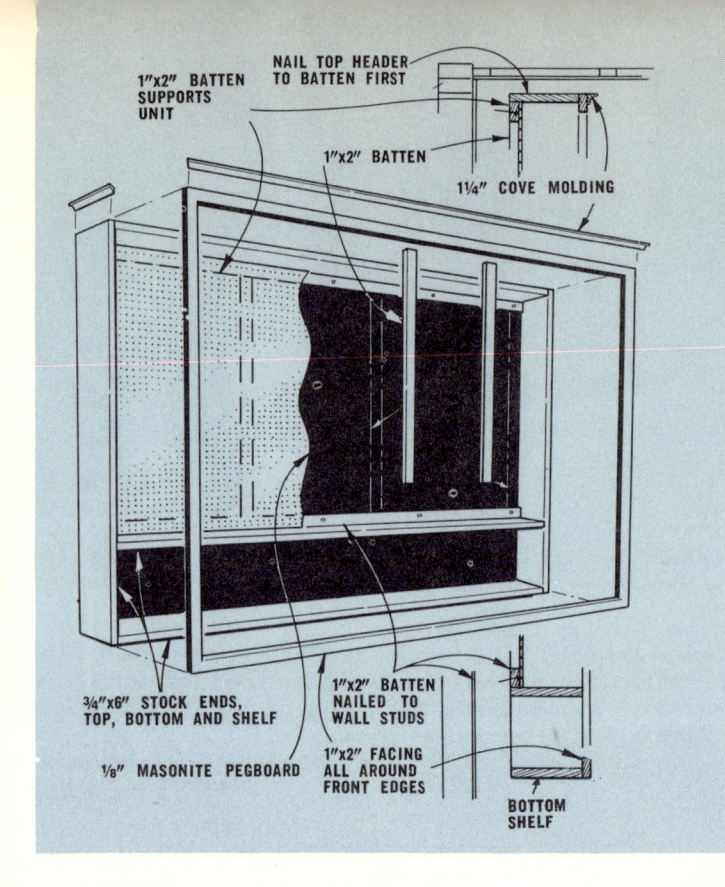

NAIL TOP HEADER TO BATTEN FIRST
1"x2" BATTEN SUPPORTS UNIT
1"x2" BATTEN
1¼" COVE MOLDING
¾"x6" STOCK ENDS, TOP, BOTTOM AND SHELF
⅛" MASONITE PEGBOARD
1"x2" BATTEN NAILED TO WALL STUDS
1"x2" FACING ALL AROUND FRONT EDGES
BOTTOM SHELF

JOINT TREATMENT (top left) calls for a slight gap between panels; nails serve as spacing guide.

CABINET TOP (left) is installed after wall panels have been nailed flush against the framework.

INEXPENSIVE LUMBER in cabinets (bottom left) is covered with panels for a smooth, neat finish.

CLEATS (below) support the deep shelves in the cabinets; they're screwed to the upright members.

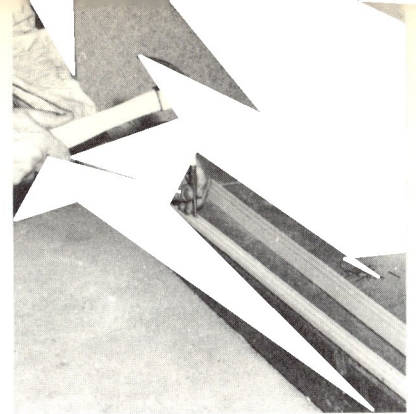

TRACK for sliding doors (above) is glued and nailed to the bottom shelf of a cabinet; it's plastic. An area of the wall is framed in (above right) for use as a tool rack. Peg board (right) is then installed to take the brackets which hold the tools.

joists, otherwise notches or holes were made in the studs. A 15-amp fuse protects the circuit, but use of No. 12 wire permits substitution of a 25-amp fuse if an electric heater is installed in the winter.

Two Despard outlets and a pilot light were installed near the workbench.

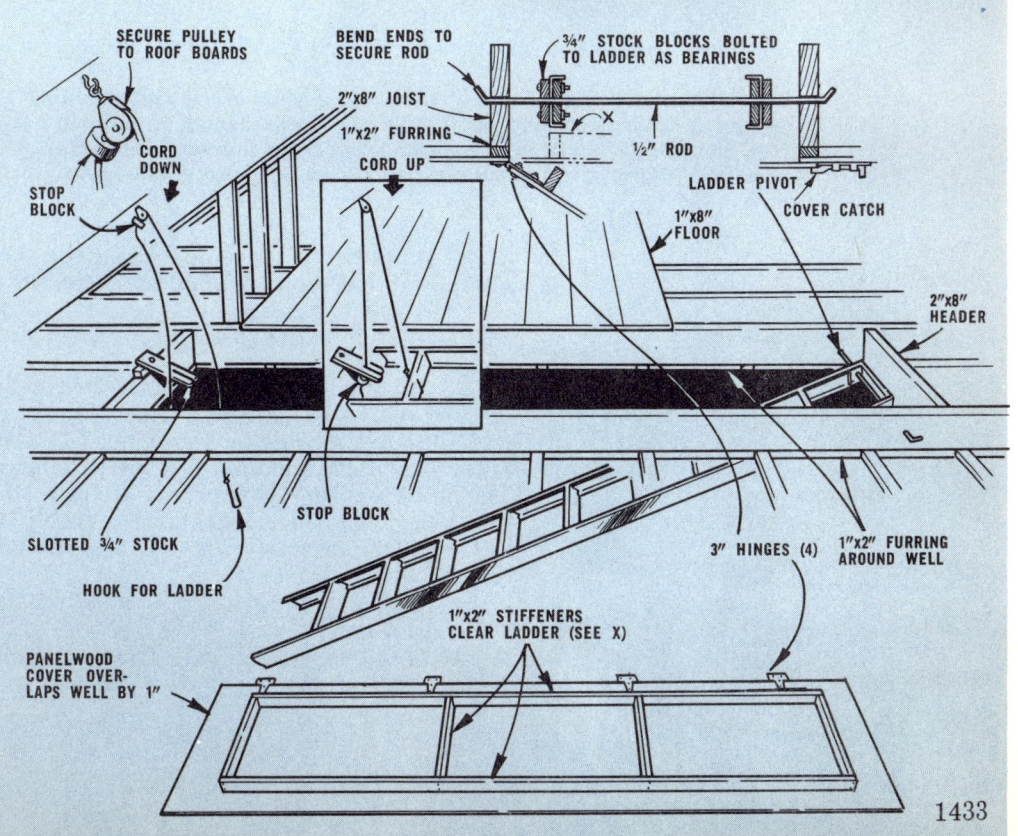

1433

LADDER is quickly lowered. Knob on cord (left) is released from slotted catch and rides up until it stops at the pulley, at which point ladder is low enough to be reached and unhooked. Pivot is a steel rod (center). A hinged ceiling panel (right) covers opening.

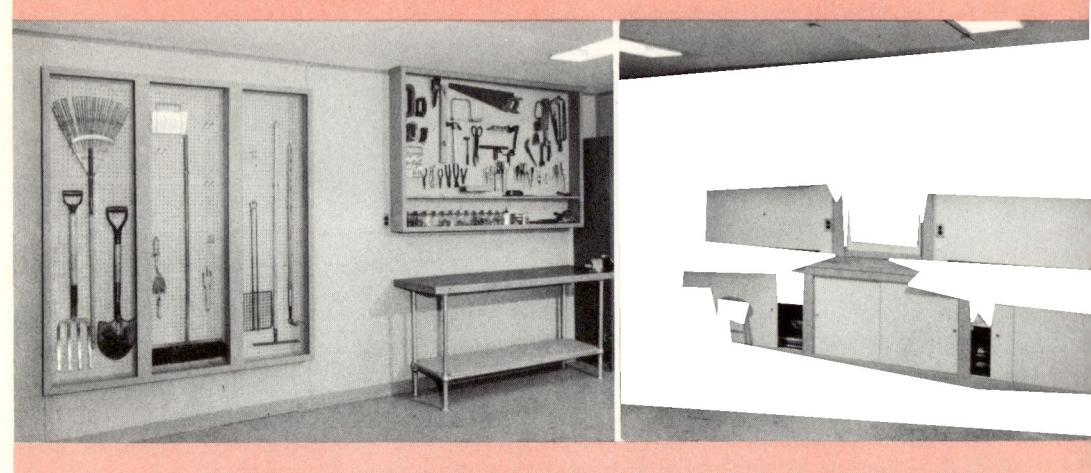

LEFT AND RIGHT WALLS of the remodeled garage are shown above. Gardening implements and other tools are stored neatly on the peg board panels; more storage space is provided in the wall and base cabinets; working areas include a bench and the base cabinet tops.

These units are very compact and the three fit a standard deep box. The pilot indicates that the outlet is hot and serves as a reminder when a soldering iron, battery charger, or some such implement is in use.

The base cabinets were framed with 2x4-in. lumber nailed as an integral part of the studs, while the framework for the upper cabinets was built as a separate unit for easier fabrication. The latter was then temporarily screwed through the upper and lower back braces into the studs. Later, when the walls were ready for covering, this cabinet was removed to permit the walls to be surfaced with sections of Panelwood.

WORKING on the car can be a pleasure if you have a bench and all the necessary tools right at hand.

FINAL STEP consists of giving the concrete floor two coats of silver grey enamel paint.

Prior to surfacing the walls and ceiling, the Panelwood was brought in and stacked for 24 hours so that it might adjust to the humidity conditions. This is best done by separating each sheet with a series of wood strips to allow free circulation.

The next operation consisted of nailing furring strips to the ceiling joists. Spaced 16 in. on centers, the furring was run lengthwise across the joists and boxed in only where a joint in the panels would occur and around the openings for the lighting fixtures.

It is worth noting how a little trick in the planning stake paid off. Since Panelwood is supplied in stock sizes of 4x8 ft., 4x10 ft. and 4x12 ft., the necessity of cutting panels was kept to a minimum by carefully positioning the opening for the ladder between the joists. Thus, with the opening for the ladder being 24 in. wide, four 12-ft. panels could be fitted in whole over a big section of ceiling.

Surfacing the ceiling was an easy job with the aid of two large T braces. Each was made by nailing a crosspiece to the end of a board slightly longer than the distance between the floor and ceiling. Wedged between the floor and a panel, they served to hold the panel securely in place while it was measured and cut for lamp openings and, most important, while it was being nailed.

A neat trick for obtaining an evenly spaced expansion joint between panels is to drive several two-inch finishing nails partly into the furring alongside a panel. The next panel is merely pushed up flush against these protruding nails and nailed into place, thus leaving the necessary $\frac{1}{16}$-in. spacing between panels.

In nailing the wall and ceiling panels, 1½-in. finishing nails were used, starting at the center and working out to prevent bulging. Recommended procedure calls for nails spaced six inches apart on intermediate supports and four inches apart around the edges. To simplify this task in working on the walls, a plumb line with small strings knotted four inches apart was hung from the top of a panel in position over a stud. A similar arrangement was used for the six-inch spacing. All nails were countersunk, puttied and sanded.

As mentioned previously, all cabinets were framed with old wood. These were subsequently partitioned and covered with Panelwood. Extruded plastic sliding door tracks were installed to accommodate Panelwood sliding doors. Two laminated table tops composed of a ¾-in. plywood core sandwiched between two pieces of Tempered Masonite were hinged to the cabinet top, one on each side of the window. The hinging was necessary to allow clearance for parking a second car. The addition of trim and molding completed the cabinets.

Both the garden and tool racks were framed with ¾x8-in. pine backed with peg board panels. Nailing the peg board to a framing of furring strip left ample backspace for manipulation of the fixtures. To finish off the interior, 1½-in. cove molding was run along all corners along with four-inch baseboard at the floor.

To adapt a 10-ft. magnesium straight ladder for access to the attic, a simple modification was necessary. Two three-inch square, ¾-in. maple plywood blocks were bolted to each side of the frame two inches from the top to reinforce it for installation of a half-inch steel rod. Threaded on both ends, this rod was bolted on each side of the joists, thus enabling the ladder to be pivoted. At the far end, a wire hook attached to a nylon cord passes through a pulley suspended from the attic ceiling. When the attic door is opened, this cord is within reach. Releasing the cord from a simple wooden catch allows the ladder to drop within reach. Release of the wire hook then makes it possible to lower the ladder to the floor. •

Garden Caddy

Tools and garden supplies can be within reach, when and where you want them, with this mobile rack.

PARTS SCHEDULE

CODE	NO. REQ'D	SIZE	PART IDENTIFICATION
A	2	31⅞"x48"	Side
B	1	16"x31⅞"	Shelf
C	1	31⅞"x31⅞"	Bottom
	12 Lin. Ft.	1"x4"	Tool Brackets
	18 Lin. Ft.	1"x2"	Edging
	5 Lin. Ft.	2"x4"	Axle Block
	4 Ea.	5" Diameter	Rubber-Tired Wheels
	2 Ea.	28" Long	Steel Axles
	4 Ea.	3"x3"	Angle Braces
	1 Ea.	½" Diameter	Axle Bolt
	10 Lin. Ft.	⅜" Diameter	Rope

Miscellaneous—6d Finish and 8d Common Nails (Galvanized)
Waterproof Glue
Screws, Staples and Washers as required

YOU'LL save yourself many, many trips between garden and tool house if you have this gardener's caddy to carry equipment, plant food, insect spray and other necessities. Roomy shelves hold flats and pots, so you also save heavy lifting.

All parts are easy to cut on a table saw. Bevel both ends of panels "A" and sides of shelf "B" to 16½ degrees. Use only plywood made with 100 per cent waterproof glue (EXT-DFPA). Join all parts with 6d galvanized finish nails and waterproof glue.

Nail the tool brackets on sides "A." (Note that the top brackets—cut from 1x4—are made with 1½-inch holes drilled before cutting, while the bottom brackets use 1¾-inch holes.) Attach a 1x2-inch cap strip to the top edge of one side, then—with sides resting on the long edge—nail the cap strip and other side together. With the sides still forming an arrowhead on the floor, nail through bottom "C" into the sides, position the shelf and nail in place. Apply mitered 1x2-inch edging around the base, install axle blocks, finish, and attach wheels or casters. •

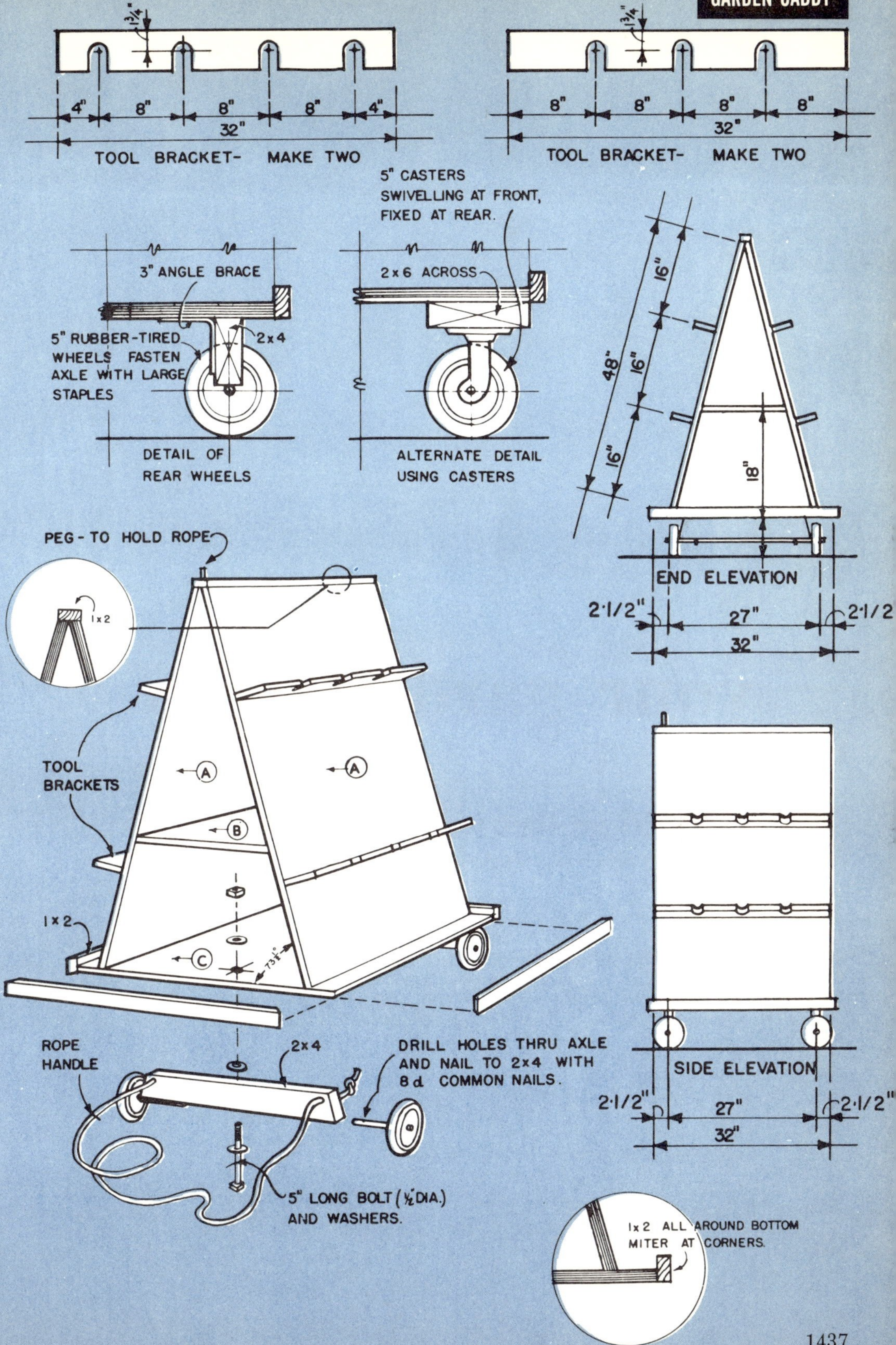
1¾"
4"
8"
8"
8"
4"
32"
TOOL BRACKET- MAKE TWO
1¾"
8"
8"
8"
8"
32"
TOOL BRACKET- MAKE TWO
5" CASTERS SWIVELLING AT FRONT, FIXED AT REAR.
3" ANGLE BRACE
5" RUBBER-TIRED WHEELS FASTEN AXLE WITH LARGE STAPLES
2x4
DETAIL OF REAR WHEELS
2x6 ACROSS
ALTERNATE DETAIL USING CASTERS
16"
16"
16"
48"
18"
END ELEVATION
2·1/2"
27"
2·1/2
32"
PEG-TO HOLD ROPE
1x2
TOOL BRACKETS
A
A
B
C
1x2
73½°
ROPE HANDLE
2x4
DRILL HOLES THRU AXLE AND NAIL TO 2x4 WITH 8d COMMON NAILS.
5" LONG BOLT (½" DIA.) AND WASHERS.
SIDE ELEVATION
2·1/2"
27"
2·1/2"
32"
1x2 ALL AROUND BOTTOM MITER AT CORNERS.

your garden plan

BY T. H. Everett

Whether you expect to remake an old garden or start a new one, make a plan before you plant.

IN creating a new garden, no matter how small it is to be, plan it first on paper and draw it to scale. But before you put pencil to paper do some serious thinking. Familiarize yourself with the area. Carefully consider its possibilities—and its limitations. No use trying to grow waterlilies in shade or rhododendrons on outcrops of limestone. Consider also the purposes you wish your home grounds to serve. Ordinarily you will need a service area to accommodate a laundry yard, delivery entrance and perhaps a separate garage or toolshed. This service area should be screened by shrubbery, hedge or maybe a vine-covered trellis.

The front yard is usually somewhat public, largely visible from the street. It should contribute its part to the beauty and landscaped effect of the community. Nothing is better than a well kept lawn as a main front feature. Appropriately placed shade trees and discreetly located shrubbery may frame the house and lot. Boundary hedges are often advantageous. A foundation planting that weds the house to the ground completes the picture.

Let restraint be the keynote. Plant too little rather than too much. Above all do not spot single bushes, trees, or flower beds indiscriminately on the lawn. Such treatment produces a confused landscape.

Avoid using too many different types of plants in the foundation planting. Be particularly wary of highly colored evergreens such as golden arborvitaes, blue spruces and the like. They do not blend well. Gazing-globes, sun-dials, statues and similar ornaments are out of place in the front yard.

1438

EACH SQUARE EQUALS 5 FEET

GARDENING

KEY TO DIAGRAM
A. hemlock or yew
B. flowering shrubs
C. berried shrubs
D. dogwood tree
E. evergreens
F. yew or hemlock hedge
G. magnolia tree
H. rhododendrons
I. flower border
J. climbing roses on trellis
K. grape on trellis
L. vegetables, herb and cut flowers
M. flowering crab apple tree
N. lilac
O. yew

Using graph paper to help scale your grounds, lay out your garden plan before planting.

The location of the driveway and of the path to the front door must be carefully considered. On a narrow lot place the driveway at one side and let the pathway branch from it near the house. A front lawn divided by a central path appears narrower than it really is.

The back garden is normally the private area—the part that you use for outdoor living. Screen it discreetly to assure reasonable privacy and to block undesirable views. A fairly spacious lawn near the house is most often desirable. This lawn should be defined in some way—by hedge, or fence or shrubbery. An open area that is not limited fails to provide a sense of enclosure and a desirable outdoor living-room effect.

You will use the back lawn for sitting and for sun bathing and for eating outdoors. A shade tree or two there will be appreciated. Flower borders may be located at its margins. A sundial, seat, statue, fountain or pool can often be placed to provide a center of interest.

The back lawn should be an outdoor extension of the interior of the home approached via a porch or terrace from the living room if possible. On larger lots the private part of the garden includes not only the outdoor living room but areas that extend beyond it to the rear and to the side of the house. These may include a rose, rock, herb, cut-flower, vegetable or other special garden as well as naturally landscaped areas.

The problems you face as a designer is to tie all parts of your home grounds into one satisfying, congruous whole, and to appropriately define its boundaries. Simplicity, livability, and ease of maintenance are points to bear in mind. Avoid the common error of setting out too many trees, shrubs and evergreens in too small areas. A few fairly sizable items may be very much more effective, not more expensive, and if well placed will not become spoiled by crowding as the years pass.

But first plan your new garden on paper. It is easier to correct mistakes there than on the ground. Graph paper ruled in small squares is useful for the purpose.

Renovating an Old Garden. If you are inexperienced and have to renovate an old garden, the task may seem to be more formidable than that of creating a new garden. But wait a minute. Maybe there is more to be salvaged than you think. In the old garden, over-crowded and long neglected though it may be, there are probably some well established trees and shrubs which, if given a reasonable chance, will become prized features. And among the tangle of weeds and overgrown shrubbery you may find perennials of various kinds that have persisted through the years of neglect and need only reasonable care to induce them to bloom freely. Bulbs of daffodils, lilies and other hardy kinds may be in the ground without, perhaps, their leaves showing at the time you view the garden. The lawn, possibly, is capable of responding to treatment less drastic than expensive remaking. An old, overgrown garden is a challenge. Meet it squarely. It can give you as much fun as making over an old house.

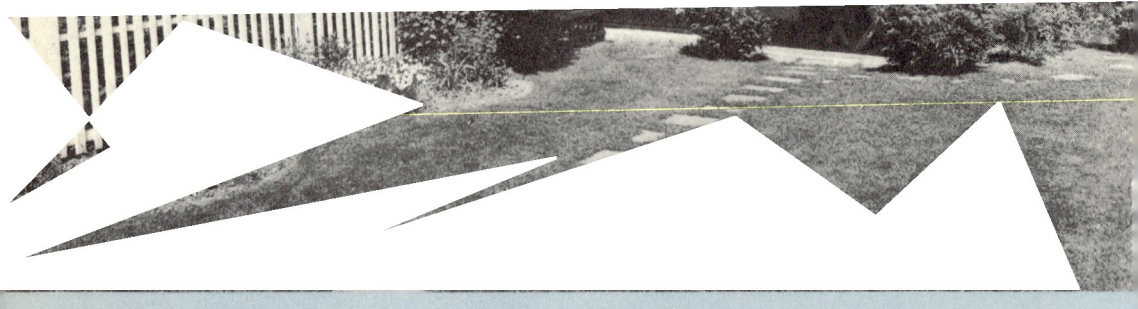

The first need of the garden renovator is patience. You cannot do it all at once. You must get to know what plants are in the garden before you discard any, and this may mean living with it through a season. Even the most experienced cannot distinguish choice lilacs from poorer kinds.

better varieties of day-lilies from semi-wild ones, or worthwhile chrysanthemums from worthless ones by examining the foliage alone. To evaluate these and many other flowers it is necessary to see them in bloom. And this probably involves waiting.

However, you need not be idle. There are surely some things that you can do right away in any neglected garden. The cleaning away of weeds, the cutting out of unwanted material and preliminary pruning, for instance. Cut out only those trees, shrubs and vines that you are certain you do not want: straggly, bare-at-the-bottom evergreens of kinds that will not respond to pruning for instance, and specimens so badly placed that you must remove them, but which you cannot, or do not want, to transplant.

Preliminary pruning must also be done cautiously if you do not know the plants. Dead branches may be cut out. Trees and

GOOD PLANNING

Bear in mind that the shrubs and trees you plant will take up more and more space as they grow.

Properly laid out, your front lawn will be neat and trim ten years later—not crowded looking.

shrubs may be moderately thinned that are obviously over-crowded. But avoid any general "butchering." An urge for tidiness may result in irreparable harm to valuable specimens.

The really important thing is to get to know what kinds of plants you have. Some you may recognize. Others may be identified for you by experienced gardeners. In still other cases it may be necessary to send samples for identification to a botanical garden or to your State Agricultural Experiment Station. Once you know what the plants in your garden are you can proceed intelligently. Each can be treated according to its needs. When renovating a garden consider basic design just as you do when making a new garden. If alteration is needed try to retain or adapt the best features of the present layout.

Pruning based on a knowledge of the plants and their needs will require attention. In some cases you may prune severely. Straggly hedges of privet or barberry may be cut nearly to the ground. Old, gangling lilacs likewise. Overgrown shrubs of many kinds may be severely thinned. Some other trees and shrubs are better if left unpruned. Read the chapter on pruning before you tackle the job.

Look the old garden over for the presence of blights and pests, black spots on roses and scale insects on euonymus, for example. Take suitable steps to bring these under control.

I have found it a good plan when making over old gardens to establish nursery areas. Into these I transplant temporarily plants or divisions of plants that cannot at the time be set in their permanent places. They grow into shapely specimens and a few months or a year later, when their permanent places are ready, they are available for re-planting. •

POOR PLANNING

A common error in landscaping a lawn is to set out too many shrubs and trees in a small area.

Thus, when the plants mature, they present an overgrown appearance and are hard to care for.

GARDENING

Photos by New York Botanical Garden

GARDEN SOILS

It's not just dirt under your feet—it's a wonderful substance that deserves the best care and attention you can give to it.

AN adequate depth of fertile soil in good condition is the basis of practically all gardening. Without it the plants you grow will be less vigorous and less healthy than they should be. Do your utmost to provide the best soil, to maintain fertility.

Nearly all soils can be improved tremendously by intelligent management. Treatments employed to do this include draining, loosening and turning, adding humus, fertilizing and liming.

Draining. Roots need air as well as moisture. Plants that grow naturally in ponds and bogs obtain air from the water in which they grow. Most plants cannot do this. Their roots rot and die if they are immersed for long. That is why sub-surface drainage of the soil is important.

If you suspect your soil is water-logged or poorly drained, dig test holes (each two feet square and two feet deep) here and there, build a ridge of soil around each to prevent surface water draining in and cover with a watertight cover. If free water stands in the holes closer than two feet to

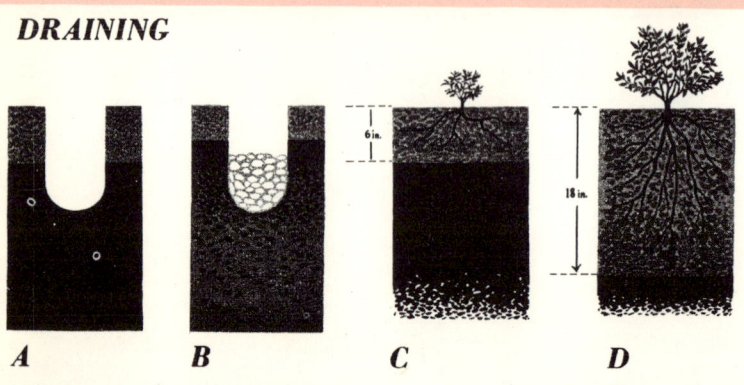

DRAINING

A   B   C   D

Dark areas in drawings at left show soil underlayer. Do not plant where underlayer is waterlogged and impervious as in A. Hole may be dug deeper, filled with stones to reach the porous underlayer, as in B. Poor root development (C) is result of only six inches between ground level and water table. For healthy plant, soil should drain to 18 inches as shown in D.

1442

GARDENING

the surface for weeks together, artificial drainage is usually needed. Agricultural drain tiles are best for providing this. First locate an outlet below the lowest point to be drained. This may be a pond, stream, ditch, sewer or other feature that permits disposal of the surplus water. Working backwards from the outlet, dig a system of ditches with bottoms that slope gradually upwards at a rate of four to six inches for each hundred running feet. At the outlet the ditch may be two to three feet deep. It should not be less than eighteen inches below ground level at any point. Make the bottoms of the ditches firm; then lay the drain tiles. Butt their ends together but use no cement because the water to be carried away must enter the drain through the joints. Cover the drain with cinders or gravel, then fill with regular soil. Space the drains from eighteen to thirty feet apart. In heavy clay soils closer spacing is needed. Drains are usually laid in herringbone pattern. The main drain may be four to six inches in bore, the

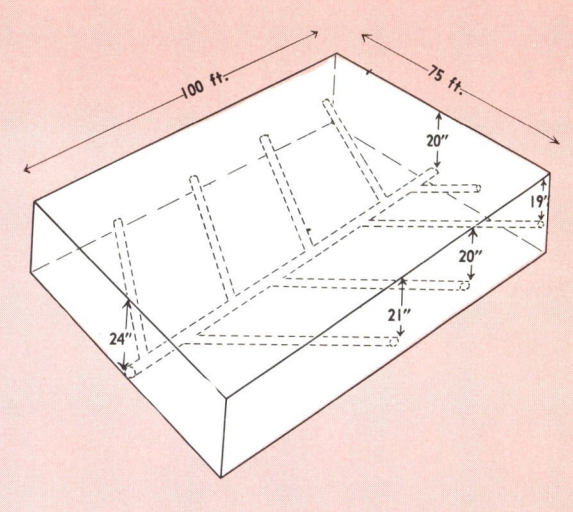

The above diagram shows a piping plan for draining a wet plot of ground measuring 100 by 75 feet.

Wet land can be much improved by draining provided a suitable outlet can be found. Here is a drainage ditch full of water before laying of drains.

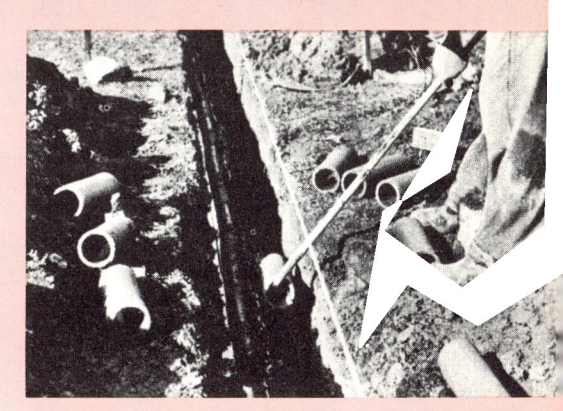

Drainpipe segments are made of tile and are here being lowered in position after which they will be covered with cinders and gravel, topped by soil.

With drainpipe segments partially covered, one of them is removed to illustrate how the water flows. This is at junction of side and main drains.

Main drains need not necessarily be made of tiles. Here is one built of stones, carefully graded. All side drains feed into this for proper soil moisture.

GARDENING
How To Dig

At one end of the plot, dig out a trench about a foot deep and a foot wide, take soil to far side.

In the bottom of the trench, place manure, peatmoss, compost or other humus-forming material.

Proper way to spade is to dig nearly vertically, putting your full weight behind each spade thrust.

In placing newly dug soil on trench that has been previously laid with compost, invert soil as shown.

side or feeder drains three to four inches.

Loosening and Turning. Loosening and turning the soil admits air, improves drainage, permits thorough mixing in of humus, brings fresh portions of the soil to the surface to be improved by weathering and buries weeds. Normally, this should be done before planting.

Soils are classified as light, medium and heavy according to the relative ease with which they may be worked. Sandy soils which break apart and fall readily before tools are "light." Clays which stick to tools and are hard to work are heavy. Medium soils (loams) come between these extremes, being *light* loams if sand clearly predominates, *heavy* if they resemble clay.

Heavy soils benefit greatly from weathering and particularly from frost. Whenever possible turn them over in fall and leave their surface rough over winter. It is usually better not to turn light soils until shortly before planting.

Shallow soils if not under-lain with solid rock, may be deepened by proper working. If your soil is shallow avoid bringing up and mixing with the topsoil more than an inch or two of poor subsoil at any one time. This, however, you may do with advantage. In other words, if your topsoil is six inches deep and overlies an infertile subsoil turn it to a depth of seven or eight inches and add plenty of humus material. In a year you will have seven or eight inches of topsoil. Then you may turn it over to a depth of nine or ten inches, again adding humus, thus again deepening the topsoil. And so on until you reach the maximum depth at which your implements will operate.

This gradual deepening works well in areas devoted to annual crops, but not where permanent crops are planted. In such places the subsoil may be improved in place, at one time, without mixing it with the topsoil, by double-digging.

GARDENING

Spade over successive strips of soil, working backwards along plot. Spade almost straight down.

On reaching the end of the plot, use soil removed from first trench to fill last. Leave soil rough.

Humus materials placed along bottom of each trench feed the organisms that make good topsoil.

In double-digging, the subsoil as well as the top layer is turned and improved by adding compost.

How to Spade. Suppose you are going to turn a piece of ground. It is too small to plow. You intend to use a spade or spading fork. First drive a stake at each corner. Next stretch a line (or piece of strong string) from stake to stake. Mark along this by chopping a groove into the ground with the bottom edge of the spade. This defines the area to be spaded. Dig a trench or ditch across one end of the plot and dump the excavated soil at the other end, just outside the marked-off area. Make the trench a foot wide and as deep as the blade of the spade is long. If the plot is weedy, skim off the weeds back from the edge of the trench eight or nine inches and throw them into the bottom of the trench. Do the same with weeds close to the ends of the trench. Spread a layer of manure, compost or other humus material in the trench and begin spading. Except in stony ground you can do better with a spade than you can with a fork.

Begin at one end of the trench. Drive the blade of the tool almost vertically into the ground six or seven inches back from the edge of the trench. Thrust the blade downwards with all your weight behind it; don't depend upon stamping or kicking. When the tool is driven in as deeply as possible, pull backwards on the handle, drop one hand down the shaft to act as a fulcrum and to provide the lift necessary. Throw the soil well forward, at the same time turning it upside down so the surface soil is underneath and soil from beneath is brought to the top. Repeat this along the edge of the trench until the end is reached. Skim the weeds off against it, spread manure or compost in it and proceed as before. Continue trench after trench until the end of the plot is reached. Fill last trench with soil from the first.

Double-digging is done in the same way

1445

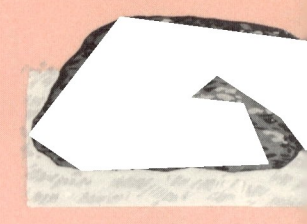

GARDENING

POOR SOIL + MANURE OR COMPOST OR GREEN MANURE + DEEP SPADING + FERTILIZER

as single-digging, except that the trench is two to two and a half feet wide and is as deep as the topsoil or the spade blade, whichever is greater. One other difference: in double-digging a four- to six-inch layer of manure or compost is spaded *into the bottom* of each trench, then another layer is spread along the bottom of the trench before the topsoil from the next trench is turned on it. In *single-digging* the soil is loosened and turned to the depth of the blade or a spade; in *double-digging* to about twice the depth.

Plows and Rotary Tillers. The plow is an agricultural rather than a garden implement. Only operators of much acreage ordinarily use plows. Rotary tillers, on the other hand, are primarily garden implements. Small models designed for gardens of modest size do first class work, taking a great deal of work out of gardening. You can turn your soil and mix humus or other needed materials with them to a depth of ten inches or so with little effort. The rotary tiller takes the place of both plow and harrow; it prepares a splendid seed bed.

Adding Humus. Humus is decayed organic matter, dark material that makes topsoil deeper in color than subsoil. Unless they contain an adequate amount of humus, light soils dry out fast and are leached of their nutrients; clay soils become compacted, fail to admit air and cake and crack under the rain and sun. Humus breaks down in the soil and supplies nourishment for both garden plants and microorganisms. Because of this its supply is constantly depleted and must be replaced. Maintenance of a suitable proportion of humus in the soil is a major problem.

Two methods of adding humus are employed: (1) using dead (and usually partially decayed) material; (2) turning under a growing crop (green manuring). Animal manure, compost, leaf-mold, peat-moss and natural humus obtained from bogs and lakes are the chief dead materials employed. Almost anything that has lived and died and decayed can be used. Be sure to use enough. In areas given over to annual crops a two- or three-inch layer turned under each year is usually not excessive. Amounts in excess of this can often be used profitably when preparing for perennial crops. If manure or other humus material is added shortly before planting see that it is pretty well decayed. Undecayed or semi-decayed material should be used only if several weeks are to elapse before planting. Never place manure close to roots unless it is thoroughly decayed. When humus materials are short, green manures are good substitutes. Most important for gardens is winter rye, which is commonly sown in fall and turned under in early spring. Both the tops and the root systems decay and

1446

GARDENING

OR PEAT-MOSS   OR NATURAL HUMUS   OR LEAF MOLD

Conversion of poor soil into good topsoil can be made by using the materials shown here in steps described in photos and drawings on the preceding pages.

AND LIME IF NEEDED   =   GOOD SOIL

turn to humus and the soil is improved immensely. Good green manures for summer are buckwheat, oats, soybeans and cow peas. Sow green manure crops whenever land is expected to be vacant for a few weeks. Turn them under while they are yet succulent and before they become too woody or otherwise difficult to handle. Always turn green manures under two or three weeks before you plant.

Fertilizers. Materials added to the soil to provide humus also supply nutrient elements. This is especially true of animal manures. Often, however, they do not supply enough, and scarcely ever do they contain the required elements in needed proportions. Fertilizers are used to correct this, and to supplement nourishment that manures, composts, green manures, etc., add to the soil. Elements most often deficient are nitrogen, phosphorus and potassium. Fertilizer that contains all of these is known as a complete fertilizer. On fertilizer containers you will find a formula consisting of three numbers. The first states the percentage of nitrogen; the second the percentage of available phosphoric acid; the third the percentage of water soluble potash. Fertilizers such as those numbered 5-10-5 or 4-12-4 are good general purpose fertilizers. For special purposes other formulae are used. There are also fertilizers that contain only one or two of the three important elements While the formula indicates the *proportions* in which nitrogen, phosphorus and potassium occur it does not show the speed with which they become available to the plant. This is particularly important with nitrogen. If the nitrogen content of a fertilizer is a quickly available salt its effect is immediate but not long-lasting; if it occurs in the form of an organic material it is much slower acting but continues to stimulate the plant over a much longer period. Most complete commercial fertilizers contain quickly available nitrogen as well as organics that provide more slowly available nitrogen. Such fertilizers are generally best for the garden. Fertilizers are not substitutes for humus nor can manure and other organic material completely or economically do the work of fertilizers. You will need both.

Liming. Do not use lime unless a soil test indicates it is needed. Have such tests made yearly for pH (acidity or alkalinity).

Lime neutralizes acidity. Most (but not all) plants get along well in a soil that is approximately neutral. Some must have distinctly acid soil. Lime is of benefit not only in correcting acidity but it also greatly improves the physical condition of heavy soils, is of help in releasing for use certain plant foods held in the soil in unusable compounds and it provides calcium. Use hydrated lime on heavy soils and ground limestone on light soils, but only in quantities that tests show are desirable. •

GARDENING

Only Man Can Plant a Tree

Shade trees and flowering trees have to be well located for healthy growth and enhancement of property values.

SHADE trees such as oaks, elms and maples and flowering trees such as magnolias, crabs and dogwoods need care. It is not enough to let them just look after themselves.

If well located they add to the beauty of your property and to its cash value. Therefore, it pays to give them the attention they need. Cultivate your trees. Don't let them take pot luck.

When planting new trees consider carefully beforehand which are best suited for your purpose. Obtain some idea of their ultimate height and shape. Are they fast-growing or slow-growing? Is their wood brittle and subject to storm damage? Are their roots likely to clog drains? Are they very subject to diseases or insects?

Get to know also if they are adapted to your soil and location and if they are easy or difficult to transplant.

You may not be able to get a tree that has every good quality but if you set up a balance sheet of comparative virtues you can choose one that rates highly.

Let price be a secondary consideration. A good tree lasts a long time. If you cannot afford the kind you want in the size you would like take a smaller specimen rather than a poor substitute. You will be amazed how quickly it will grow if you look after it. And it's fun watching the development of a tree you plant yourself.

Don't skimp on preparing the hole for a new tree. Dig it wide enough to accommodate the roots when fully spread out

1448

1

After digging hole deep enough to accommodate the roots (1) spade the bottom (2) and mix in generous amounts of manure, peat-moss, other humus.

2

6

With roots spread in a position of natural growth, fill hole with good topsoil (5) mixed with compost, peat-moss or humus, tamp firmly around edges.

3

7

Put tree in place (3) and remove burlap from roots as shown below. Bottom sacking is left to rot. In bare-rooted trees, the burlap is removed entirely.

8

Water thoroughly several times (7) letting drain for a couple of hours, then add more soil and top with mulch. The guy-wires make tree more secure.

GARDENING

Good Shade Trees

Photos courtesy, Arnold Arboretum, Jamaica Plain, Mass.

In planting shade trees, choose the ones that are best suited to your purpose, bearing in mind the ultimate size. Here is a small-leaved linden tree.

The Chinese elm is medium-sized, fast-growing and leafy, well suited for either city street or open yard. Its wood is strong and resistant to storms.

Good Shade Trees

PAPER BIRCH (Betula papyrifera)	Handsome white bark. Moderate size. Needs fairly moist, well-drained soil. Must be transplanted carefully.
CHINESE ELM (Ulmus pumila)	Moderate size. Fast grower. Good city tree.
SASSAFRAS (Sassafras albidum)	Tall but quite slender. Good fall color. Difficult to transplant. Set out young trees only. Prefers light soils.
HONEY LOCUST (Gleditsia triacanthos)	Large, of same form as American elm and best substitute for it. Flowers fragrant. A thornless as well as normal thorny type is available. Good city tree.
SMALL-LEAVED LINDEN (Tilia cordata)	Large, but stands pruning well. Will not thrive in dry soil. Flowers fragrant. Good city tree.
JAPANESE PAGODA TREE (Sophora japonica)	Large, round headed, branches spreading. Showy white flowers in summer. Stands heat and drought well.
RED MAPLE (Acer rubrum)	Large. Like all maples, roots at surface; hence difficult to grow anything under. Attractive in bloom and in fall color. Thrives in moist or wet soils.
PIN OAK (Quercus palustris)	Large but comparatively narrow. Grows fairly fast. Will thrive in moist soil. Good city tree.
RED OAK (Quercus borealis)	Large, round-headed. Grows fairly fast. Good fall color.

with at least a foot extra all around, and more if it is a big specimen or if the soil is poor. Break the bottom of the hole with a spading fork and mix plenty of rotted manure or compost with the under soil. Prepare the hole in advance of planting.

Make sure the tree is dug with an ample mass of healthy roots. The more roots that can be saved the better. The fine fibrous feeding roots are especially important. With most deciduous (non-evergreen) trees of ordinary planting size it is not necessary to move a ball of earth. The roots are shaken or combed free of soil. Protect the bare roots from drying by wrapping them in moist burlap, wet hay or similar material. If you cannot plant such trees right away heel them in (set them closely together and cover the roots with soil). Specimens of deciduous trees larger than ordinary planting size are usually dug with a large ball of earth and then the outer portion is combed with a fork so that a comparatively small center ball remains with bare roots protruding all around. Wrap these roots to keep them moist.

At planting time cut off cleanly any broken root ends. Reduce the top some-

Good Flowering Trees

GARDENING

Flowering trees provide blossoms in spring, shade in summer and fruit in the fall. A popular member of this group is the crab-apple tree shown above.

The flowering crab at top blooms every spring with white or pink petals. Chinese fringe tree, above, grows slowly but has lacy white flowers in summer.

what by removing unwanted branches and by shortening side branches back somewhat. In some cases the "leader" or central growing shoot may be shortened slightly also.

Set the tree at the same depth or perhaps an inch deeper than it was in the nursery. Work good topsoil enriched with humus and perhaps a little bone meal among its roots but do not use fertilizer. Pack the soil firmly. Do not complete the surface levelling at once. Leave a slight depression where the hole was and fill this with water two or three times to settle the soil about the roots.

Staking or guying with three wires (threaded through old rubber hose where they go around the trunk) may be needed to make the newly planted tree secure, as shown.

To complete the job, mulch the soil with a layer of compost, old manure or peatmoss.

The best time to plant is during leaf drop in fall or in spring two or three weeks before the buds burst. Choose cloudy weather, if possible. Sun and wind dry the roots. •

Good Small Flowering Trees

FLOWERING DOGWOOD (Cornus florida)	White or pink flowers in spring. Red berries and good foliage color in fall. Needs fairly moist good soil. Transplant with ball of earth.
JAPANESE FLOWERING DOGWOOD (Cornus Kousa)	White flowers. Blooms one month later than native flowering dogwood. Less stiff in habit. Attractive raspberry-like fruits.
ENGLISH HAWTHORN (Crataegus oxyacantha Pauls Scarlet)	Pink flowers in spring.
WASHINGTON THORN (Crataegus phaenopyrum)	White flowers in spring. Long lasting red fruits in fall.
SILVER BELL (Halesia monticola)	White flowers in spring. Likes good soil.
WITCH-HAZEL, CHINESE (Hamamelis mollis)	Yellow flowers in late winter.
WITCH-HAZEL, JAPANESE (Hamamelis japonica)	Yellow flowers in late winter.
MAGNOLIA (Magnolia soulangeana)	Large pink or purple-pink flowers in spring. Transplant in spring only.
FLOWERING CRABS (Malus)	White or pink flowers in spring. Many excellent varieties. Attractive in fruit. Good kinds are spectabilis, hupehensis, niedzwetsckyana and scheideckeri.
JAPANESE CHERRIES (Prunus)	White or pink flowers in spring. Many excellent varieties. Good kinds are Kwanzan, Fugenzo and Shirofugen. Difficult to transplant except when small.

GARDENING

Deutzia Lemoinei

Photos by New York Botanical Garden

Shrubs for the Home Garden

SHRUBS that drop their leaves each fall are deciduous. In every garden there is a place for some deciduous shrubs. You may use them in borders and beds and as informal screens. Most of them flower attractively and many of them fruit profusely. They change with the seasons more than evergreens do. They provide lightness and grace. Many, such as lilacs and mock oranges, are good cut flowers.

Select your shrubs with care. Find out before planting how large each eventually gets to be and allow space for its development.

Scotch Rose

Fragrant Viburnum

Royal Azalea

Hydrangea Paniculata

Fothergilla Monticola

GARDENING

This shrub is to be transplanted.

Prune away one-third of the top.

Or thin out one-third of the branches.

Dig trench past natural spread of branches.

Comb most of the soil from outer root mass.

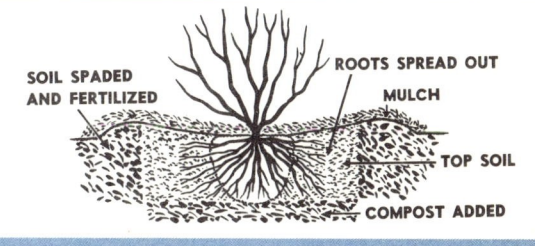

Ridge, depression around shrub holds water.

SOIL SPADED AND FERTILIZED — ROOTS SPREAD OUT — MULCH — TOP SOIL — COMPOST ADDED

When you "heel in," shovel soil over the roots, tread it and put in another row of shrubs.

Nondescript, ragged-looking shrubberies result from choosing poor kinds, and setting the plants too closely together.

Most shrubs grow remarkably fast if given a reasonable chance. Because of this it is usually best to plant young, vigorous specimens. Only in the case of such slow-growing kinds as azaleas does it pay to buy bigger plants to start. Not that large shrubs cannot be moved safely. Most of them can. But the labor involved adds to the cost, and is usually unwarranted.

Prepare the ground well. Spade the entire area if a bed or border is to be planted. Dig a large-sized hole for a single specimen. Better a dollar-sized plant in a three dollar hole than vice versa.

The planting directions given for trees apply here also. Follow them carefully, except that shrubs rarely require staking or guying. Many, however, are better if pruned rather severely at planting time. Reduction of the top growth compensates for the loss of roots inevitable in transplanting. The best times to transplant shrubs are early fall and early spring. •

1453

A SELECTION OF THE BEST

Type of Shrubs	For Very Dry Soils	For Moist or Wet Soils	For Ordinary Soils	Approximate Height in Feet	Flower Color	Blooming Season	Good Fall Foliage Color	Attractive in Fruit	Needs Full Sun	Good for Shade	Withstands Light Shade	Kills Back But Renews Self Each Year in Cold Climates
Glossy Abelia (Abelia grandiflora)			✓	3 to 6	blush (fragrant)	summer & fall	✓	✓			✓	✓
False Indigo (Amorpha fruticosa)	✓			12	purple	late spring			✓		✓	
Red Chokeberry (Aronia arbutifolia)		✓		10	white	spring		✓			✓	
*Korean Azalea (Azalea mucronulata)			✓	6	rosy lavender	early spring					✓	
*Flame azalea (Azalea calendulacea)			✓	10	orange to scarlet	spring					✓	
*Pinxter-Flower (Azalea nudiflora)			✓	6	blush to pink (fragrant)	spring					✓	
*Royal Azalea (Azalea schlippenbachii)			✓	6 to 7	pink (fragrant)	spring					✓	
*Pinkshell Azalea (Azalea vaseyi)		✓		6	pink	early spring	✓				✓	
*Torch Azalea (Azalea kaempferi)			✓	6	orange-salmon	spring					✓	
*Swamp Honeysuckle (Azalea viscosa)		✓		8	pink or blush (fragrant)	early summer	✓				✓	
Japanese Barberry (Berberis thunbergii)			✓	6	yellow	spring	✓	✓			✓	
Fountain Buddleia (Buddleia alternifolia)			✓	15	lavender (fragrant)	early summer			✓			
Butterfly Bush (Buddleia davidi)			✓	15	white, pink, red & purple (fragrant)	summer & fall			✓			✓
Beauty-berry (Callicarpa dichotoma and Callicarpa japonica)			✓	4 to 5				✓	✓			✓
Bluebeard or Blue Spirea (Caryopteris incana)			✓	4	blue	fall			✓			✓
Dwarf Flowering Quince (Chaenomeles japonica)			✓	3	pink & red	spring		✓				
Japanese Quince (Chaenomeles lagenaria)			✓	8	pink, red & white	spring		✓	✓			
Sweet Pepperbush (Clethra alnifolia)		✓		10	white (fragrant)	summer	✓				✓	
Tatarian Dogwood (Cornus alba sibirica)		✓		8					✓			
Golden Twig Dogwood (Cornus stolonifera flaviramea)		✓		10								
Winter Hazel (Corylopsis pauciflora)			✓	6	yellow (fragrant)	early spring	✓				✓	
Cotoneaster												
(Cotoneaster hupehensis)			✓	6	white	spring	✓	✓	✓			
(Cotoneaster racemiflora)			✓	8	white	spring		✓	✓			
(Cotoneaster horizontalis)			✓	3	pink	spring	✓	✓	✓			
(Cotoneaster salicifolia floccosa)			✓	10	white	spring	✓	✓	✓			
Broom (Cytisus nigricans)	✓			4	yellow (fragrant)	summer			✓			
Scotch Broom (Cytisus scoparius)	✓			8	yellow (fragrant)	summer			✓			
Deutzia (Deutzia gracilis)			✓	4	white	late spring			✓			
(Deutzia lemoinei)			✓	6	white	late spring			✓			
Enkianthus (Enkianthus campanulatus)		✓		15	yellowish brown	spring	✓				✓	
(Enkianthus perulatus)		✓		6	white	spring	✓					
Corkbark Evonymus (Evonymus alatus)			✓	8			✓		✓			
(Evonymus alatus compactus)			✓	5			✓		✓			
Forsythia (Forsythia intermedia spectabilis)			✓	10	yellow	early spring			✓			
(Forsythia ovata)			✓	8	yellow	early spring			✓			
(Forsythia suspensa)			✓	10	yellow	early spring			✓			
Honeysuckle (Lonicera morrowii)			✓	6	white	spring		✓			✓	
(Lonicera standishii)			✓	6	white (fragrant)	early spring					✓	
(Lonicera tatarica)			✓	10	white or pink	spring		✓			✓	
Snowberry (Symphoricarpos albus)			✓	5	white	summer		✓		✓		
Starry Magnolia (Magnolia stellata)			✓	15	white	spring			✓			
Neillia (Neillia sinensis)			✓	5	white or	spring					✓	

*Require acid soil.

SHRUBS FOR THE GARDEN

Type of Shrubs	For Very Dry Soils	For Moist or Wet Soils	For Ordinary Soils	Approximate Height in Feet	Flower Color	Blooming Season	Good Fall Foliage Color	Attractive in Fruit	Needs Full Sun	Good for Shade	Withstands Light Shade	Kills Back But Renews Self Each Year in Cold Climates
Flowering Crab (*Malus sargentii*)			✓	6	white	spring		✓	✓		-	
Snow Wreath (*Neviusia alabamensis*)			✓	5	white	late spring					✓	
Mock Orange (*Philadelphus coronarius*)			✓	10	white (fragrant)	late spring					✓	
(*Philadelphus virginalis*)			✓	6	white (fragrant)	late spring					✓	
Beach Plum (*Prunus maritima*)	✓			10	white	spring		✓	✓			
Flowering Plum (*Prunus triloba*)			✓	6	pink	spring			✓			
Jetbead (*Rhodotypos tetrapetala*)			✓	6	white	late spring		✓			✓	
Shrub Roses (*Rosa rugosa*)	✓			6	pink, red & white (fragrant)	late spring		✓	✓			
(*Rosa spinosissima altaica*)	✓			6	white (fragrant)	late spring		✓	✓			
Spireas (*Spirea prunifolia plena*)			✓	6	white	spring			✓			
(*Spirea vanhouttei*)			✓	6	white	spring			✓			
(*Spirea Anthony Waterer*)			✓	2½	pink	summer & fall			✓			
Sweetleaf (*Symplocos paniculata*)			✓	20	white (fragrant)	spring		✓			✓	
Fothergilla (*Fothergilla gardeni*)		✓		3	cream (fragrant)	spring (fragrant)	✓				✓	
(*Fothergilla monticola*)		✓		6	cream (fragrant)	spring (fragrant)	✓				✓	
Rose of Sharon (*Hibiscus syriacus*)			✓	12	white, pink, lavender, blue & red	summer & fall			✓			
Hydrangea (*Hydrangea paniculata*)			✓	15	white	summer & fall					✓	
†(*Hydrangea macrophylla*)			✓	8	white, blue & pink	summer & fall				✓		
(*Hydrangea arborescens grandiflora*)			✓	10	white	summer				✓		
St. Johns Wort (*Hypericum frondosum*)			✓	4	yellow	summer & fall					✓	
Winterberry (*Ilex verticillata*)		✓		10				✓				
Sweet-spire (*Itea virginica*)		✓		8	white (fragrant)	summer	✓		✓			
Jasmine (*Jasminum nudiflorum*)			✓	8	yellow	early spring						
Kerria (*Kerria japonica*)			✓	6	yellow	late spring	✓				✓	
Beauty Bush (*Kolkwitzia amabilis*)			✓	8	pink	summer			✓			
Spice Bush (*Lindera benzoin*)		✓		12	yellow	early spring	✓		*	✓		
French Lilacs (*Syringa vulgaris*)			✓	20	white, lilac & purple (fragrant)	spring			✓			
Persian Lilac (*Syringa persica*)			✓	8	pink & lavender (fragrant)	spring			✓			
Tamarisks (*Tamarix parviflora*)	✓			15	pink	spring			✓			
(*Tamarix odessiana*)	✓			6	pink	late spring			✓			
(*Tamarix pentandra*)	✓			15	pink	summer			✓			
Viburnums (*Viburnum carlesi*)			✓	10	white (fragrant)	spring			✓			
(*Viburnum tomentosum*)			✓	10	white	late spring		✓			✓	
(*Viburnum dilatatum*)			✓	7	white	late spring		✓				
Weigelia (*Weigelia florida hybrids*)			✓	8	pink	spring			✓			

†Do not thrive in dry soils.

GARDENING

Every Garden Should Have Evergreens

It isn't always summer—and without evergreens your grounds may be bare and bleak for more of the year than they need be.

THERE is a solidity and feeling of permanence about evergreens that is not quite supplied by deciduous trees and shrubs. They seem to provide security and stability in the garden scheme of things.

As backgrounds to show off flowering plants to good advantage evergreens are superb. Many are unsurpassed as subjects for use in foundation plantings. Single specimens of pines, spruces, hollies, boxwood and many others can be breathtakingly magnificent. We use evergreens as hedges and as groundcovers and as screens both to give privacy and to close out undesirable views. The friendly evergreens, as one writer has dubbed them, are needed in every garden, so let's get to know something about them and how to use them.

Evergreens are divided into two great groups—the broad-leaved and the narrow-leaved. These designations are roughly descriptive but not entirely so. A few broad-leaved evergreens (such as heather) actually have foliage that is narrower than the leaves of some narrow-leaved evergreens, for example the plum-yew (*Cephalotaxus*). But these are exceptions.

True narrow-leaved evergreens are all conifers (using the term in its broad sense). They do not have flowers. Here belong the pines, spruces, firs, yews, junipers and arborvitaes.

Broad-leaved evergreens normally bear flowers and these are often very beautiful, as for example those of rhododendrons, mountain laurel and camellias. Where winters are severe the number of broad-leaved evergreens that can be grown is strictly limited. In more favored climates the garden maker has a much wider choice.

Evergreens for hedges and groundcovers are discussed elsewhere in this book. Here we shall consider their other uses and one of the chief of these is in foundation plantings.

Choose the kinds you use for this purpose with great care. Where permanently low plants are wanted don't set out young specimens of tall growing kinds. If you do they will become so overgrown in a few years that they will have to be removed and replaced. It's wiser and less expensive to plant suitable varieties in the beginning: kinds that will remain low, or at least that can be kept low by proper pruning. And remember, not all evergreens can be pruned.

GARDENING

In arranging your foundation planting avoid using too many different kinds of plants. To do so gives a "spotty" effect. And above all do not splurge on highly colored types. Golden arborvitaes and silver cypresses that look cute in the nursery surrounded by lots of their kind or by oceans of green can be mighty hard to live with near your own frontdoor. They shout too loud. They don't give their neighbors a chance.

Evergreens in a foundation planting should blend and form comfortable billowy masses with taller accents only where needed as, for example, at the corners of the house.

If the house reaches high from the ground, tall corner accents are usually advantageous but long low houses are improved by sticking to plants of more horizontal habit. The evergreens in your foundation planting must not only blend, but also provide a suitable background for whatever flowering plants you use—azaleas, tulips or geraniums perhaps. Think of that when you plan your planting.

One more point. Don't overplant. Leave room for the newly set evergreens to grow. At a later date, if they do begin to crowd, transplant some of them or chop out a few if need be. Few plants are spoiled as quickly as evergreens that are crowded. The trick is to do something about it before they are harmed, before they have lost their foliage on one or more sides.

As informal screens and windbreaks evergreens possess the supreme advantage of remaining good the year around. Such plantings are often preferable to strictly sheared hedges because they divide the landscape less sharply.

For screening choose kinds that retain their lower branches. Select such plants also with an eye to their ultimate height and to the type of soil and location they prefer. Pines, junipers and some others simply must have plenty of light and air. Hemlocks and rhododendrons typify kinds that need,

Courtesy of L. C. Chadwick, Ohio State University

A tall evergreen at the corner of this house has softened the corner line. Two yews flank the door.

Common boxwood is used here to provide accents on either side of this otherwise formal threshold.

A charming foundation planting is achieved around this chimney by evergreens and deciduous shrubs.

Broad-leaved and narrow-leaved evergreens are combined here to frame a window decoratively.

GARDENING

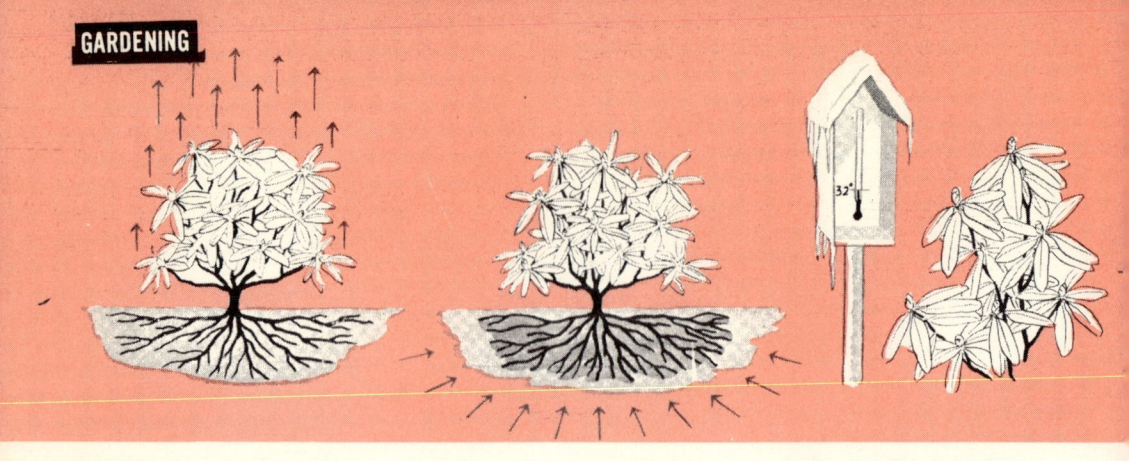

Like all plants, evergreens give off water vapor through leaves.

Normally this loss is taken up by water absorbed by roots.

But in winter when the ground freezes water isn't plentiful.

As a result of losing more and more water, leaves "burn"

To prevent this, plant on north or west of buildings, in shade.

North or west facing slopes are also good, under shade trees.

If exposed to wind, protect with a burlap screen, as shown.

Be sure to keep well watered if the late summer and fall is dry.

A mulch of leaves or peat-moss keeps soil from deep-freeze.

or at least will stand, shade. It's no use planting acid soil plants in alkaline regions or lovers of moisture in dry, thirsty soils.

And in making screen plantings bear in mind that plants grow and need more room. To obtain a reasonably quick screen you may set out large plants to begin with and space them fairly wide apart; or set out smaller specimens closer together than is good for them to be ultimately, than thin them out later. The latter sounds attractive but the labor involved in transplanting plus a very natural disinclination to disturb an arrangement that still looks good often prevents it from being done. Too often plantings made with the intention of thinning them out later are left to deteriorate for lack of timely attention.

But it is not only as screens and background that evergreens may be grouped. The smaller kinds are also lovely in beds and borders in the fore- and middle-

A SELECTION OF BROAD-LEAVED EVERGREENS

Name of Shrub	For Full Sun	Prefers Light Shade	For Sun or Shade	Needs or Prefers Acid Soil	Needs Fairly Moist Soil	Needs Well-Drained Soil, Not Too Dry	Has Attractive Fruits	Color of Flowers	Blooming Season	Hardy North	Needs Sheltered Position or Protection North	Suitable for Mild Climates Only	Height in Feet
Wintergreen Barberry (Berberis julianae)			✓			✓		yellow	spring		✓		6
Warty Barberry (Berberis verruculosa)			✓			✓		yellow	spring		✓		3
Japanese Boxwood (Buxus microphylla japonica)			✓			✓					✓		15
Common Boxwood (Buxus sempervirens)			✓			✓					✓		18
Camellia (Camellia japonica)		✓		✓	✓			white, pink and red	spring			✓	20
(Camellia sasanqua)		✓		✓	✓			white, pink and red	winter			✓	15
Mexican-orange (Choisya ternata)	✓					✓		white (fragrant)	summer			✓	10
Rock-rose (Cistus ladaniferus maculatus)	✓					✓		white and red	summer		✓		5
(Cistus laurifolius)	✓					✓		white	summer			✓	8
Japanese Oleaster (Elaeagnus pungens)			✓			✓	✓	cream (fragrant)	summer			✓	10
Cape Jasmine (Gardenia florida)			✓	✓		✓		white (fragrant)	summer			✓	6
English Holly (Ilex aquifolium)			✓		✓	✓	✓				✓		30
Dahoon (Ilex cassine)			✓		✓	✓						✓	25
Chinese Holly (Ilex cornuta)			✓			✓	✓				✓		12
Japanese Holly (Ilex crenata)			✓			✓					✓		20
Inkberry (Ilex glabra)			✓	✓	✓					✓			6
American Holly (Ilex opaca)			✓		✓	✓	✓				✓		40
Mountain Laurel (Kalmia latifolia)		✓		✓		✓		pink	late spring	✓			20
Drooping Leucothoe (Leucothoe catesbaei)		✓		✓	✓			white	spring	✓			5
Japanese Privet (Ligustrum japonicum)			✓			✓	✓	white	summer			✓	12
Bull Bay (Magnolia grandiflora)			✓			✓		white	summer			✓	80
Oregon Grape-holly (Mahonia aquifolium)		✓				✓	✓	yellow	spring		✓		4
Nandina (Nandina domestica)			✓		✓		✓	white	early summer			✓	6
Osmanthus (Osmanthus ilicifolius)			✓			✓		white (fragrant)	summer			✓	20
Mountain Andromeda (Pieris floribunda)		✓		✓	✓			white	spring	✓			5
Japanese Andromeda (Pieris japonica)		✓		✓	✓			white	spring		✓		10
Laland Firethorn (Pyracantha coccinea lalandi)			✓			✓	✓	white	spring		✓		8
Japanese Pittosporum (Pittosporum tobira)			✓			✓		cream (fragrant)	spring			✓	10
Cherry Laurel (Prunus laurocerasus)			✓			✓		white (fragrant)	summer			✓	20
India Hawthorn (Raphiolepis indica)			✓			✓		pink	spring			✓	5
Carolina Rhododendron (Rhododendron caroliniana)		✓		✓	✓			pink	spring	✓			6
Catawba Rhododendron (Rhododendron catawbiense) and its hybrids.		✓		✓	✓			white, pink, and red	late spring	✓			8
Rosebay Rhododendron (Rhododendron maximum)		✓		✓	✓			white or pink	early summer	✓			25
Indian Azaleas (Rhododendron indicum)		✓		✓	✓			white, pink, red	spring			✓	6

It is usually necessary to have male and female plants of hollies growing near together to ensure fruiting.

GARDENING

Narrow-Leaved Evergreens

FIRS. Need rich moist soil and unpolluted atmosphere. Not good for city conditions. Splendid as single specimens. Attain heights of 75 feet and more. Among the best are White Fir, Nordmann Fir and Nikko Fir.

DOUGLAS-FIR. Thrives in ordinary soil. An attractive fast-growing evergreen tree. Withstands city conditions fairly well. Not a true fir.

SPRUCES. Require good soil, neither wet nor excessively dry. Most form sizable trees but also many dwarf varieties. Among the best are Engelmann Spruce, Oriental Spruce and White Spruce. For windbreaks, Norway Spruce. Colorado Blue Spruce is popular.

PINES. Mostly adapted for dryish soils and exposed situations. Stand city conditions fairly well. Among the best are White Pine, Swiss Stone Pine, Austrian Pine, Red Pine and Scotch Pine. Mugho Pine is a good dwarf. Japanese Black Pine is excellent for seashore.

JUNIPERS. Need good drainage and thrive in rather poor, dry soils. They need full sun. Many kinds are available in a wide assortment of forms, shapes and colorings. Among the best are Chinese Juniper, Pfitzer Juniper, Sargent Juniper, Meyer Juniper and Eastern Red-cedar.

CYPRESSES (Including Biotas and Retinisporas). Need protection from sweeping wind. They stand some shade. Among the best are Sawara Cypress, Hinoki Cypress, Dwarf Hinoki Cypress, Nootka Cypress and, for mild climates, Lawson Cypress.

CEDARS. Need warm, rich soils. Magnificent as specimens. Tenderest is the Deodar. A hardy form of the Cedar of Lebanon thrives in Massachusetts. The Atlantic Cedar is intermediate in hardiness.

HEMLOCKS. Need fairly moist, well-drained soils, protection from sweeping winds. Stand shade better than most narrow-leaved evergreens. All are excellent. Sargents Weeping Hemlock is low and attractive.

ARBOR-VITAES. Need moist soil. American aborvitae is hardiest of evergreens. Many varieties available. Most discolor in winter.

YEWS. Thrive in ordinary soils. Stand sun or shade. Withstand city conditions well. Numerous varieties available. Most important are Upright Japanese Yew, Spreading Japanese Yew, Dwarf Japanese Yew, Hick's Yew and Spreading English Yew, The Upright English Yew and the Irish Yew are less hardy.

---

foreground. Flowering evergreens such as heathers and Daphne Cneorum are especially effective when so used.

Specimen evergreens, well located and free standing, add immensely to the garden picture. Under these circumstances their beauty, grace and dignity is emphasized. They are not just part of a "planting." They are individuals. Such specimens need careful placing so they will have room to develop symmetrically.

When full grown they should be in scale with the property and with the garden picture. Don't plant a couple of Norway spruces which later may have a spread of fifty feet on a frontplot measuring fifty by twenty-five feet. Select something smaller.

Planting. Planting evergreens differs from planting non-evergreens in one important particular. Except in the tiniest seedling sizes they should never be handled bare-rooted. They should always have a good ball of earth attached to their roots. And this ball should not be broken or disturbed. Do not comb the roots around the outside of the ball free of soil as is recommended for deciduous trees and shrubs. Keep the ball intact.

To ensure this see that the ball is wrapped tightly in burlap and handle the plant carefully so there is no danger of the soil cracking across or loosening or breaking apart.

Never pick up an evergreen, or indeed any other balled plant, by its top or trunk. Always take hold of the ball itself when the plant has to be lifted or moved.

If evergreens cannot be planted immediately after they are dug stand them closely together in a shady place, away from sweeping winds, and pack the balls around with moist leaves, straw, hay or similar

WHITE PINE · BLUE ATLANTIC CEDAR  · BLUE SPRUCE

material. Sprinkle the tops with water two or three times a day.

It is not usual to cut back evergreens at planting time and with many kinds it is not practicable. But some evergreens can be so treated and it is advantageous if they must be moved to cut them back with a comparatively small root ball. This may also be done if they are straggly, unshapely specimens.

Dig the holes plenty large. Allow a foot or more of space around the outside of the ball for packing in new soil. Break up the bottom of the hole and add plenty of humus material. Set the plant so that when planted it will not be more than an inch deeper than it was before. Unwrap the burlap and cut it away so that the piece immediately beneath the ball remains undisturbed. It will rot in the soil. Pack firmly around the ball some good top-soil mixed with about one-third part humus, compost, peat-moss or very rotted manure. Do not use fresh manure.

When the hole is three-quarters filled with soil fill it with water three or four times and allow it to drain for an hour or two before completing the job. Then fill in more soil and finish off the surface so there is a slight depression around the trunk and a rim around the outside of the hole-that-was. This facilitates future waterings.

Always mulch evergreens after planting. A two or three inch layer of leaf-mold, compost, peat-moss or other suitable material keeps the soil evenly moist and encourages favorable root action.

The most favorable times to transplant evergreens are in spring just before new growth begins or in late summer or early fall after the season's new growth has matured and become firm.

It is especially important that newly-planted evergreens never suffer for lack of moisture during the first year after planting.

GARDENING

Caring for Evergreens. All evergreens benefit if the soil around them is kept mulched. Digging or otherwise disturbing the roots of evergreens is very harmful. If the late summer and fall is dry see that evergreens are well watered. Watch out for lace-bug on rhododendrons, red spider on spruces, junipers and hemlocks and for first signs of other pests and diseases and take prompt remedial measures if they appear. It's no use spraying unless the plants are threatened. •

INDIA HAWTHORN

HOLLY

DWARF MUGHO PINE

DWARF PINE   Photos by New York Botanical Garden

What About Groundcovers?

These plants thrive where grass will not grow, protecting the surface of your soil from erosion and extremes of temperature.

EXCEPT in cultivated areas which are kept hoed or mulched, it is desirable to keep the surface of the soil covered with some kind of low vegetation. This keeps down weeds, prevents erosion and protects the roots of trees and shrubs from extremes of heat and cold. If appropriately done it also adds charm to the garden picture, showing off trees and shrubs and flowering plants to best advantage. Such greenery appears cool in summer and gives relief to the eye from the brighter colors in flower beds and borders.

Lawn is the most universally used green groundcover. For some purposes it is unsurpassed. No other groundcover that is practicable to maintain will stand the walking upon and the wear that grass will. If well cared for no other groundcover is as generally admired.

Because of this some gardeners make the mistake of attempting to solve all their groundcover problems by sowing grass seed. This just doesn't work. There are places where a lawn is certainly *not* the answer to the groundcover problem. In deep shade, for example, and on steep banks where it is almost impossible to use a lawnmower effectively. Also, where a perpetual battle to maintain grass has to be faced, even if you do succeed in establishing it, and in places where tree roots rob the soil of food and moisture.

In spots such as these try using some other groundcover. There are not many to choose from, it's true, but there are some mighty good ones. There are plenty of low carpeting plants, of course, but few have the qualities of an acceptable groundcover.

Such a groundcover must provide a rather complete mantle for the soil surface. It must be perennial. It must be vigorous enough to maintain itself and keep down most weeds, but not so rampant that it crowds out its neighbors. It must require little maintenance.

Also, it should be inexpensive to purchase. This is a desirable quality indeed because it often takes a large number of plants to cover even a moderate area. But don't sacrifice quality and suitability for price considerations. All good groundcovers can be increased rather easily and most of them surprisingly quickly. So if you can't, or don't feel inclined to buy *all* the plants you need, then buy some.

Lay in a stock sufficient to plant part of the area you want to cover. And then begin a program of propagation. Within a year or two your stock will have increased many-fold.

Early spring and early fall are the best times to set out groundcover plants. If you are planting on steeply sloping land the former is decidedly to be preferred, since there is less chance of erosion before the plants take hold. When planting such areas mulch the surface with coarse compost or litter, just as a precaution.

Some groundcovers are evergreen, others die down during the winter. Most important in making a selection is to choose one highly adapted to the soil and situation you have to face. To look well, a groundcover must be in flourishing condition, not just hanging on. •

GARDENING

These Are The Best Groundcovers

PACHYSANDRA *(pachysandra terminalis)*. Evergreen. Height 6 inches. Foliage yellow-green. Flowers white, rather inconspicuous. Forms a thick carpet and an interesting leaf pattern. Spreads slowly. Apt to "burn" in exposed places in winter. Set plants 6 or 7 inches apart. Propagate by division, cuttings, or root-cuttings. If in sun needs fairly moist soil. Thrives in wide range of soils.

CREEPING MYRTLE *(vinca minor)*. Evergreen. Height 3 or 4 inches. Foliage deep glossy green. Flowers blue or white, attractive. Forms a flat mat. Spreads rapidly. Set one-year or two-year old field-grown plants 12 inches apart each way. Propagate by division or cuttings. Grows well in poor soils.

PURPLELEAF WINTERCREEPER EUONYMUS *(euonymus fortunei coloratus)*. Evergreen. Height 9 to 12 inches. Foliage deep green, becoming purple in winter. Flowers inconspicuous. Forms a somewhat loose spreading mat. May be kept more compact by shearing each spring. Spreads rapidly. Much less subject to scale insects than most euonmyuses. Set plants 2 feet apart. Propagate by cuttings or by transplanting self-rooted stems. Thrives in wide variety of soils.

CARPET BUGLE *(ajuga reptans)*. Not evergreen. Height 2 or 3 inches. Foliage deep green or bronze. Flowers blue, attractive. Forms dense mat. Spreads rapidly. Set plants 9 to 12 inches apart. Propagate by division. Needs moderately moist soil.

DWARF LILY-TURF *(ophiopogon japonicus)*. Evergreen. Height 9 to 12 inches. Foliage deep green. Flowers lilac, attractive. Forms dense turf. Spreads slowly. Set plants 10 to 12 inches apart. Propagate by division. Any ordinary soil.

BIG BLUE LILY-TURF *(liriope muscari)*. Evergreen. Height 9 to 12 inches. Foliage deep green or variegated with yellow. Flowers lilac. Forms dense turf. Spreads slowly. Set plants 10 to 12 inches apart. Propagate by division. Any ordinary soil.

For Sun

MEMORIAL ROSE *(rosa wichuraiana)*. Not evergreen. Height 18 inches. Foliage medium-green. Flowers white, attractive. Forms tangled, thorny carpet. A vigorous grower, spreads fairly quickly. Set plants 3 to 6 feet apart. Propagate by cuttings. Not particular as to soil. Shear or prune back each year after blooming. Good for banks.

ROSE "MAX GRAF." Not evergreen. Height 1 foot. Foliage medium green. Flowers pink, attractive. A vigorous trailer. Spreads fairly quickly. Set plants 3 to 6 feet apart. Propagate by cuttings. Any well-drained soil. Shear occasionally if needed. Good for banks.

BEARBERRY *(arctostaphylos uva-ursi)*. Evergreen. Height 4 inches. Foliage dark green. Flowers white or pinkish. Berries red. Forms thick mat of trailing stems. Set plants one foot apart. Use pot-grown plants only. Propagate by cuttings. Needs acid soil. Thrives on sandy and gravelly soils.

MOSS PINK *(phlox subulata)*. Evergreen. Height 4 inches. Foliage light- to medium-green. Flowers white, lilac, pink, and red, showy. Forms dense mat. Spreads moderately fast. Set plants one to one and a half feet apart. Propagate by cuttings and division. Any well-drained soil.

CREEPING JUNIPERS *(juniperus horizontalis, and Bar Harbor juniper Waukeegan juniper and some others)*. Evergreen. Height 12 inches. Foliage green or blue-green. No flowers. Form dense mats. Spread rapidly. Set plants 2 to 3½ feet apart. Propagate by cuttings. Any well-drained soil.

STONE-CROPS *(sedum album, sedum hybridum, sedum rupestre, sedum acre, sedum sexangulare, sedum stoloniferum and others)*. Heights 4 to 9 inches. Foliage green. Flowers white, pink, red, or yellow. Form mats. Spread rapidly. Propagate by division or cuttings. Any well-drained soil.

For Shade

ENGLISH IVY *(hedera helix)* and
BALTIC IVY *(hedera helix baltica)*. Baltic ivy has smaller leaves and stands severe cold better than English ivy. Otherwise similar. Evergreen. Height 6 inches (climbs high if given support). Foliage dark green. Forms mat of trailing, rooting stems. Spreads rapidly. If exposed to sun or sweeping winds foliage "burns" badly in winter. Set plants 18 to 24 inches apart. Propagate by cuttings or by transplanting self-rooted stems. Needs moderately moist soil containing fair amount of humus.

LILY-OF-THE-VALLEY *(convallaria majalis)*. Not evergreen. Height to 6 inches. Foliage medium green. Flowers white, fragrant, highly attractive. Forms thick cover. Spreads slowly. Set plants 6 to 8 inches apart. Propagate by division. Needs rich, moist, humusy soil. Plants should be lifted, divided and replanted every few years.

EUROPEAN WILD GINGER *(asarum europeum)*. Evergreen 6 to 8 inches. Foliage dark lustrous green, very handsome. Flowers inconspicuous. Forms neat cover. Spreads slowly. Set plants 8 or 9 inches apart. Propagate by division and seeds. Needs rich, reasonably moist soil.

BARRENWORT *(epimedium—any kind)*. Not evergreen. Height 6 to 9 inches. Foliage green or bronzy-green. Flowers white, pink or yellow; handsome. Forms a dense cover. Does not spread. Grows slowly. Set plants 10 to 12 inches apart. Propagate by division. Needs fairly moist soil rich with humus. Very choice.

Hedges and groundcovers are used here to define boundaries of lawn, give architectural effects.

HEDGES—how to plant and maintain them

Walls of living green serve a variety of purposes and give your home garden that mark of distinction.

HEDGES are used to mark boundaries, to provide backgrounds, to insure privacy and to afford protection from wind, animals and the neighborhood kids, also to give architectural character.

They may be sheared and strictly formal, lightly trimmed and semi-formal, or untrimmed. Hedges are evergreen or deciduous, low or tall, wide or narrow.

No one plant offers all these variations. Decide upon the particular virtues you would like your hedge to have, then select the plant most likely to provide them. Consider not only what *you* want from the plant but also what *the plant needs* to succeed. Can you offer the soil and situation that the plant you have in mind must have?

Before you plant a hedge decide upon its ultimate height. The minimum width at maturity of a tall hedge is greater than that of a low hedge of the same kind. This width at maturity is something to consider, especially if you are planting along the boundary of neighboring property.

The wisest plan is to set hedges so that they will not intrude when fully grown. This means that the center of the hedge must be well inside the property line, the exact distance inside to be determined by the width of the hedge at maturity, which in turn is dependent upon the kind of plant used and the height it reaches.

Having decided upon the kind of hedge you want, locate a source of supply. Young, vigorous hedge plants are nearly always best although older plants can sometimes be used successfully for informal hedges and occasionally it is necessary to employ them to create immediate effects. Usually, plants 1 to 3 feet tall are preferred.

Planting. Plants in a hedge are crowded and need every help possible. Prepare the soil well. Dig a trench at least a foot deep and of ample width to take the roots without crowding. Spade plenty of manure or compost into its bottom. Mix humus and bone meal with the good topsoil packed about the roots.

Don't set hedge plants too far apart. For most deciduous kinds a foot apart in a single row or a foot and a half apart in a double is best. Because of their cost it is often necessary to space evergreens at twice this distance.

Cut back newly-planted deciduous hedges to within six inches of the ground. This takes courage but results in vigorous growth and a dense hedge well furnished to its base. Less severe treatment often results in an open bottom. After this initial pruning don't trim the hedge again during its first season. The following spring cut it back to about a foot high and begin regular trimming. Prune newly-planted evergreen hedges lightly.

Privet hedge, square cut and with vertical sides. This is well placed, not too near the sidewalk.

These round-form hemlock hedges had originally been planted almost too close to one another (below).

Deciduous hedge loses its leaves in winter. Here it forms an effective border for roadway.

Care of Hedges. Hedges need fertilizing, watering, spraying and other care normally afforded shrubs and evergreens. They also need trimming (unless they are completely informal).

Never shape a hedge so that its top is wider than its base. Strong growing types such as privet may have vertical sides but it is better to taper the hedge gradually to the top. The top may be flat, rounded or pointed.

Trim formal hedges with hand or electric hedge shears. A knife or pruning shears is best for semiformal ones.

During the years the hedge is developing, shorten all strong growing shoots several times during each season. This encourages bushiness and is especially important with evergreens.

Mature hedges need trimming once or twice a year only. •

GARDENING

Good Hedge Plants

Deciduous

GLOSSY ABELIA *(Abelia grandiflora)*. Good sheared or unsheared. Semi-evergreen. 2 to 4 feet tall, 1 to 3 feet wide. Dark green. Pink flowers. In harsh climates winter kills, but the plant renews itself each summer. Sun or light shade.

FIVE-LEAVED ARALIA *(Acanthopanax sieboldianus)*. Good sheared. 2 to 5 feet high, 1½ to 3 feet wide. Medium green. Stems thorny, forming impenetrable hedge. Stands shade and city conditions well.

MENTOR BARBERRY *(Berberis mentorensis)*. Good sheared or unsheared. Semi-evergreen. 2 to 5 feet tall, 1½ to 4 feet wide. Dark green. Stems thorny, forming impenetrable barrier. Stands heat and drought well.

JAPANESE BARBERRY *(Berberis thunbergi)*. Good sheared or unsheared. 1½ to 5 feet tall, 1 to 3 feet wide. Light green. Variety *atropurpurea* reddish-plum colored. Flowers yellow. Berries red, long-lasting. Stems thorny, forming a good barrier. Stands shade, dryness and poor soil.

BOX BARBERRY *(Berberis thunbergi minor)*. Identical with Japanese barberry but lower and smaller leaves. 9 to 15 inches high, 6 to 9 inches wide.

TRUEHEDGE COLUMNBERRY *(Berberis thunbergi erecta)*. Identical with Japanese barberry but more erect. Suitable for narrow hedges.

DWARF-WINGED EUONYMUS *(Euonymus alata compacta)*. Good sheared or unsheared. 2 to 5 feet tall, 2 to 5 feet wide. Foliage green, brilliant red in fall. Stands some shade.

BEECH (American Beech, *Fagus grandifolia* and European Beech, *Fagus sylvatica*). Good sheared. 6 to 12 or more feet tall, 4 to 6 feet wide. Medium green. American Beech stands more cold than the European Beech, is somewhat more difficult to transplant. Both have surface root systems. Difficult to grow flowers near them.

COMMON BUCKTHORN *(Rhamnus cathartica)*. Good sheared. 4 to 10 feet tall, 3 to 5 feet wide. Medium green. Thorny. Very hardy. Succeeds in shade and in dry places perhaps better thany any other hedge plant.

GLOSSY BUCKTHORN *(Rhamnus frangula)*. Not quite so dense as Common Buckthorn but more handsome. Otherwise similar.

PRIVET (Several Kinds). Good sheared. 3 to 6 feet or more tall, 3 to 4 feet wide. Dark green. Quick growing. Stands shade. Amur Privet *(Ligustrum amurense)* is hardiest. California Privet *(Ligustrum ovalifolum)* has brighter foliage. Stands shade and other difficult conditions. Good under city conditions. Roots exhaust soil for some distance around. Difficult to grow flowers near.

Evergreen

KOREAN BOXWOOD *(Buxus microphylla koreana)*. Good sheared or unsheared. 2 to 2½ feet tall, 2 to 3 feet wide. Dark green. Slow growing. Hardier than Common Boxwood.

JAPANESE BOXWOOD *(Buxus microphylla japonica)*. Identical with Korean Boxwood but taller. 3 to 4 feet tall, 2½ to 4 feet wide.

COMMON BOXWOOD *(Buxus sempervirens)*. Good sheared or unsheared. 3 to 15 feet tall, 2 to 9 feet wide. Dark green. Slow growing. The choicest boxwood.

EDGING BOXWOOD *(Buxus sempervirens suffruticosa)*. Identical with common boxwood but dwarfer. 1 to 2 feet tall, 1 to 2 feet wide.

ITALIAN CYPRESS *(Cupressus sempervirens)*. Good sheared or unsheared. 4 to 12 feet or more tall. 2 to 3 feet wide. Dark green. For mild climates only.

JUNIPERS (Chinese Juniper, *Juniperus chinensis*; Red-cedar, *Juniperus virginiana*). Good sheared or unsheared. 4 to 12 feet or more tall, 3 to 4 feet wide. Green or blue green. Stand dryness well. Need full sun.

GLOSSY PRIVET *(Ligustrum lucidum)*. Good sheared. 6 to 12 feet or more, 3 to 6 feet wide. Dark glossy green. Suitable for mild climates only. Very handsome. Exhausts nearby soil of fertility and moisture. Difficult to grow flowers near.

PITTOSPORUM *(Pittosporum tobira)*. Good sheared or unsheared. 3 to 6 feet tall, 3 to 5 feet wide. Dark green. Fragrant flowers. Suitable for mild climates only.

DOUGLAS-FIR *(Pseudotsuga douglasi)*. Good sheared. 6 to 12 feet or more high, 4 to 6 feet wide. Dark green.

JAPANESE YEW *(Taxus cuspidata and varieties)*. Good sheared. 3 to 6 feet or more tall, 2 to 4 feet wide. Variety *nana* (often listed as *brevifolia*) best for low hedges. Dark green. Stands shade. One of the best hedges.

ENGLISH YEW *(Taxus baccata and varieties)*. Similar to Japanese Yew but suited only for mild climates.

AMERICAN ARBORVITAE *(Thuya occidentalis)*. Good sheared. 4 to 12 feet or more tall, 3 to 6 feet wide. Dark green. Stands some shade. Needs fairly moist soil.

HEMLOCK (Canada Hemlock, *Tsuga canadensis*; Carolina Hemlock, *Tsuga caroliniana*). Good sheared. 4 to 12 feet or more tall, 4 to 8 feet wide. Dark green. Stands light shade. Among the finest of hedge plants.

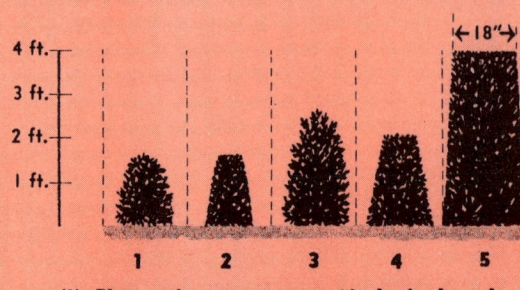

---

(1) Plant only evergreens with leafy branches even with the ground. (2) Trim lightly. (3) First year growth. (4) Encourage bushiness by shortening all growing shoots several times each season. (5) Shear hedge once or twice every year.

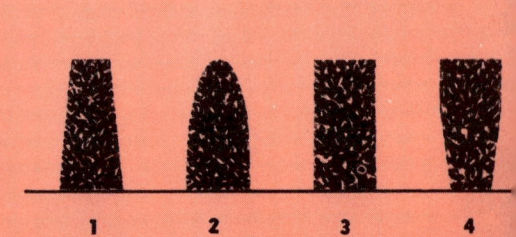

(1) and (2) are good hedge shapes because the top is narrower than the bottom. In (3) the vertical sides are all right for strong-growing varieties such as privet. (4) shows what to avoid —the top should never be wider than the bottom.

Training Deciduous Hedge

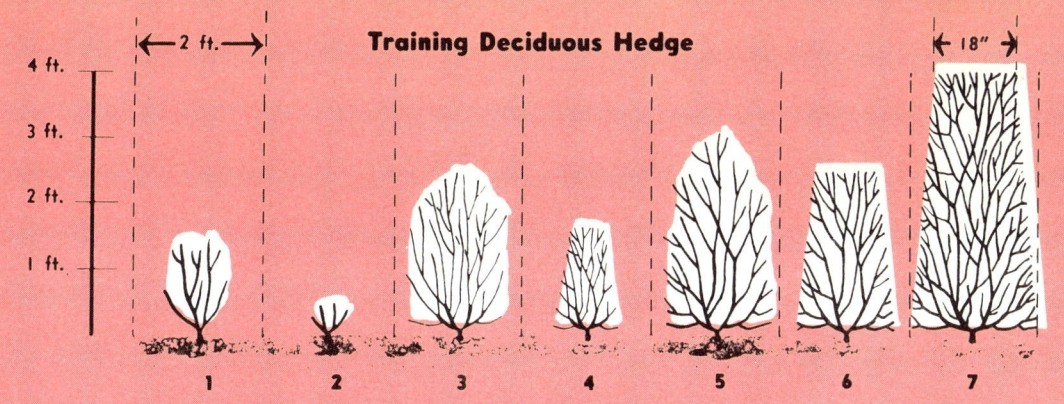

(1) When planted, hedge is 18" high. (2) After planting, prune to only 6". (3) Don't trim again during the first season. (4) The following spring cut to height of 1 foot, begin regular trimming. (5) Shorten strong growing shoots. (6) In trimming, taper gradually to top. (7) Mature hedge.

In planting deciduous hedge, first stretch line where you are going to place the hedge.

Dig the trench a foot deep, using the spade. The width of the digging should be ample.

Spade compost or manure into the bottom of the trench. Be sure to use adequate amount.

...ove burlap around roots, ...each in a straight line ...pre-determined distance.

Note the fine root system of this young hedge plant, which is Japanese Barberry variety.

Fill trench around the roots, using only good soil that is mixed with humus materials.

...own the earth around ...plant, treading firmly upon ...the overturned chunks of soil.

Fill in additional soil and finish the surface so it is level and without foot marks.

Take a pair of shears and cut the newly-planted hedge back to within 6" of the ground.

GARDENING

Vines in Variety

There's a vine for every purpose but be sure that the vine you choose is the proper one for what you may have in mind.

YOU certainly have a place in your garden for a vine—to screen a porch, to clothe a pergola, to climb a chimney, to soften architecture, to relieve the monotony of wall or fence.

There is a vast number of vines from which you can choose. Select those best suited for your purpose.

To do this intelligently you must know something about how these plants climb. If you do not you may make the mistake of planting a kind that permanently attaches itself, such as Virginia-creeper or evergreen euonymus, against a wooden house and have to tear it down next time the house is painted. Or you may court disappointment by planting a vine of restrained growth such as the five-leaved akebia in hopes that it will cover a tall chimney.

Stickers. Vines that cling or stick by aerial roots or by sucker-like discs should never be planted against supports that need painting. They belong only on masonry, brick or concrete walls, or against the trunks of trees. They are ideal for situations where tall climbers are needed, because they need no special supports.

1468

Perennial Vines

GARDENING

FIVE-LEAVED AKEBIA. Height 12 ft. or more. Flowers rather inconspicuous, fragrant. Foliage dark green, of refined appearance. Free of pests and diseases. Soil, rich. Position sunny, will stand light shade moderately mild climates (twiner).

DUTCHMAN'S PIPE. Height 30 ft. Flowers insignificant. Foliage bold, handsome, forming a dense screen. Grows rapidly. Almost any soil and situation. Dies to ground each year (twiner).

TRUMPET CREEPER (Trumpet Vine). Height 30 ft. Flowers red, orange or yellow. Summer. Foliage light green. Ordinary kind (Campsis radians) attaches itself by aerial rootlets, Chinese kind (Campsis chinensis) has few or none. Rich moist soil and sunny position. Attracts humming birds. Prune back young growths fall or spring.

BITTERSWEET. Height 25-30 ft. Flowers inconspicuous. Fruits orange, decorative. Male plants do not fruit. Set male and female plants near together. Difficult to transplant, cut back severely when transplanted. Soil, ordinary. Sun or light shade. Prune young growths severely fall, winter or spring. Much subject to infestations of scale insects (twiner).

CLEMATIS (Many Kinds). Height 6 to 15 ft. Flowers large or small, white, blue purple, pink or red. Among best are Jackmani (purple), paniculata (white, fragrant) and montana rubens (pink). First two may be pruned low, each spring, last should be lightly thinned only. Soil deep, cool, well drained, not acid. Keep mulched with compost or leafmold. Position sunny, with roots shaded from sun. Paniculata easiest to grow, is small flowered, blooms in fall. Seeds are attractive. Twines leaf stalks around supports.

CINNAMON-VINE. Height 10 to 25 feet. Flowers small white, fragrant. Foliage, dark green. Grows rapidly, stems die to ground each winter. Any ordinary soil. Sun or shade (twiner).

EVERGREEN EUONYMUS. (Bigleaf Wintercreeper). Height 30 feet. Handsome foliage. Fruits resembling those of bittersweet. Subject to infestations of scale insects. Any location. Ordinary soil, but in rich soil becomes established sooner. To encourage climbing provide supports from beginning. The hardiest evergreen vines (aerial rootlets).

ENGLISH IVY. Height 50 feet or more. Evergreen. Handsome foliage. Flowers rather insignificant, fruits blue-black. Many varieties of which "Baltica" is hardiest. Likes rich, fairly moist soil. Thrives in shade, also in sun provided soil is not dry (aerial rootlets).

CLIMBING HYDRANGEA. 30 feet or more. Handsome foliage. Showy white flowers. Slow-growing when young. Plant against north or west-facing walls in deeply prepared rich soil. Excellent for sea-side. Both Hydrangea petiolaris and the rarer Schizophragma hydrangeoides are good. Prune back previous years growths winter or spring (aerial roots).

PERENNIAL PEA. Height 6-7 feet. Flowers pink or white, resembling sweet peas but not fragrant. Rather difficult to transplant, always take ball of earth when moving them. Dislikes acid soil. Full sun. Very hardy (tendrils).

HONEYSUCKLE. Height 10-25 feet or more. Several kinds. Flowers white, apricot, red, etc., fragrant. Prune by thinning in spring. Soil ordinary. Position sunny. Halls honeysuckle which stands shade is apt to become a pest, difficult to eradicate (twiner).

CLIMBING ROSES. Height 6-20 feet. All colors except lavender, purple and blue. Fragrant. For culture see chapter on Roses (scramblers).

MOONSEED. Height 8 feet. Flowers inconspicuous. Fruits black, resembling small grapes. Foliage attractive. Dies down almost to ground each winter. Likes moist soil. Shade or sun (twiner).

BOSTON-IVY. Height 50 feet or more. Foliage handsome, brilliantly colored in fall. Often takes a year or two to begin climbing. Any ordinary soil. Sun or shade (discs on tendrils).

VIRGINIA-CREEPER. Height 50 feet or more. Foliage handsome, brilliantly colored in fall. Any ordinary soil. Sun or shade. In damp, shaded places often is disfigured by mildew in fall (discs on tendrils).

SILVER LACEVINE. Height 25 feet. Flowers white in foamy masses. Foliage attractive. Prune back to live wood each spring. Any ordinary soil. Sun (twining).

WISTERIA. Height 50 feet or more. Flowers blue, lavender or white, fragrant. Foliage attractive. Plants in shade or growing too vigorously often fail to bloom. Excessive vigor may be checked by root-pruning and by strict attention to summer pruning (see page 103). Plants raised from seeds often fail to bloom for many years. Get grafts from plants of known flowering ability. Somewhat difficult to transplant. Set plants from pots. Needs stout supports (twining).

Cup of Gold will thrive outdoors in warm climates only.

Canary Creeper is an annual, has daintily fringed blooms.

Climbing Hydrangea is a fine floral vine for north wall.

Boston Ivy is good on masonry but shouldn't be used on wood.

Passion Flower is bright blue, clings to support by tendrils.

Sweet Peas thrive only in cool weather. Sow early in wet soil.

GARDENING

Annual Vines

BALLOON VINE. Height 5-10 feet. Flowers inconspicuous. Fruits decorative, resembling miniature balloons. Sow outdoors when all danger of frost has passed. Likes a warm sunny situation (tendrils).

BALSAM-APPLE AND BALSAM-PEAR. Heights 15-20 feet. Fruits curious, colorful and ornamental. Foliage attractive, deeply lobed, rich green. Sow outdoors when trees begin to leaf or earlier indoors in pots and transplant later. Rich soil and sunny location desirable. Need plenty of moisture (tendrils).

BLACK-EYED SUSAN VINE. Height 4 to 8 feet. Flowers orange, yellow, or white with purple-black throats. Tends to crawl on the ground. Good for window boxes, porch boxes, urns etc. Sow outdoors when soil is warm or better indoors early and transplant to garden later. Full sun and ordinary soil (twiner).

CANARY CREEPER (Canary-Bird Vine). Height 10-12 feet. Flowers clear yellow attractively fringed. Foliage deeply lobed, light green. Requires same treatment as nasturtium to which it is related (twiner).

CARDINAL CLIMBER. Height 15 feet. Flowers scarlet, resembling small morning glories, opening shortly after dawn, closing at night-fall. Foliage glossy green, attractively dissected. Culture same as for Cypress vine (twiner).

CUP-AND-SAUCER VINE (Cobaea). Height 15-20 feet. Flowers large, bell-shaped, purple, or white, good for cutting. Start in pots indoors 6 weeks before plants are to be set in open ground, set seeds on edge, scarcely cover them with soil. Avoid keeping too wet. Set plants in garden when weather is settled and warm. Likes full sun and warm, rich soil but will grow in partial shade (tendrils).

CYPRESS VINE. Height 10-15 feet. Flowers scarlet or white, star-shaped, open only at night and very early and very late in the day. Foliage green, fern-like, very dainty. Sow outdoors after soil has warmed up or indoors (twiner).

GOURDS. Height 8-12 feet. Fruits colorful and highly ornamental. Can be preserved for winter decoration indoors. Sow indoors in pots 6 weeks before ground is warm and weather is settled enough to transplant to open garden, or sow outdoors after all danger of frost is passed. Cutworms are apt to attack young plants. Rich soil best. Position sunny (tendrils).

HYACINTH BEAN. Height 10 feet. Flowers white, lavender, purple, good for cutting. Fruits highly ornamental, white or purple. Sow outdoors after danger of frost has passed, or early indoors in pots and transplant outdoors later. Avoid disturbing roots when transplanting. Full sun. Any reasonably good soil (twiner).

JAPANESE HOP VINE. Height 20-25 feet. Female plants have yellowish-green catkins. Foliage attractively lobed, often variegated with white. Very fast grower. Sow early spring. Will stand some shade as well as heat and drought. Any reasonable soil (twiner).

MOON-VINE. Height 20 feet. Flowers large, white fragrant, open in the evening and at night only. Foliage heart-shaped, attractive. Soak seeds in tepid water for 24 or 48 hours before sowing. Sow indoors in pots 6 weeks before transplanting to open ground which is done after weather is settled and warm. Soil ordinary. Full sun. Needs plenty of moisture when actively growing (twiner).

MORNING GLORY. Height 8-20 feet. Flowers white, pink, red, purple, blue, and variegated. Leaves heart-shaped, dark green. Sow directly outdoors in spring or start early indoors or in frame in pots and transplant to garden when danger of frost is over. Grows in any fair soil but responds to good conditions. Soak seeds in water for a few hours before sowing. Full sun (twiner).

NASTURTIUM. Height 6 feet. Flowers buff, yellow, orange red, maroon. Highly attractive. Foliage light green. Sow outdoors when ground is warm. Soil should not be rich in nitrogen otherwise excessive foliage develops at expense of blooms. Full sun. In many sections extraordinarily subject to infestations of aphids (twiner).

SCARLET RUNNER BEAN. Height 8-15 feet. Flowers scarlet. Beans edible if taken from pods before fully matured. Sow seeds outdoors after ground has warmed somewhat. Keep soil dryish until seedlings are well up. Plants require copious supplies of water during summer. Good soil and full sun (twiner).

SWEET PEA. Height 5-8 feet. Flowers all colors, except yellow. Fragrant, splendid for cutting. A cool weather annual, dies when hot, humid, weather comes. In favored sections sow outdoors in late fall, elsewhere at earliest date in spring it is possible to have the ground in condition. May also be started indoors or in frame in pots early and later transplanted. Soil deeply prepared, rich. Water freely during growing season. Fertilize generously. Keep all faded flowers picked (tendrils).

Twiners. Twining vines twist themselves tightly around their supports by rotating the tips of their stems as they extend themselves. The important things to remember is that they cannot twine around objects that are too thick, trunks of trees for example. They need supports of lesser diameter such as stakes, wires, strings, or slender posts.

A few of the more vigorous, including wisteria and bittersweet, manage to scramble up tall trees, twisting two or three of their own stems to form sturdy upward extenders.

Some twiners rotate always in a clockwise direction as do the Japanese hop and the honeysuckle, but the majority, like the morning-glory, twine themselves from right to left, or counter-clockwise.

If you are starting the stem of a twining vine around a support be sure you wind it in the right direction, otherwise it must reverse itself before it can climb.

Tendril-Twiners. The sweet-pea, cup-and-saucer vine and many others grip their supports by means of special organs called tendrils. These sensitive devices coil around strings, wires, brushwood, canes, and other objects of small diameter. They cannot take hold of thick supports. Similar in character are vines such as nasturtium which coil the stalks of their leaves around their supports.

Scramblers. Not all vines attach themselves. Climbing roses for example do not. They just scramble upwards, aided in the case of roses by their down-pointed thorns. But jasmines have no thorns. Neither do some others of their class. Scramblers weave their branches among each other and attain height in that way.

For convenience of culture we may consider vines as annuals and perennials. The annuals like other annual flowers are raised from seed each year. The perennials, if

GARDENING

hardy to the locality, once established are there indefinitely.

Perennial Vines. Because perennial vines are luxuriant growers give them the best you can in the way of soil preparation. Work the soil deeply. Add lots of compost or rotted manure and mix in a generous drenching of bone-meal. Beware particularly of soil around the foundations of a house. It is apt to be poor sub-soil, covered with four or five inches of better soil. Excavate and discover what the conditions are before you plant.

Except in milder parts of the country plant in spring rather than fall, because the vines take hold of their supports quickly then and are less likely to be damaged by storms.

If you are planting English-ivy, trumpet-creeper or other vine that clings by rootlets or sucker-like discs, cut it down to within a few inches of the ground. In fact it pays to prune all perennial vines severely back at planting time. Set the plants as close to the support as possible.

Be sure that you water newly planted vines thoroughly during their first season or two whenever there is need for it. Especially, beware of the soil drying if they are planted against a building that has an overhanging roof. Give attention also to watering established vines in dry weather. Don't do this merely when they are blooming.

Annual Vines That Soon Cover. Vines that you can grow and bloom in one summer with no more trouble or expense than buying a packet of seeds and sowing them in spring are invaluable. You can use them for temporary screens and backgrounds, to decorate fences and walls and to give height and interest to the flower border. Some are fragrant and many provide excellent flowers for cutting. Such are the annual vines.

None cling by means of rootlets or sucker discs. All attach themselves either by tendrils, as does the sweet pea, or by twining stems as does the morning glory. Therefore they must be provided with sticks, trellises, openwork fences, strings or wires.

Vines For Warm Regions. The milder the climate the greater is the variety of perennial vines.

Most showy among the flowering ones are yellow allamanda, pink coral-vine, pink, red and apricot bougainvilleas, yellow and orange bignonias, beaumontia (white flowers like Easter-lilies), fragrant mignonette-vine, white and red clerodendron or glorybower, lavender cryptostegia, golden hibertia, yellow and white jasmines, beautiful passion-flowers in red, blue and other colors, purple wreath or petrea with lavender and purple flowers, scarlet rangoon-creeper, cup-of-gold with huge chalices that change from cream to deepest gold, handsome lavender potato-vines, sweetly fragrant white stephanotis, yellow orchid-vine, and many others. •

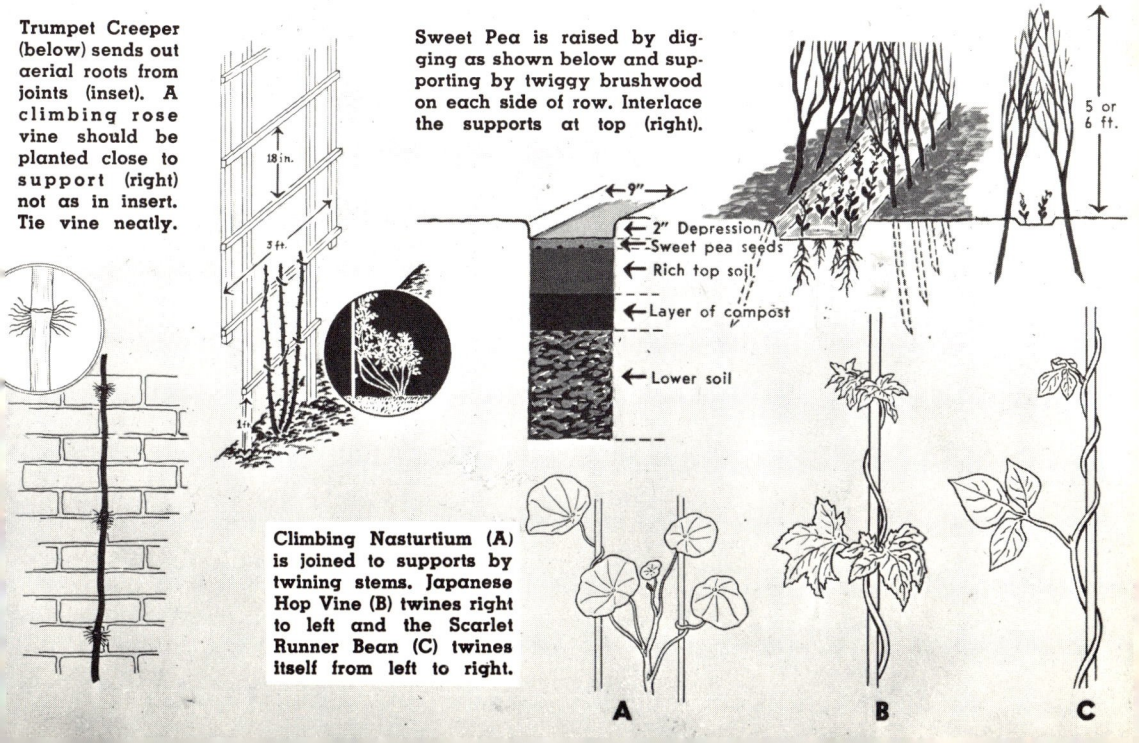

Trumpet Creeper (below) sends out aerial roots from joints (inset). A climbing rose vine should be planted close to support (right) not as in insert. Tie vine neatly.

Sweet Pea is raised by digging as shown below and supporting by twiggy brushwood on each side of row. Interlace the supports at top (right).

Climbing Nasturtium (A) is joined to supports by twining stems. Japanese Hop Vine (B) twines right to left and the Scarlet Runner Bean (C) twines itself from left to right.

GARDENING

Here is a border of annuals showing phlox in front, salvia farinacea behind it and sunflowers at right rear.

ANNUALS—for quick returns

A small investment brings a generous short-term yield when you can sow the seeds and enjoy the flowers that very year.

THE quickest return on a minimum investment that your garden gives is provided by annuals. These plants bloom the year you plant them. You sow the seeds, care for the crop, enjoy the flowers and discard the plants all within the space of a few months or even weeks. And next year you begin all over again. It's as simple as that.

Annuals are musts for the short-term garden. If you rent rather than own and don't want to spend too much on the garden, annuals are for you. If you want to improve your soil over a period of years by turning it each fall and adding humus, grow annuals. If you seek variety among cut flowers or want to brighten the garden during the summer try zinnias, marigolds, petunias and other annual flowers.

No plants are easier to grow once their simple requirements are understood. Almost all need plenty of sun; a few stand light shade. All grow well in a freely-drained fertile soil that would produce good vegetables. Some succeed in poorer soil.

Many can be sown outdoors. Others are usually started indoors or in a frame and are later transplanted to the garden.

Give annuals room to develop. Keep them free of weeds, pests and diseases, water and stake them when necessary and they will reward you grandly.

It's important to select the kind of annuals best adapted to your purpose. Don't sow larkspurs or gaillardias, if what you want is an all-summer display because they bloom lavishly but briefly in early summer and die when the first real hot weather comes. Yet they are splendid as early sum-

MARIGOLD   SWEET SULTAN   VINCA   HYBRID NASTURTIUM

Annuals: These Bloom from Seed the First Year — GARDENING

Flower	White	Cream	Yellow	Orange	Brown	Red	Pink	Lavender	Purple	Blue	Suitable for Hot, Dry Places	Dies Out in Hot, Humid Weather	Will Stand Some Shade	Height in Inches	Approximate Distance Apart in Inches	Sow Outdoors Early	Sow Outdoors When Weather Is Settled	Short Blooming Season	Sow Indoors and Transplant for Early Bloom	Good as a Cut Flower	Sow June or Early July for Late Season Bloom	Sow Sept.–Nov. in Deep South	Difficult to Transplant. Sow Where to Bloom
Ageratum							✓	✓		✓	✓		✓	6–24	8–12	✓			✓	✓			
Arctotis (African Daisy)							✓				✓	✓		15–20	9–12	✓			✓	✓			
Aster	✓	✓				✓	✓	✓	✓					9–36	9–12		✓		✓	✓			
Babysbreath	✓						✓							12–18	4–6	✓		✓		✓		✓	
Balsam	✓					✓	✓	✓					✓	9–18	9–10		✓		✓		✓		
Browallia	✓							✓						12–18	6–9		✓		✓	✓			
Calendula		✓	✓	✓										9–18	8–10	✓			✓	✓	✓		
California-Poppy		✓	✓	✓		✓	✓			✓				6–12	4–6	✓				✓		✓	✓
Calliopsis			✓	✓	✓	✓				✓	✓			12–30	6–9	✓			✓	✓			
Candytuft	✓						✓	✓					✓	6–12	4–6	✓				✓			
Carnation	✓	✓	✓			✓	✓	✓						8–18	6–10		✓			✓			
Celosia		✓	✓	✓		✓	✓							12–36	12–24		✓		✓	✓			
Chrysanthemum	✓		✓							✓				12–18	8–10	✓			✓	✓			
Cornflower	✓					✓	✓	✓	✓	✓				12–30	8–10	✓				✓		✓	
Cosmos	✓		✓	✓		✓	✓				✓			36–72	12–24		✓			✓			
Four O'Clock	✓	✓	✓			✓	✓			✓				20–24	15–18		✓			✓			
Gaillardia			✓	✓		✓					✓	✓		12–18	6–9	✓		✓		✓		✓	
Globe Amaranth	✓					✓	✓				✓			12–18	9–12		✓		✓	✓	✓		
Ice Plant	✓						✓				✓			4–6	4–6	✓							
Larkspur	✓						✓	✓		✓				12–30	6–10	✓		✓		✓		✓	✓
Leptosyne			✓											12–24	6–12	✓		✓		✓			
Linaria	✓	✓	✓			✓	✓	✓	✓	✓				12–18	6–8	✓		✓		✓		✓	
Lobelia	✓						✓	✓		✓			✓	4–8	6–8				✓				
Love-in-a-Mist	✓								✓	✓				8–12	6–8	✓		✓					
Marigold, African			✓	✓										24–42	12–24	✓			✓	✓			
Marigold, French			✓	✓	✓									6–18	8–12	✓			✓	✓			
Mexican Tulip-Poppy			✓											15–24	6–9	✓				✓			✓
Mignonette		✓										✓		6–12	4–6	✓		✓		✓			
Nasturtium		✓	✓	✓		✓					✓			9–15	6–9		✓		✓	✓			
Nicotiana	✓					✓							✓	18–48	6–24		✓		✓	✓			
Petunia	✓	✓				✓	✓	✓	✓	✓	✓			6–12	6–9		✓		✓	✓			
Phlox	✓	✓	✓			✓	✓	✓	✓	✓				6–12	4–6		✓			✓		✓	✓
Poppy	✓	✓				✓	✓						✓	18–36	6–9	✓		✓		✓		✓	✓
Portulaca	✓	✓	✓	✓		✓	✓				✓			4–5	2–3		✓						
Rudbeckia (Blanket Flower)			✓	✓	✓						✓			20–24	8–10	✓		✓		✓			
Salpiglossis	✓	✓	✓	✓	✓	✓	✓	✓				✓		24–34	6–8		✓		✓	✓			
Salvia	✓					✓	✓		✓					24–42	10–15		✓		✓				
Sanvitalia			✓								✓			3–4	3–4	✓							
Scabious	✓					✓	✓	✓	✓					30–36	8–10		✓			✓	✓		
Snapdragon	✓	✓	✓	✓		✓	✓							8–36	8–10		✓		✓	✓		✓	
Snow-on-the-Mountain	✓								✓					24–36	10–15	✓			✓				
Spider Flower	✓						✓						✓	36–48	9–10		✓		✓				
Star of Texas			✓							✓				15–20	8–9	✓			✓				
Statice	✓	✓	✓			✓	✓	✓	✓	✓				12–24	6–9		✓		✓	✓	✓		
Stock	✓	✓	✓			✓	✓	✓	✓			✓		12–25	9–12	✓			✓	✓		✓	
Strawflower	✓	✓	✓	✓		✓	✓							24–36	9–10		✓	✓	✓	✓			
Sweet Alyssum	✓						✓							4–8	3–4	✓					✓	✓	
Sweet Sultan	✓	✓	✓				✓					✓		30–36	8–10	✓				✓	✓		
Sunflower		✓	✓	✓	✓									36–96	18–24		✓			✓	✓		
Tassel Flower			✓			✓					✓			15–18	6–9	✓							
Tithonia				✓										96	36		✓		✓	✓			
Torenia	✓							✓					✓	10–12	5–7		✓		✓				
Verbena	✓					✓	✓	✓	✓	✓				6–9	8–9		✓		✓	✓			
Vinca	✓					✓	✓							9–15	8–9		✓		✓				
Wax Begonia	✓					✓	✓			✓			✓	8–12	8–9				✓				
Zinnia	✓	✓	✓	✓		✓	✓	✓			✓			9–36	6–10		✓		✓	✓	✓		

GIANT IMPERIAL STOCKS   MEXICAN TULIP-POPPY   LOBELIA   WONDER LARKSPUR

Photos courtesy, W. Atlee Burpee Co.

PINK SPIDER-FLOWER	WHITE NICOTIANA SYLVESTRIS	TALL CRIMSON CELOSIA	LEMON YELLOW AFRICAN MARIGOLD	WHITE EARLY FLOWERING COSMOS	PINK SPIDER FLOWER
BLUE SALVIA FARINACEA	TALL PALE YELLOW ZINNIA	TALL BLUE AGERATUM	TALL RED ZINNIA	STAR OF TEXAS	TALL PALE PINK ZINNIA
BLACK MAROON SCABIOUS	SNOW-ON-THE-MOUNTAIN	CRIMSON GLOBE AMARANTH			
TORENIA	SWEET ALYSSUM WHITE	YELLOW CALIFORNIA POPPY	PINK PHLOX DRUMMONDI	MEXICAN TULIP-POPPY	BROWALLIA	BRONZE FRENCH MARIGOLD	DWARF BLUE AGERATUM

mer cut flowers. On the other hand globe-amaranth and begonias bloom all summer and are fine for garden display, but are of little use for cutting. And so it goes.

Sowing. There is no special trick to sowing annuals The procedures are described in "How To Sow Seeds." It is important to select appropriate dates. Sow those that you start indoors so that the plants are just ready to put out when the weather is warm enough to permit this. Do not let them get crowded and starved while awaiting transplanting. Avoid sowing so late, however, that your plants are undersized at setting-out time. Amateurs commonly make indoor sowings too early.

On the other hand they are apt to delay outdoor sowing too long. The seeds of many annuals should be gotten into the ground on the first occasion in spring when the soil is workable. With others wait until danger from frost has passed. And in still other instances successive sowings to insure an extended season of bloom are desirable.

Care of Seedlings. From the time annuals sown directly out-of-doors break through the ground give attention to surface cultivation. Keep down all weeds and maintain the top inch of soil in a loose condition. Never cultivate deeper than this. If you do you will injure delicate feeding roots. Stir the soil each time rain packs it,

In planting annuals, lay stick where each group is to be, after carefully making your plans on paper.

not immediately after the rain ends but as soon as the soil has dried to the extent that it does not stick to shoes and cultivator.

You must thin the young plants too. Whether you sowed the seeds broadcast or in drills the seedlings will (or should) come up more thickly than the mature plants are to be. There are maybe four times as many seedlings as you need in the area, or even more. Remove the surplus before they harm their neighbors by crowding.

If possible choose cloudy weather for thinning out. Don't remove all the surplus plants at one time. Spread the operation over three or four weeks. At the first thinning pull out the weakest seedlings of those that are beginning to crowd. When the plants left begin to touch thin again, once more take out the weakest (so far as you can make such a selection) and still leave those standing correctly spaced.

The ultimate spacing will depend upon the kind of annual you are thinning. A very approximate rule suggests that the plants should be spaced finally at distances equal to half their height. This is not exact because some kinds are naturally more spready than others. But it serves fairly well as a guide.

You may have sown some annuals of easily transplantable kinds such as asters or stocks in a seed bed outdoors with the idea of moving them to their flowering quarters when big enough. This is a good

Take plants out of flats by lifting them from the bottom. Try to break away without damaging roots.

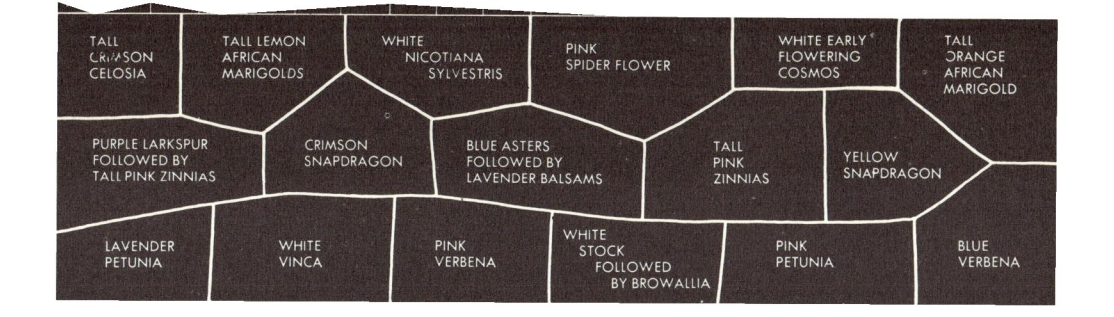

TALL CRIMSON CELOSIA	TALL LEMON AFRICAN MARIGOLDS	WHITE NICOTIANA SYLVESTRIS	PINK SPIDER FLOWER		WHITE EARLY FLOWERING COSMOS	TALL ORANGE AFRICAN MARIGOLD
PURPLE LARKSPUR FOLLOWED BY TALL PINK ZINNIAS	CRIMSON SNAPDRAGON	BLUE ASTERS FOLLOWED BY LAVENDER BALSAMS		TALL PINK ZINNIAS	YELLOW SNAPDRAGON	
LAVENDER PETUNIA	WHITE VINCA	PINK VERBENA	WHITE STOCK FOLLOWED BY BROWALLIA		PINK PETUNIA	BLUE VERBENA

plan if the place where they are to bloom is not ready at sowing time. Dig such plants up and transfer them when their second pair of leaves are well developed. Do not break the roots.

Planting. Cloudy weather is best for planting but you will not always be able to wait for this. Under exceptional conditions when you transplant in bright hot weather you may have to shade the plants temporarily after they are moved. Usually this is not necessary. Water the plants thoroughly to settle the soil about their roots.

If plants are overgrown and "leggy," in most cases they will be improved if you "pinch them back." Pinching back consists of cutting off or nipping off between the thumbnail and forefinger the tips of the growing shoots. This is successful only with such plants as petunias, snapdragons and verbenas that form side branches.

Summer Care. After the plants are set out keep the surface soil cultivated regularly as advised for annuals sown directly outdoors.

Tall-growing plants will need support of some kind. Staking should be done neatly and securely and well before the plants grow crooked or have been damaged.

Unless you intend to collect your own seed keep all faded flowers picked. This prolongs the blooming season. Seed production seriously drains the plant's energy.

Sweet alyssum blooms better if sheared back when it begins to get straggly.

Supplementing Annuals. We may consider along with garden annuals such plants as geraniums, fuchsias, heliotropes, lantanas, coleus and alternanthera. Like recognized annuals these garden plants are set out in spring, decorate the garden for a single season and in fall are dug up.

Grow these plants in pots. They transplant better from pots than from flats. Do not plant them outdoors until all danger of frost has passed and the weather has become settled and fairly warm. Their summer care is the same as for regular annuals. •

Grow These Annuals For Their Attractive Colored Foliage

Name	Color	Sowing
Castor Oil Plant	green or bronze	Sow outdoors when weather is settled. 3 feet apart.
Dusty Miller (Centaurea gymnocarpa and Centaurea candidissima)	grey	Sow early indoors and transplant or sow early outdoors.
Amaranthus "Molten Fire"	scarlet	Sow early indoors and transplant or sow early outdoors.
Amaranthus tricolor (Joseph's Coat)	red, yellow & green	Sow early indoors and transplant or sow early outdoors.
Perilla	red-purple	Sow early indoors and transplant or sow early outdoors.

Make a hole large enough to accommodate the plant without crowding. Put it in by its soil ball.

Fill hole around annual with soil and press firm. Take special care not to break or damage the stem.

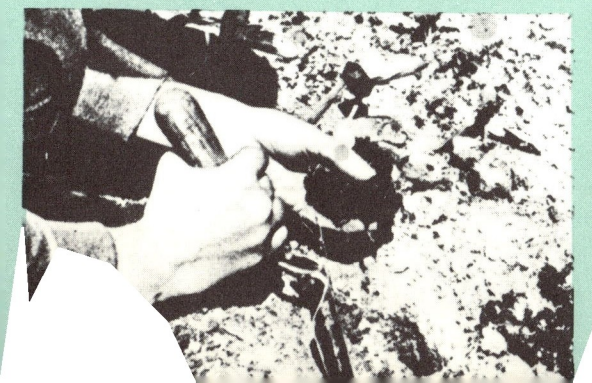

Photos by New York Botanical Garden

HOLLYHOCKS   CANTERBURY BELLS   FOXGLOVES

These Take Two Years

Photos by New York Botanical Garden

Biennials bloom but once, and then only in their second year—so give them good growing conditions.

BIENNIALS are plants that make substantial growth in their first year and in their second bloom and die. In addition to true biennials gardeners find it advantageous to grow on a biennial schedule a few plants that are technically perennials. Such plants are considered here as biennials.

Some biennials are completely hardy and may be grown out of doors at all times. Others, in severe climates, need the protection of a cold-frame during the winter.

It is most important to sow the seeds at the right time. The sowing date should allow the plants to attain good size before winter but not to become so large that they tend to run to flower in the fall, nor to become so leafy and soft that they are likely to be killed in winter.

Sowing dates vary in different parts of the country. Because a

Some biennials need a seedbed kept in shade.

When seedlings grow second pair of leaves, transplant to nursey beds. Keep soil shallowly cultivated.

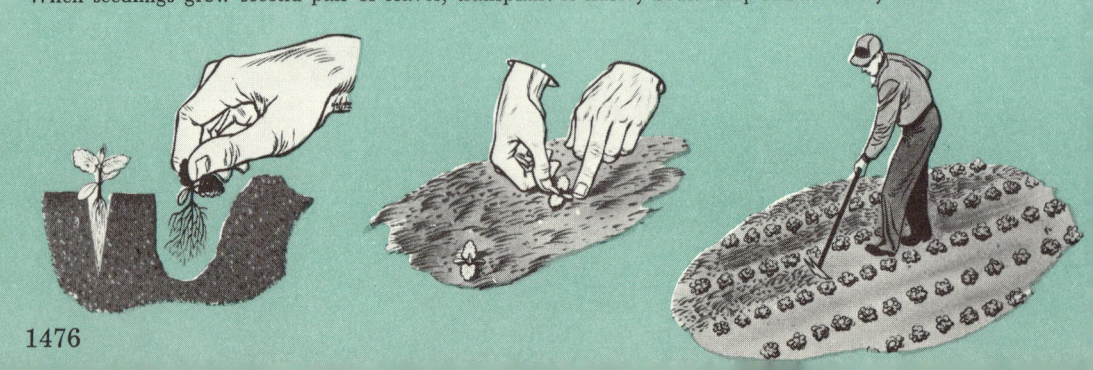

1476

GARDENING

week or two one way or the other may make considerable difference, the best date to sow a particular biennial in your garden may differ by a week or more from the best date for a garden only a few miles away. Find the most favorable dates for your garden by experiment.

Biennials are all sown in the summer months. Sow them either in an outdoor bed or in a bed in a cold-frame. Make sure the ground is not likely to wash or erode if heavy rains come. The bed should be level. Take care that it is not under the drip of trees. In any case, prepare the soil very well and scatter the seeds in shallow drills spaced three or four inches apart.

After sowing, protect the seed bed with lath shades or with burlap tacked to light wooden frames to raise it a few inches above soil level. Such protection is necessary for shade-loving biennials such as foxgloves and forget-me-nots and is desirable for others. Tiny seedlings are easily harmed by fierce summer sun. Do not keep glazed sash on cold-frames at this time of the year; shades alone are necessary.

The seed-bed must never become dry. Inspect it daily. When the young plants show above ground, gradually accustom them to stronger light if they are sun-loving kinds such as wallflowers. Begin by removing the shades both early and late and putting them in position only during the brightest part of the day. Then, after a few days, take them off altogether.

If the plants are kinds that need shade, leave the shades in place as long as necessary. The important thing is not to shade so heavily that the plants become "drawn" or "leggy" or weak. Keep the seed-bed weeded and lightly cultivated.

This sowing-in-a-special-seed-bed technique is practically essential to success in raising biennials. I have seen many beginners sow their biennials in a patch in the perennial border or in the front of the shrub border or in some other place among other plants. It never works.

Not only must they have a good seed-bed but you must also arrange for nursery-beds (or cold-frames) in which to grow them on. Biennials are grown almost to full size before they are transferred to the locations where they are to bloom. Rarely if ever will they develop satisfactorily if they are set out among other plants when small.

Biennials bloom in spring and early summer and then die. •

GARDEN BIENNIALS

CANTERBURY BELLS. For borders and cut flowers. Height 3 to 4 feet. Blooms in June-July. White, pink, lavender, purple. Sow in June. Space 12 by 9 inches in nursery beds. Full sun.

ENGLISH DAISIES. For edgings and beds. Height 6 inches. Blooms in early spring to beginning of hot weather. White, pink, red. Sow in June. Space 6 inches each way in nursery beds or cold-frames. Full sun.

FORGET-ME-NOTS. For beds and borders. Height 6 to 9 inches. Blooms in spring. Blue, white, pink. Sow in late July. Space 8 inches apart in nursery beds or frames. Needs light shade when growing. Stands full sun at flowering time.

FOXGLOVES. For borders and cut flowers. Height 3 to 6 feet. Blooms in June-July. White, pink, purple. Sow in June. Space 15 by 10 inches in nursery beds. Sun or light shade when in nursery beds; lightly shaded for flowering.

HOLLYHOCKS. For borders. Height 5 to 7 feet. Blooms in July. White, yellow, pink, red, maroon. Sow in June. Space 15 by 12 inches in nursery bed. Full sun. When grown as biennials they are not much affected by rust disease.

HONESTY. For borders and cutting. Blooms in May. Attractive seed pods follow. White, purple. Sow in June. Space 12 by 9 inches apart. Light shade.

MULLEINS. For borders. Height 2 to 6 feet. Blooms in early summer. White, pink, purple, yellow. Sow in June. Space 12 by 10 inches in nursery beds. Light shade.

PANSIES. For beds and borders. Height 6 inches. Blooms in spring until coming of hot weather. All colors and mixtures except bright red. Sow in late July or early August. Space 6 to 8 inches apart. Light shade. Will stand full sun in flowering quarters.

ROSE-CAMPION. For beds and borders. Height 2 to 3 feet. Blooms in June-July. Crimson. Foliage white-wooley. Sow in June. Space 12 by 10 inches in nursery beds. Full sun.

SWEET WILLIAMS. For beds, borders and cutting. Height 1 to 2 feet. Blooms in late spring. White, pink, red, variegated. Sow in June-July. Space 12 by 9 inches in nursery beds or cold-frames. Sun or light shade.

After ground freezes apply light layer of loose material. In spring lift plants with fork, plant in borders.

GARDENING

Photos by New York Botanical Garden

Perennials for Permanence

HARDY perennials are the backbone of the flower garden. They come in immense variety. Some, such as daylilies, are so good-natured and tenacious in their attachment to life that the most inexperienced beginner cannot fail with them. Others, including the rarer primroses and the New Zealand forget-me-not, are so difficult to satisfy that it is unusual for the most skilled gardener to bring them to bloom. Between these extremes is a vast number of easy-to-grow and reasonably easy-to-grow kinds, from among which you can select those that suit your needs.

When choosing perennials consider the purposes for which you need them. For cut flowers? To plant alone in a bed? As a group in a border or by the waterside? As an edging?

What height should the plants be? Upright or spreading? When do you want them to bloom?

The Perennial Border. Let's suppose you want to make a perennial border, which is a popular way of using these plants. You wish a variety of flowers you would like bloom from spring to fall and you want pleasing color arrangements.

First choose the location. The ideal has soil that is deep, rich and well drained, receives sunshine practically the whole day (light shade from the hottest mid-day sun would be splendid), and is sheltered from sweeping winds. You may have to settle for less. But at least strive.

Don't attempt a perennial border in unimproved subsoil from a cellar excavation, in soil that is exhausted of nourishment and moisture by nearby trees, or in dense shade. If your ground is waterlogged, drain it or try some of the common bog plants.

Locate your border so that it fits pleasingly into the garden plan, so it can be seen from the terrace or from one of the principle windows, or as a boundary to the lawn. Or part of a formal garden.

If possible provide a background—a hedge, a wall or a fence. Without such support a border is rarely as effective as with it. Walls of all kinds are good, especially if partially vine-clothed. Hedges, particularly evergreen hedges, are excellent except that greedy rooting kinds (such as privet) so rob the soil that perennials planted close to them suffer. Periodic root pruning of the hedge and additional fertilization and watering for the perennials is a partial answer. Informal backgrounds of evergreens or shrubs can be lovely.

Borders may be straight or curved or undulating but they must end somewhere. Just as backgrounds are important so are logical endings, and here again walls, fences, hedges or well-chosen groups of evergreens or shrubs suggest themselves.

Make the border not less than six feet wide. Eight or nine is better if tall plants are used. Long borders in the large gardens should not exceed twelve feet in width.

Before you plant fix up the soil. Once the plants are in you won't be able to do much more than tickle its surface for three or four years. So go to town at the beginning. If it is very poor remove the soil to a depth of at least a foot and replace it. Or crop it for a couple of years with annuals and improve it between crops by turning it and mixing in lots of humus. This will delay the planting of perennials but the results should be worth it.

Most perennials bloom for a compara-

GARDENING

tively short season. When not flowering their foliage takes up space and needs light and air and their roots need moisture and fertility. Interplanting of kinds that bloom at different seasons is helpful but is limited by these circumstances.

If you settle for less than a seasonlong riot of color you can have a good perennial border. Here's how. Use a few reliable standbys and repeat these, in different colors perhaps, along the border.

See that these basic items include kinds that bloom at different seasons and types that reach different heights.

In June, for example, clumps of peonies, irises and pinks may give character to your border. In high summer the main show might be phlox, daylilies and veronicas. For fall color rely upon asters and chrysanthemums in varying colors and heights. Between groups of these basic plants set others to give diversity and interest. Choose kinds that bloom for a long time when possible. Plant hardy bulbs also: for spring, daffodils, tulips, hyacinths and others; for summer, the hardy amaryllis.

Planting and Replanting. By following the above suggestions you will have the best possible border of a type that does not need new planting each year. This does not mean that once planted the garden will go on forever without replanting. Perennials grow and exhaust the soil and crowd their neighbors. Make over your border every third or fourth year. Dig up the plants. Fix the soil by turning it deeply and conditioning it with humus, lime if needed, and fertilizer. Replant after dividing those perennials that need such treatment. If this is too much to do at one time then make over a third or fourth of the area each year so that the entire border is done every three or four years.

You may wonder *when* the border should be remade. You have read that irises should be transplanted in early summer, peonies in late summer, phlox in fall and anemones in spring. How then can you remake a border containing all these at one time? The truth is that these recommended planting seasons are rules for perfection. Apply them if you have beds or borders given over to one kind of plant or if you are buying new plants that come as small divisions and have been out of the ground for some time. But in fall, after the first frost, and while the ground is still warm enough to encourage new roots, you can transplant almost any perennial in your own garden successfully. And that's the time to remake your border. Start as early as possible.

Although any perennial *can* be transplanted successfully, in early fall there are a few that prefer not to be moved at any time. It is better to dig around these and leave them undisturbed.

After the plants are lifted, heel them in (that is, plant them very closely together in rows) in some out of the way corner while the soil improvement is in progress. Be sure to label them carefully. If possible complete the soil work rapidly and replant immediately. If it is not possible to do this in time for the plants to make new roots before the ground freezes up delay replanting until spring. The plants will be all right heeled in if the soil where they are is well drained. Cover them with leaves, salt hay or evergreen branches over winter. Or, if you prefer, keep them in a cold-frame.

Before you plant make a plan. It's easy

When ready for replanting, divide perennials, providing good quantity of roots, sound "eyes."

See that the hole is plenty big enough and that the plant is at the right depth when planting.

Mark on ground location of each group. Use a trowel or spade in planting, depending on plant.

Add more soil, level off the surface, leaving no foot marks. No watering needed if soil is moist.

to do this on graph paper. Arrange the plants in irregular groups or drifts. Use occasional single specimens of bold subjects such as peonies and gas-plants; in most cases set three, five or more plants of a kind together.

At replanting time divide the plants that need it, and most will. When planting spread the roots and work the soil well in between them. Don't set the plants too high or too low. In nearly all cases their crowns should be about an inch below the surface. Make the soil firm about the roots. No watering is necessary unless the soil is really dry, which is unlikely to be the case. Take care to keep the soil surface neat and level and cultivate it lightly when the planting is finished. After the ground has frozen apply a winter covering.

Care of Perennials. Routine work with perennials consists of removing the winter covering when spring arrives. Don't do this too early. Better leave the covering in position until you are sure winter has departed. Don't leave it in place so long that the plants are harmed, however. If the covering is heavy remove it gradually. Choose weather that is dull and moist rather than sunny and windy for this task.

Keep the soil cultivated regularly or mulch with leaf-mold, peat-moss or other suitable material when the weather begins to get really warm. Don't mulch too early. Water in dry weather. Soak the soil to a depth of six inches or more. Then give no more until it is dry again. In hot weather this may be in four or five days. Do not hesitate to water in sunshine if the plants are in need of moisture.

Other Ways of Using Perennials. The perennial border is a favorite garden feature. Perennials can also be grown in beds by themselves, as edgings, occasionally as solitary specimens and in other ways. Details of their planting and care are the same. If you need cut flowers in quantity establish a special cutting garden and there line your perennials out in rows as you would shrubs in a nursery or vegetables in the kitchen garden. In this way you can grow many other flowers with the same effort.

Propagation. Division is the simplest way to increase most perennials. Cuttings and root-cuttings are used for some. Seeds, sown in a cold-frame or out-of-doors in the same way as biennials, are successful with many, but highly developed garden varieties cannot be propagated in this way. Progeny raised from their seed is almost always very inferior. If a perennial is a named variety don't raise from seed. •

A Selection of Good Perennials

Blooming times of the early season ones will be earlier in the South and later in the Northernmost parts of the country than indicated here.

THESE BLOOM APRIL-MAY

Name	How to Propagate	Color	Height in feet	Remarks
Anemone pulsatilla (Pasque Flower)	seed	lavender	1	Attractive in seed as well as in bloom.
Arabis albida (Rock Cress)	seed, division, cuttings	white	1	The double-flowered kind is especially good. Single flowered kind can be raised from seed.
Brunnera macrophylla (Forget-me-not Anchusa)	seed, division	blue	2	Good for shade and moist soils.
Euphorbia myrsinites	seed, division	yellow	1	
Viola odorata (Sweet Violet)	division	purple, violet, white	½	Needs fairly moist humusy soil and location that is shaded and cool in summer. North side of wall is good place.

THESE BLOOM MAY

Name	How to Propagate	Color	Height in feet	Remarks
Alyssum saxatile (Basket-of-Gold)	seed	yellow or lemon	1	Old plants are not easy to transplant. Easy to raise young ones.
Amsonia tabernaemontana	seed, division	pale blue	1½	Good for partial shade.
Anchusa azurea (A. italica)	root-cuttings, divisions, seed	pale blue	4	Some individuals are much better than others. Select the best seedlings and propagate by root-cuttings or division.
Aquilegias (Columbine)	seed	white, yellow, blue, red, lavender	2-4	Short lived. Raise a few plants from seed each year. Likes light shade.
Armeria maritima lauchneana (Thrift)	division	rose-crimson	½	Good for edgings. Does well in hot, dry places. Good for Seaside.
Cerastium tomentosum (Snow-in-Summer)	seed, division	white	1	A lover of sunshine.
Convallaria majalis (Lily-of-the-Valley)	division	white	3/4	Needs shade and rich fairly moist soil.
Dicentra spectabilis (Bleeding Heart)	division	pink	2-3	Foliage dies down middle of summer.
Doronicum (Leopardbane)	division	yellow	1½	
Helonias bullata (Swamp-pink)	division	pink	2	Likes moist or wet soil.
Iberis sempervirens (Evergreen Candytuft)	seed, division	white	3/4	Shear back lightly after flowering.
Iris (many kinds)	division	white, yellow, blue, purple	½-3	
Linum (Flax)	seed	white, yellow, blue	1½	Need full sun. Stand dry soils. Flowers drop early in afternoon.
Mertensia virginica (Virginia Bluebell)	seed, division	blue or pink	2	Foliage disappears in summer.
Phlox divaricata (Blue Phlox)	seed, division	blue, purple-blue	1	Does well in light shade.
Phlox subulata (Moss-pink)	division, cuttings	white, red, pink, magenta	½	Needs full sun. Stands dry soil.
Polemonium reptans	division	blue	3/4	Good carpeter.
Polygonatum multiflorum (Solomons-Seal)	division	white	3	Good for shade.
Primula (Hardy Primroses)	seed, division	yellow, orange, pink, red, blue	½-3	Require moist soil rich with humus, and light shade.
Trollius (Globe Flower)	seed, division	yellow, orange	1-3	Best in deep, rich moist soil.

THESE BLOOM JUNE

Name	How to Propagate	Color	Height in feet	Remarks
Allium tuberosum (A. odorum)	seed, division	white	2½	Fragrant.
Aster alpinus "Goliath"	seed, division	blue-purple	1	
Campanula glomerata	division	purple	2½	
Astilbe many kinds (Spiraeas)	division	white, red, pink	2	Need moist soil. Will stand light shade.
Campanula persicifolia in variety (Peach leaved Bell Flower)	seed, division	white, blue	2-3	

COLUMBINE

THRIFT

BLUE PHLOX

THESE BLOOM JUNE — Continued

Name	How to Propagate	Color	Height in feet	Remarks
Belamcanda chinensis (Blackberry-lily)	seeds	orange spotted with black, ornamental seeds	2-3	Full sun.
Chrysanthemum coccineum (Pyrethrum or Painted Daisy)	seed, division	red, pink	2	Need light well drained soil.
Coreopsis lanceolata grandiflora (Tickseed)	seed, division	yellow	3	
Delphinium hybrids	seed	lavender, purple, blue, white	6	
Dianthus plumarius (Cottage Pink)	seed, cuttings	red, white, pink	1	Needs full sun. Fragrant.
Dianthus gratianopolitanus (D. Caesius) (Cheddar Pink)	seed, cuttings	red, white, pink	1	Needs full sun. Fragrant.
Dicatmnus albus (Gas Plant)	seed, division	white, pink, red	3	Resents transplanting. Leave undisturbed if possible.
Filipendula hexapetala (Dropwort)	division	creamy-white	3	Low ferny foliage.
Gaillardia (Blanket Flower)	seed	yellow, orange, red	2	
Geum (Avens)	seed	yellow, orange, red	1½-3	
Gypsophila paniculata (Babys-Breath)	seed, grafting	white	3	Needs sun. Do not transplant oftener than necessary.
Helenium Hoopesii (Helen's Flower)	division	yellow	1½	
Hemerocallis (Daylily)	division	lemon, yellow, orange deep red	2-3	Easy anywhere. Stand light shade.
Heuchera (Allum-root)	division	white, pink, red	1-2	
Iris (several kinds)	division	all colors except red	2-3	
Lychnis Viscaria (German Catchfly)	seed, division	magenta	1½	Difficult color to place. Use near whites or where green predominates.
Nepeta Mussini	division cuttings	pale blue	2	Needs sun. A good edging plant.
Nepeta "Souvenir de Andre Chaudron" ("Blue Beauty")	division, cuttings	blue	2	Needs sun.
Oenothera missouriensis (Ozark Evening Primrose)	division	yellow	1	Full sun.
Papaver orientale (Oriental Poppy)	root-cuttings	pink, red white	3	Foliage dies down in summer. For full sun and well drained soil.
Phlox carolina (P. suffruticosa)	division, cuttings	white, pink,	2½	Sun or light shade.
Polemonium coeruleum (Jacobs Ladder)	division	blue	2	
Salvia pratensis	seed	lilac, white, pink	3	
Thalictrum aquilegifolium (Meadow-rue)	seed, division	white to purple	3	
Thermopsis caroliniana	seed	yellow	5	Like a tall yellow lupine.

THESE BLOOM JULY

Name	How to Propagate	Color	Height in feet	Remarks
Achillea Ptarmica "The Pearl"	division	white	2	
Althea rosea (Hollyhocks)	seed	white, yellow, pink, red	6	These are better grown as biennials. When kept as perennials are disfigured by rust disease.
Betonica grandiflora (Betony)	division seed	rose purple	2-3	
Chrysanthemum maximum (Shasta Daisy)	division	white	2-3	Needs full sun and rich soil. Divide every two years.
Clematis davidiana	seed, division	blue	3	These are bush types.
Clematis mandchurica	seed, division	white	3	These are bush types.
Echinops Ritro (Globe Thistle)	seed, division	blue-gray	4	
Erigeron speciosus (Fleabane)	division	lavender	2	

NEPETA NERVOSA

THESE BLOOM JULY — Continued

Name	How to Propagate	Color	Height in feet	Remarks
Hemerocallis (Daylily)	division	yellow, orange, brown	2-3	Easy. Stand light shade.
Monarda didyma (Bee-balm)	seed, division	white, pink, scarlet	2-3	Stands moist soil and some shade.
Penstemon barbatus (Beard-Tongue)	seed, division	scarlet	3	
Platycodon (Balloon-flower)	seed, division	blue, or white	2	
Rudbeckia (Coneflower)	seed, division	yellow, red purple, or white	3-6	
Stokesia cyanea (Stoke's Aster)	seed, division	blue, white	1	Needs sharp drainage.
Thalictrum glaucum (Meadow-rue)	division	yellow	3-4	Blue-grey foliage, fragrant.
Valeriana officinalis (Garden Heliotrope)	seed, division	pink, white, lavender	4	Fragrant.

THESE BLOOM AUGUST

Name	How to Propagate	Color	Height in feet	Remarks
Aconitum (Monkshood)	division	blue, or blue-white	4	Appreciate a little shade and rich, moderately moist soil.
Anemone hupehensis	seed, root-cuttings	lavender, rose-	2	Do not transplant oftener than necessary.
Asclepias tuberosa (Butterfly-weed)	seed	orange	2-3	Difficult to transplant.
Eryngium (Sea-holly)	seed	blue	2-2½	
Hosta (Plantain-lily)	division	white, lavender, blue	1-2	Good for shade.
Hibiscus (Rose-mallow)	division	white, pink, red	4-5	Needs full sun and moist soil.
Liatris (Blazing Star)	seed, division	pink, white	3-5	
Phlox paniculata (Hardy Phlox)	division, cuttings	white, pink, red	3-4	Much subject to disease.
Salvia Pitcheri	seed, division	blue	4	

THESE BLOOM SEPTEMBER

Name	How to Propagate	Color	Height in feet	Remarks
Aconitum (Monkshood)	division	blue-violet	5	Stand light shade, fairly moist soil. Do not transplant unless necessary.
Anemone (Japanese Anemone)	division, or root-cuttings	white, pink, red	2-4	Moist soil, light shade. Do not transplant unless necessary.
Aster (Michaelmas Daisy)	division	white, lavender, pink, red, blue	1-6	
Eupatorium coelestinum (Mist-Flower)	seed, division	blue	3	Comes up very late in spring.
Helianthus multiflorus fl. pl. (Perennial Sunflower)	division	yellow		Blooms resemble those of double dahlias.
Helenium (Helen's Flower)	seed, division	yellow, copper-red	3-5	
Hosta (Plantain-lily)	division	white, lavender,	1-2	Good for shade.
Physostegia "Vivid" (False Dragonhead)	division	white, pink, red	2-4	Spreads rapidly.
Sedum spectabile	division, cuttings	pink, red	2	For full sun and dry soils.

THESE BLOOM OCTOBER

Name	How to Propagate	Color	Height in feet	Remarks
Chrysanthemum arcticum	division, cuttings	white	2	
Chrysanthemums, hardy	division, cuttings	white, cream, yellow, bronze, red	2	One of the most effective fall flowers.
Cimicifuga simplex	division,	white	2-4	Give rich soil, full sun and divide and replant each spring.
Tricyrtis (Toad-lily)	division, seeds	lavender, spotted purple,	2-3	Rich woodsy soil and shade.

GARDENING

Cannas are easy to plant and come in many colors. They grow to considerable height.

Photo by New York Botanical Garden

beauty from bulbs

There's no mystery involved in getting good results from your bulb planting. Intelligent handling pays off in fine, healthy blooms.

First step in planting tulip bulbs is to prepare the bed by spreading bone-meal liberally on soil.

After treading on the bed to consolidate it, rake it fine and level and establish a finished grade.

Next, fork the bed over deeply, mixing the bone-meal thoroughly with soil. Bulbs thrive on this.

If no other spring-flowering plants are to be set between them the bulbs are placed six inches apart.

GARDENING

Some Unusual Bulbs

ATAMASCO OR FAIRY LILY (*Zephyranthes*). For garden decoration. 6-12 inches. White or pink. Plant in the spring, 2-3 inches deep, about 2 inches apart. Full sun. Warm, well-drained soil. *Zephyranthes candida* is hardy in New York. Others are more tender.

AUTUMN CROCUS (*Colchicum*). For garden decoration. 6-9 inches. Flowers are white or pink, in the summer or fall. Large, coarse leaves appear in the spring and die by summer. Plant where dying foliage will not be unsightly. Likes good soil and good drainage. Plant in August-September with tops of bulbs 2-3 inches below the surface. Space 4-6 inches apart.

BELLADONNA LILY (*Amaryllis belladonna*). For garden decoration and cutting. Flower is white or pink. Plant in July-August, 8 to 9 inches deep in warm, fertile, well-drained soil. Leaves appear after flowering. Not reliably hardy north of Washington, D. C.

CRINUM. For garden decoration and cutting. Here belong the "milk-and-wine lilies" of the South. All need full sun, rich soil and plenty of water when actively growing. *Crinum Powelli*, the hardiest, lives outdoors in sheltered positions in New York. Plant in spring, 12 inches apart with tips of bulbs just beneath the surface.

FLOWERING ONION (*Allium*). For garden decoration. Many very different kinds. Among the best are *moly* (yellow), *neapolitanum* (white) and *albopilosum* (blue-gray). All need well-drained soil, and most require full sun. *Moly* stands shade.

HARDY AMARYLLIS (*Lycoris*). For garden decoration and cutting. 2-3 feet. Flowers lavender lilac in August. Plant in July. Leaves appear in spring, die down before flowers appear. Full sun. Fertile, well-drained soil.

ORNITHOGALUM. For garden decoration and cut flowers. White, gray or yellow. For garden decoration. Several distinct kinds. *Nutans* is one of the hardiest; *arabicum* is one of the best but it is hardy in fairly mild climates only. Plant 4 inches deep in rich soil, in sun or light shade.

SPRING STAR-FLOWER (*Triteleia* or *Brodiaea uniflora*). For garden decoration. 3 inches. Pale blue. Plant in light, well-drained soil, in a sunny position. Hardy in sheltered locations in New York.

STERNBERGIA. For garden decoration. Resembles bright yellow crocus. 3-4 inches. Give sunny sheltered position and well-drained soil. Plant in the spring.

THE group of plants that the gardener knows as bulbs is a vast one. Not all are dealt with here but a great many of the best and most popular are. You will find others discussed in the chapter on Rock Gardens.

The requirements of bulbs are various but one thing is certain: most are harmed if fresh manure is near them. Because this is well known, many beginners are scared about fertilizing at all. This is a mistake. Bulbs respond to intelligent fertilizing as do other plants. Some, such as cannas, elephant's ears and crinums are big feeders.

Nearly all revel in compost, leafmold and similar mild forms of humus. Mix these liberally with your soil. I know of no bulb that does not find bonemeal to its liking. Use it at the rate of half a pound to a pound to each square yard and work into soil.

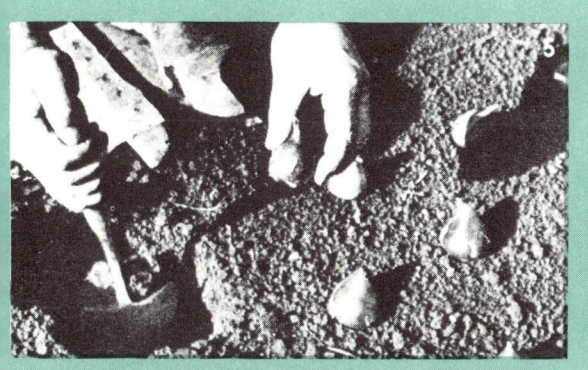

Stand on a piece of board and stab trowel deeply into the bed, drawing soil up and out toward you.

With a bulb planted, fill the hole and press earth down firmly, finishing surface off nice and level.

When the hole is deep enough place the bulb in it and push it into the loose soil at bottom of hole.

Do not use a dibble (below) in planting bulbs, as bulb may not rest in bottom of hole, as it should.

GARDENING

Spring-Flowering Bulbs

HYACINTH. For formal beds and borders. Group in front of a perennial border. Very fragrant. All colors. Good when planted near or inter-planted with other spring-blooming plants such as arabis, alyssum saxatile, pansies, English daisies and forget-me-nots. Available in several grades. Buy "bedding" size (17-18 centimeters or 2¼ inches in circumference). Lift after foliage dies; the bulbs bruise easily. Handle carefully. Store one layer deep in cool, dry, airy place. Plant in October. Hyacinths need sun and light and rich, extremely well-drained soil.

SPANISH AND ENGLISH BLUEBELLS. For grouping in borders. For woodland gardens. For cutting. Blue, pink and white. Fragrant. Spanish bluebell (Scilla campanulata) is more vigorous than the English (Scilla nutans). Lift and replant only when obviously overcrowded. Plant in September-October. Deep, reasonably moist soil. Shade.

CROCUS. For naturalizing in grass and along fringes of shrubbery. For growing in perennial border. All colors except red and pink. Lift and replant only if overcrowded or if bulbs work their way to the top of the ground. Plant in September-October. Light, well-drained soil preferred. Sun or light shade.

CAMASSIA. For woodland gardens. For grouping in borders. For cutting. White, light and deep blue-purple. Culture is exactly the same as Spanish bluebells. Shade or sun.

SUMMER SNOWFLAKE. For perennial border. For naturalizing among shrubbery. For cutting. White. Plant in fall as soon as obtainable. Do not lift and replant unless overcrowded. Sun or light shade.

SNOWDROP, GRAPE-HYACINTH, SQUILL (Scillas), GLORY-OF-THE-SNOW, WINTER ACONITE. For naturalizing beneath shrubbery. For perennial border. For rock-gardens. Snowdrops are white; grape hyacinths are blue and white; squills and glory-of-the-snow are blue, pink, and white; winter aconites are yellow. Easy and permanent. Plant in fall as soon as you can obtain them. Sun or light shade. Winter aconite needs reasonably moist soil, stands more shade.

TULIPS. For grouping in perennial border. Alone in beds or with such plants as forget-me-nots, English daisies, pansies and primroses. For cutting. Various types, including the short-stemmed single earlies and double earlies, cottage, breeders, lily-flowering, rembrandts and darwins, which bloom later and have longer stems. Almost every color except real blue. Plant in early November. Protect where winters are severe by mulching after ground has frozen. After foliage dies lift and store in cool, dry, airy, shady place until fall, or leave undisturbed and plant shallowrooted annuals such as portulaca or sweet alyssum over them. Every third year lift, grade and plant in new ground. Don't plant tulips in ground from which tulips have been taken for three years. Full sun.

NARCISSI (Including Daffodils). For naturalizing in grass, open woodlands and among shrubbery. For grouping in the perennial border. For cut flowers. Less well adapted than tulips or hyacinths for solid beds, but can be so used. Many types. White, through all shades of yellow and orange; some are nearly pink. Many are highly fragrant. Best to leave them in ground all summer. Lift, grade and immediately replant in July every third to fifth year. Plant new bulbs as early as they can be obtained (usually in September or in early October). Fertilize established plantings each year in early spring. Prefer light shade.

SPANISH, DUTCH AND ENGLISH IRISES. For grouping in perennial borders. In beds and borders alone or with other flowers. For cutting. All colors except red and pink. Lift and store like tulips each year. Not extremely hardy. In the north plant in a warm sheltered place (close to a south-facing wall, for example) and cover through the winter with a six- or eight-inch layer of leaves or salt-hay. Full sun.

Stagnant water is disastrous to most bulbs. They must have good drainage. Yet they require liberal supplies of moisture while growing, whenever their leaves are green and above ground.

Spring-flowering Bulbs for Fall Planting.
These hardy bulbs are all easy to grow. See that the soil is deeply prepared and adequately drained. Plant at the right depth and at the right time. Bulbs planted in grass need no additional protection during winter. If planted in bare ground most benefit from a mulch of leaves, litter, salt-hay or evergreen branches applied *after* the ground has frozen. If you put the mulch on too early you invite mice to take up winter quarters. Do not let bulbs suffer from drought at any time when they have green leaves showing. Never remove foliage until it has yellowed.

Tender Bulbs for Summer Bloom.
These bulbs bloom outdoors in summer or fall and are usually stored indoors during the winter. Their tenderness varies. Unless you garden in a decidedly favorable climate do not set these in the open garden until the weather is settled and fairly warm. Lift them at the first killing frost. •

These Real Lilies are Easy

Only plants that bear the botanical name Lilium are true lilies. Others such as day-lilies, plantain-lilies, water-lilies and lily-of-the-valley, are not.

Some lilies are very difficult to grow, others thrive without trouble. Among the easiest are:

	Blooming Season	Color	Stem-Rooting
Lilium candidum (Madonna lily)	July	white	no
Lilium elegans	July	red	yes
Lilium hansoni (Hanson's lily)	June-July	yellow	yes
Lilium henryi (Henry's lily)	Aug.-Sept.	yellow-orange	yes
Lilium pardalinum	July	orange	yes
Lilium pumilum	June-July	red	yes
Lilium regale (Regal lily)	July	white	yes
Lilium speciosum	Aug.-Sept.	white or pink	yes
Lilium testaceum (Nankeen lily)	July	apricot	no
Lilium trigrinum (Tiger lily)	August	orange	yes
Lilium umbellatum	July-Aug.	yellow-orange	yes

Buy lily bulbs that are disease-free, plump, fresh and with live roots. Plant in fall (Madonna lily in August) or early spring in well drained soil that contains plenty of humus. Lilies appreciate light shade from hot sun. In summer mulch with peat moss or leaf mold, in winter with partly rotted leaves or salt hay.

1486

GARDENING

Hardy Bulbs to Plant in the Fall

Ground Level	Tulips	Narcissi and Daffodils and Summer Snowflake	Hyacinths	Crocuses	Grape-Hyacinths, Squills, Snowdrops, Glory-of-the-Snow, Winter-Aconite	Spanish, Dutch, and English Irises	Spanish and English Bluebells	Camassia
1"								
2"								
3"								
4"								
5"								
6"								
7"								
8"								
9"								
Distance Apart	6"	7"–8"	7"–8"	3"–4"	2"–3"	4"–5"	3"–4"	5"–6"

Showing depth below surface tip of bulb should be and distances between bulbs.

PLANTING LILY BULBS

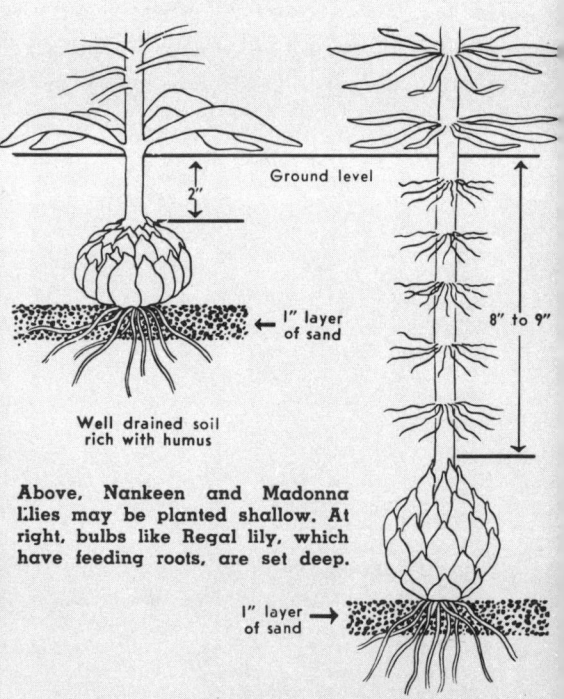

Above, Nankeen and Madonna Lilies may be planted shallow. At right, bulbs like Regal lily, which have feeding roots, are set deep.

Courtesy, W. Atlee Burpee Co.

1487

GARDENING

Tender Bulbs for Summer Bloom

ACIDANTHERA. For cutting and garden decoration. 2-2½ feet. Flowers white, marked purple, in late summer. Fragrant. Needs long season of growth. Not suitable for outdoor garden where fall frosts come early. Plant 3 inches deep, 3-4 inches apart. Culture and storage as for gladiolus. In mild climates leave in ground over winter.

AMARCRINUM. For cutting and garden decoration. 3 feet. Flowers pink, fragrant, in late fall. Set 18 inches apart in light, rich well-drained soil. Position: sunny. Lift after first frost; leave soil on the roots. Store in light cool cellar or deep, well-protected frame.

CALADIUM, FANCY-LEAVED. For "tropical" effects. 1½-2 feet. Splendidly colored leaves. Plant tubers or started pot plants 12-15 inches apart after the ground is really warm. Requires rich humusy soil, shade, plenty of moisture and shelter from sweeping winds. After the first touch of frost, lift and handle like begonias. Store in 50 to 60 degree temperature.

CANNA. For beds and borders. 2 to 6 feet. Flowers cream, yellow, orange, red. Start root divisions indoors 12 weeks before planting out time if it is to be potted, 4-5 weeks before if it is to be set in garden from flats. Plant with "eye" or growing bud 2 inches or less below the surface. Set plants 18 inches apart. After first frost lift, cut stems back to a length of 6 inches. Leave soil dry and store in single layer packed with sand or dry soil in 40-50 degree temperature.

ELEPHANTS EAR (*Colocasia*). For "tropical effects." 6 to 8 feet. Large, handsome leaves. Separate and start tubers in pots indoors 8 to 10 weeks before setting them in the garden. Don't plant in the open until the soil is warm and the weather is settled. Choose sheltered, partly shaded locations. Provide very rich, moist soil. Store in winter like cannas.

MONTBRETIA. For cutting and garden decoration. 2½ to 3½ feet. Flowers yellow, orange or red. Treat like gladiolus. Plant 3-4 inches deep, 4-5 inches apart.

OXALIS BOWIEANA. For beds and borders. 6-9 inches. Flower is pink; in late summer and fall. Treat like gladiolus. Plant 2-3 inches deep, 3-4 inches apart.

PERUVIAN DAFFODIL (*Ismene*). For garden decoration and cutting. 2 feet. Flowers white or pale yellow, fragrant. Plant 8-10 inches apart in sunny place in well-drained, fertile soil. Cover bulbs with three times their own depth of soil. Store in winter in 60-degree temperature.

SUMMER HYACINTH (*Galtonia*). For beds and borders. 3-5 feet. Flowers cream. Same culture as gladiolus. South of Philadelphia may be left in ground all winter.

TIGER-FLOWER (*Tigridia*). For beds and borders. 1-2 feet. Flowers white, tawny yellow, pink, red, variously spotted and blotched. Plant 5-6 inches apart. Cover bulbs to a depth of 3 inches. Culture as for gladiolus. Store, with foliage still attached, in 55-60 degree temperature. Need warm sheltered situation.

TUBEROUS BEGONIA. For beds and borders. 1 to 1½ feet. Flowers white, cream, yellow, pink and red. Start indoors 6-8 weeks before time to transfer plants outdoors, after the ground is warm and the weather is settled. Tubers planted one inch deep directly outdoors when soil is warm bloom later. Space 10 to 12 inches apart. Tuberous begonias need soil rich with humus, shade from strong sun and shelter from strong winds. Keep soil always fairly moist. Lift at first light touch of frost. Do not remove stems or foliage, keep earth on and place in warm light place for two or three weeks to encourage tops to dry, then clean off tubers and store packed in peat-moss in temperature of 50-55 degrees.

TUBEROSE. For cut flowers and garden decoration. 2-3 feet. Flowers white, fragrant. Plant strong bulbs in rich soil in warm, sunny location when the weather is settled. Set 5-6 inches apart and cover to a depth of 3 inches. A long growing season is needed. In North it may be started indoors in pots. Remove all small offsets from blooming size bulbs before planting. Do not remove foliage at lifting time. Treat like tuberous begonias but store dry with soil attached to their roots in 60-degree temperature throughout the winter.

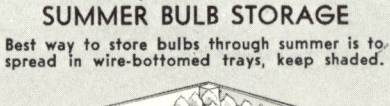

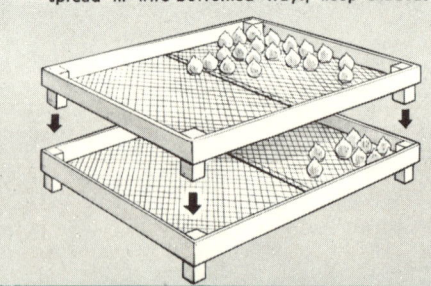

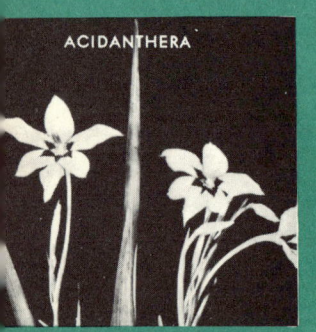

OXALIS BOWIEANA

SUMMER BULB STORAGE
Best way to store bulbs through summer is to spread in wire-bottomed trays, keep shaded.

ACIDANTHERA

ORNITHOGALUM ARABICUM

PERUVIAN DAFFODIL

GARDENING

LIFE CYCLE OF A BULB

If you slice a bulb in half you can see through a magnifying glass that it has a complete plant in embryo. If not present, bulb will not bloom.

Planted at the right time and depth the bulb develops mass of new roots. Winter covering of mulch (top) helps bulb to grow.

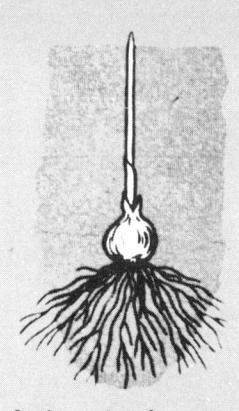

In the spring the stem pushes upward through the ground covering. At this time remove winter protection gradually.

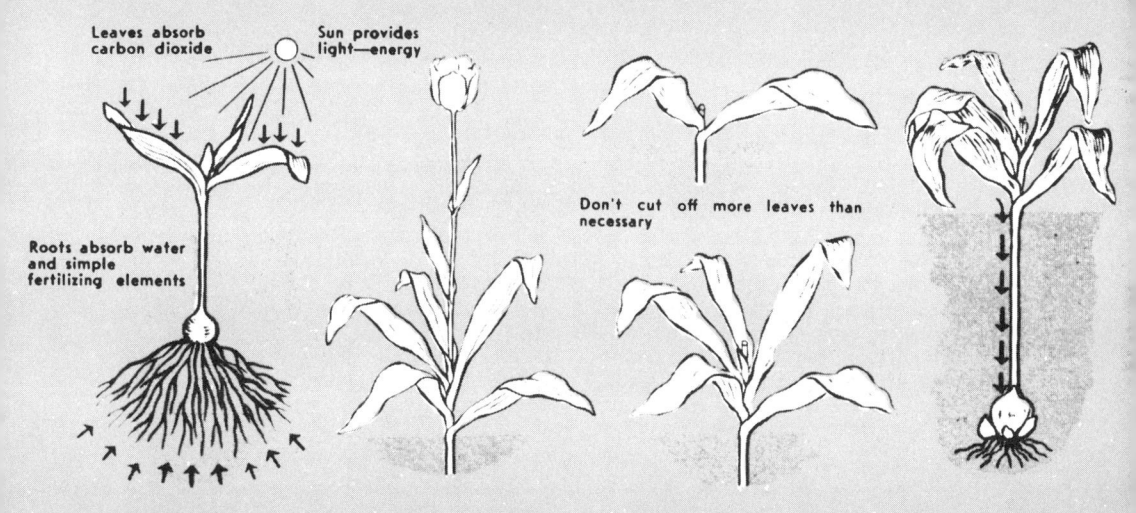

Leaves absorb carbon dioxide
Sun provides light—energy
Roots absorb water and simple fertilizing elements

Don't cut off more leaves than necessary

As it emerges into the sun its green leaves make food from water and carbon dioxide, thus furthering the growth of bulb.

After bulb blooms, do not take off leaves as these prepare food that is kept in bulb for use in blooming next year.

If leaves are brown and dead they may be removed, but when cutting flower leave them on (bottom), not off as at top.

Whether or not bulb will bloom next year is determined largely by amount of food made by leaves and stored.

TUBEROUS BEGONIA

DAFFODILS

Rock Gardens

Photos by New York Botanical Garden

GARDENING offers nothing finer than a well planned, skillfully planted rock garden, nothing more atrocious than a bad one. The peanut-brittle type of bank, border or bed studded with regularly placed rocks that stand more or less on end represents an all-time low in poor landscaping. Don't inflict it on your friends and neighbors. Justify your rock garden either on the ground that your land is rocky or sloping and hence is a "natural" for this type of development, or on the basis that you wish to grow a variety of plants not easily accommodated in ordinary beds and borders Rock gardens in level, rockless parts of the country are not out of place if well done, and if they serve this latter purpose.

Your rock garden may be (1) entirely natural; (2) completely artificial, or (3) a mixture of both. Natural outcrops can often be planted attractively with no preparation other than clearing away unwanted trees, brush and coarse herbage, and deepening and filling with porous, fertile soil whatever pockets and crevices exist in and between the rocks.

Place rocks so strata lines run in same direction.　　For incline, no rocks should overhang those below.

RIGHT

WRONG

RIGHT　　**WRONG**

A rock garden may have a winding path leading through it, as pictured.

A cascade or waterfall, with pumps to recirculate water, adds to garden.

Variation on path theme may be made by flowers, rocks.

Monotony of rocks may be relieved by grass where setting is artificial.

Rocks may also be used as a staircase leading down to paved patio.

A pool adds charm to any man-created rock garden.

Judicious removal of soil from around an outcrop will sometimes reveal beautiful rock previously buried. By baring portions you may be able to add to the extent and impressiveness of your garden.

Often natural rockwork can be improved by constructing additional ledges and outcrops near it. Let such additions be of native stone arranged to blend perfectly with the natural feature. When assembling stone for a constructed rock garden, choose pieces with well-weathered surfaces, of a character and coloring that suggest great age. Avoid newly quarried rocks, round, hard boulders and thin, flat slabs. These are difficult to arrange convincingly.

Best of all are water-worn limestone, soft sandstone and rocks of similar porous character. Tufa is light and easy to handle, but except in desert regions it usually looks a little out of place. In naturally rocky regions it is generally best to employ the type of rock natural to the locality.

Before you begin construction have in mind a clear idea of the feature you are trying to create. You need not copy any

Source of waterfall should be higher than cascade. **RIGHT**

Fall should not begin from highest garden point. **WRONG**

Properly mixed soil is even more important than the rocks. Soil should be at least a foot deep.

The rocks are now in place. Although carefully planned, the effect is one of great naturalness.

specific piece of natural rockwork, but if your garden is of the "naturalistic" type it should appear as if it *could* have been created by Nature. Don't let it look as if a couple of truckloads of rocks had been dumped on the ground and filled over with soil.

A mistake commonly made is to have the rocks all about the same size. Don't do this. It gives the garden a mechanical appearance. Even a few big rocks skillfully located give character. Use streamers, ledges and minor outcrops of lesser rocks to complete the picture. Don't dot rocks over the entire area. Flats, gentle slopes and flower-decked meadows may occupy the spaces between the rocky outcrops. You may have read rules to the effect that one-third, one-half, or two-thirds of each rock should be beneath the soil surface. Nonsense. The important thing is that the groupings *look* as if they are part of outcropping bed rock and as if they were connected one to the other underground. If you succeed it does not matter what proportion of each individual rock is buried. A *feeling* of stability is essential. Loose pieces on or at the surface should be used only as they might occur in rocky country, as if broken from the parent bed rock.

Be very careful to keep the parallel strata lines that show on the faces of most rocks running at about the same angle and in the same direction throughout the garden. If tilted slightly from the horizontal these usually give the most satisfactory effect. Begin building the rock garden at the lowest part and work upward and backwards. Expose the weathered face of the rocks to view and, wherever it can be done without losing effectiveness, tilt the rocks so their top surfaces carry water back to the roots. Pack the soil firmly around each rock; don't leave air pockets. Arrange simple stepping-stone or other appropriate paths so that reasonable access to the plants is possible.

Water in the form of a cascade, stream or pool adds tremendously to the delight of a rock garden. It gives life to the picture and attracts birds. It also gives logical reason for growing a few bog plants near the margins of the water. Fit the water feature compatibly into the design. See that a pool occupies a natural looking hollow and that cascades do not spout from the tops of rocks but originate part way down a slope.

Naturalistic rock gardens fit well into natural landscapes. It is also possible to have delightful formalized rock gardens, banks or terraces obviously constructed, not intended to imitate nature, and paved paths with tiny plants in the crevices. Tastefully planted dry walls (walls in which soil substitutes for cement) fit well into developments of this kind.

ROCK FOILS   **GRAPE HYACINTHS**   **CROCUS IMPERATI**   **ALPINE BELLFLOWERS**

This is the same rock formation after the plants that have been set in it have become established.

The soil must drain freely. See that it is gritty and porous. If heavy, the addition of one-third part by bulk of coarse sand or coal cinders is helpful. Use plenty of humus, leaf-mold or peat-moss and some bone-meal. A soil of this character suits most plants; modify it locally to meet the requirements of highly specialized kinds if this seems desirable. Try to have a foot or more of prepared soil wherever you plant. Rock plants root deeply. Spring or early fall are the best planting seasons. Set most of the plants out in natural-looking drifts and groups rather than singly or evenly spaced in regular shaped patches. Never let the plants dry out. Spread their roots carefully at planting time and firm the soil well about them. Water thoroughly immediately after planting.

One cannot generalize about the needs of rock plants. There are thousands of different kinds from which a selection can be made for almost any situation. Study dealers' lists carefully. Try to choose wisely. Give consideration to the known requirements of particular plants. Let this consideration take priority over color arrangement or other purely aesthetic matters.

Once constructed a rock garden does not call for much hard work. Its upkeep is relatively easy. In spring give attention to uncovering, to pushing back plants that have heaved and to dividing and re-setting. •

GARDENING

Rock Garden Plants

A Selection of Rock Garden Plants For Sun

Achillea serbica
Achillea tomentosa
Adonis amurensis
Aethionema grandiflorum
Aethionema pulchellum
Aethionema Warley Hybrid
Alyssum saxatile
Alyssum saxatile luteum
Alyssum montanum
Androsace lanuginosa
Androsace sarmentosa
Anthemis montana
Aquilegia flabellata nana
Arabis albida
Arabis procurrens
Arenaria montana
Armeria caespitosa
Bellium minutum
Campanula garganica
Campanula portenschlagiana
Campanula poscharskyana
Campanula cochlearifolia
Ceratostigma plumbaginoides
Dianthus caesius
Dianthus alpinus
Dianthus arenarius
Dianthus superbus
Erinus alpinus
Geranium cinereum
Geranium lancastriense
Gypsophila repens
Gypsophila fratensis
Gypsophila cerastioides
Helianthemums (many kinds)
Iris cristata
Iris pumila
Linaria aequitriloba
Linaria pilosa
Linum alpinum
Linum salsoloides
Lychnis alpina
Mazus reptans
Papaver alpinum
Phlox subulata (many kinds)
Polemonium reptans
Potentilla verna nana
Saponaria ocymoides
Saxifraga macnabiana
Sedum (many kinds)
Sempervivums (many kinds)
Silene alpestris
Silene maritima
Thymes (many kinds)
Tunica Saxifraga
Valeriana supina
Veronica armena
Veronica filifolia
Veronica repens
Veronica rupestris
Veronica pectinata

Rock Plants For Shade

Aquilegia canadensis
Arenaria balearica
Asperula odorata
Campanula rotundifolia
Chrysogonum virginianum
Corydalis lutea
Cotula squalida
Dicentra exima
Epimedium (many kinds)
Ferns (many kinds)
Hepaticas (many kinds)
Houstonia coerulea
Mertensia virginica
Myosotis palustris semperflorens
Myosotis sylvatica
Nierembergia rivularis
Phlox divaricata
Podophyllum peltatum
Polygonatum biflorum
Primula denticulata
Primula japonica
Primula Sieboldi
Primula veris
Primula vulgaris
Primula vulgaris coerulea
Pulmonaria angustifolia
Sanguinaria canadensis
Sedum ternatum
Silene pennsylvanica
Silene virginica
Thalictrum kiusianum
Thalictrum minus
Vancouveria hexandra
Violas (many kinds)

Bulbs For The Rock Garden

For Sun
Allium cyaneum (and other dwarf kinds)
"Botanical" tulips
Crocus species
Dwarf Narcissi
Glories-of-the-snow
Grape hyacinths
Snowdrops
Squills

For Shade
Allium moly
Anemones (many kinds)
Bellwort
Blood-root
Dutchman's Breeches
Jack-in-the-Pulpit
May-apple
Rue Anemone
Spring beauties
Squirrel Corn
Trilliums
Trout-lilies

Dwarf Evergreens

(All except the yews, rhododendrons and hemlocks need full sun.)

Alberta spruce
Dwarf Mugho pine
Dwarf yews
Dwarf arborvitaes
Dwarf firs
Creeping junipers
Dwarf hemlocks
Dwarf rhododendrons
Heaths and heathers
Spike-heath
Sand-myrtle
Brooms (many kinds)
Santolina
Dwarf barberries

SUN ROSES   CROCUS VERSICOLOR   ANDROSACE VILLOSA   CAMPANULA CARPATICA

GARDENING

The Garden Pool

Water-lilies in an informal pool.

J. Horace McFarland Co.

Pools may be geometrically formal or naturalistically informal.
Either way they add much to the beauty of your garden landscape.

NOWHERE can water-lilies be grown to greater perfection than in the U. S. For this reason and because water is such an interesting landscape element have a garden pool, if you can. Its value as a mirror, the feeling of coolness and tranquility it gives, and the opportunity it provides to accommodate goldfish and such-like are appealing.

Water plants are easy to grow, need no cultivation, staking, tying or watering. Weeding is almost non-existent and they are free from diseases and insects.

If you have a natural pond or if one can be made by damming a stream you are fortunate. Otherwise you must construct a pool. Usually this will be of concrete, although a clay-bottomed pool may do. A miniature pool can be made of a sawed-off tub sunk into the ground.

Two basic problems must be met: (1) Assure yourself of a supply of water. (2) Make certain the pool can be drained.

Still water suits aquatics best. But water is needed and occasionally it must be replenished and changed.

This formal pool has special pockets for soil in its bottom to hold lilies, other aquatic plants.

Same pool after plants and water have been added. Included are water hyacinths and umbrella palms.

GARDENING

The size of the pool should be in scale with the surrounding landscape.

Pools may be formal, geometrical and with neat curbs defining them, or they may be informal and naturalistic. In formal surroundings the former is better; in naturalistic surroundings the latter is usually preferred.

Before you make a decision outline your proposed pool on the ground, with stakes linked together with strings or garden hose.

Small pools can be filled conveniently by the garden hose. For larger ones it is better to pipe water to them. Make sure that (1) the supply lines are buried well below frost level or (2) provision is made to drain them in winter. The first is safer. Do not install fountains that cause much inflow.

A drain that also serves as an overflow is ideal. It may lead to sewer, ditch, stream, dry well or to some place below the level of the pool bottom where the water may seep away or evaporate.

All pipes that lead into or away from the pool should be in position before concrete is poured.

Small pools can be emptied by siphoning the water away through a hose. Fill it with water. Do not let air enter. Place one end in the pool, the other at a lower level. Open the lower end.

A depth of two feet is desirable for pools that are to contain water-lilies in tubs; twenty inches is a minimum. If planted in soil placed on the bottom of the pool, fifteen inches is enough. Roots should be eight to twelve inches under water.

Water-Lilies. Hardy water-lilies may be left out all winter if they are under so much water that their tubers do not freeze or if, after the pool is drained, they are protected from freezing by a thick layer of leaves placed over them. They may be taken indoors and buried in moist sand where a 40 to 50 degree temperature is maintained. Tropical water-lilies are not winter-hardy except in the warmest areas; ordinarily they must be replaced yearly.

Water-lilies are gross feeders. They like a rich loamy soil. Good garden soil mixed with half its bulk of rotted cow-manure and a pint of bonemeal and a pint of dried blood or tankage added to each bushel is ideal. If you cannot get rotted cow-manure, use dried sheep manure, with one part to ten parts soil.

Plant hardy water-lilies in spring just before the trees open their buds; tropical water-lilies only when the weather is warm and settled. Do not plant tropicals unless the water has been warmed. •

Other Aquatics

THE LOTUSES. Looking like great tropical-lilies but with huge shield-like leaves and large flowers that rise out of the water to a height of two or three feet the lotuses are grand plants for the garden pool. They require the same treatment as hardy water-lilies. The American lotus has yellow flowers, the Egyptian, pink, the Japanese, white, the Chinese, red, and Shiroman, white. All have decorative seed pods.

SHALLOW WATER PLANTS. For planting in shallow water —where the soil is covered to a depth of from one to three inches make a selection from the following:— Arrowhead, Floatingheart, Flowering-rush, Marsh Marigold, Pickerel-rush, Sweet Flag, Wild Calla, Water-snowflake, Parrot-feather, Water-poppy, Water-clover, and Velvet Leaf. All of these grow well in any good garden soil. The first seven are hardy outdoors. The other five should be wintered indoors in a pool or aquarium in the North.

FLOATING PLANTS. You will like for your pool some of the following plants which float freely on the surface and need not be planted in soil. In the North all of these should be taken indoors during the winter. Azolla, water-fern, Water-lettuce, and Water-hyacinth.

SUBMERGED PLANTS. These submerged plants oxygenate the water, keep it pure, and improve it for fish:— Anacharis, Cabomba, Coon-tail, Milfoil, Needle-leaf Ludwigia, and Tape Grass. Plant them in soil in containers, in the bottom of the pool or in shallow water.

BOG PLANTS. Plants that naturally grow in bogs are appropriate for planting at the margins of pools. Among the most suitable are:—Yellow flag iris, Marsh iris, Water forget-me-not, Cardinal flower, Bog bean and Narrow leaved cat-tail, all of which are hardy, as well as such tender plants as Papyrus, Taro, Crinum-lily, Ginger-lily, Thalia and Umbrella palm.

Section through a typical garden pool of reinforced concrete. Note shelves for shallow plants. One square equals half foot.

Nymphae "Conqueror." Here is a close-up of this charming plant.

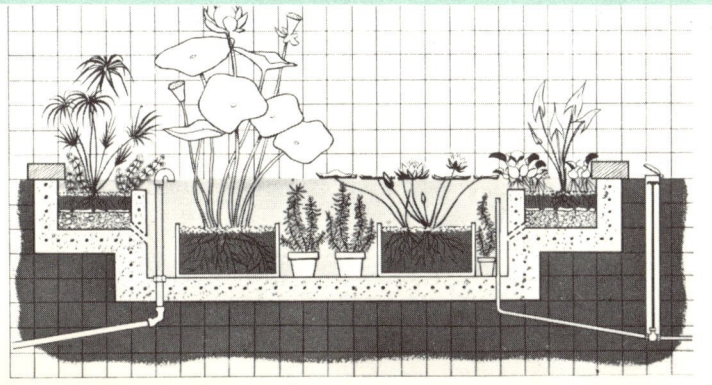

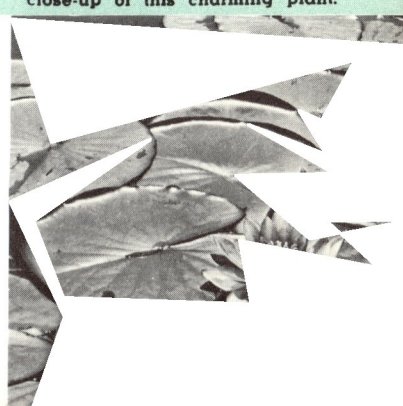

Your Own Vegetable Garden

Maybe you can buy them cheaper, maybe you can't. But at least you have the satisfaction of having grown your own.

THE production of crops to eat has been of primary concern since man ceased to depend upon wild vegetation and hunting as a means of sustenance. It is still basic to his existence.

Because cultivating a vegetable garden gives opportunity to participate in food production it satisfies a fundamental urge latent in every normal individual.

Those who say "I can buy vegetables cheaper" simply miss the point, for the values one gets from cultivating a kitchen garden are not expressable in terms of money. Furthermore they are rarely right. For with properly directed effort you can, in any reasonable garden soil and situation, grow a variety of vegetables far cheaper than you can buy them. Always supposing of course, that you do not charge for your own labor. Modern freezing methods make it easy to store excess. There need be no waste.

The requirements for a successful vegetable plot are: a fairly good soil or one that can be made so, a reasonably level, sunny, situation, a water supply, and know-how with the ability to apply it.

A vegetable garden must be well drained. If the water table is so high that the soil is saturated to within a foot or so of the surface you face serious difficulties.

Apply yourself diligently then to conditioning and improving the soil during the time when it is free of crops. Dig, manure,

Kohlrabi is prepared by trimming off the roots and leaves. These may be ruined by bad harvesting.

Early sown lettuce is ready shortly after tomatoes (planted against stakes at right) have been set up.

Vegetables Not Ordinarily Grown From Seed

Vegetable crops are mostly annuals raised from seeds. A few are propagated in other ways and a few are perennials. The most important of these are:

ARTICHOKE, GLOBE. Perennials. For fairly mild climates only. Propagate spring, by suckers from base of old plants. Space 3 feet apart, in rows 4 feet apart. Soil, light, rich, well drained. Plants remain productive 3 or 4 years.

ARTICHOKE, JERUSALEM. Grows well even on poor soil. Plant tubers 4 to 6 inches deep (whole or cut), 1½ to 2 feet apart in rows 3 feet apart. Crop does not store well. Dig and use it as needed. Not recommended for small gardens.

ASPARAGUS. Hardy perennial. Remains productive 12-20 years. Needs rich mellow soil. Often grown in rows five or six feet apart but for small garden plant in beds as shown in diagrams. Set one year old roots in spring. Do not cut crop first year and but lightly second year. Never cut later than mid-summer. Fertilize freely. Protect with mulch in winter.

POTATO. Plant tubers (whole or cut) 10 to 12 inches apart, in trenches 4 inches deep and about 3 feet apart. Draw earth up to lower parts of stems as they grow. Dig earlies as soon as large enough to use, lates after foliage has withered. Store in cool, dark frost-proof place.

SWEET POTATO. Tender. Needs four months of warm weather to grow well. Set out rooted cuttings after all danger of frost has passed in deep, warm, sandy loam soil. Space rows 30-36 inches apart. Allow 15-18 inches between plants.

RHUBARB (Pie Plant). Hardy. In good soil with proper care rhubarb remains productive 10 or 20 years. Plant root divisions in rows 4 feet apart. Plant with 2½-3 feet between plants in the rows. Prepare ground deeply and well. Fertilize established plantations liberally.

---

fertilize, and lime it as occasion demands, and as opportunity occurs.

Look after your soil at other times too. Don't walk upon it more than is absolutely necessary when it is wet, especially if it is at all heavy. To do so compacts it and destroys its texture.

Size. It is a mistake to attempt too large a garden. A plot fifty by forty feet is about the maximum that an able-bodied person can care for adequately in their spare time. This will require an average of thirty hours of labor a month through the season.

Gardens worked with hand tools can be much more closely cropped than is possible where machine tools are used. Under such intensive cultivation the weight of crops obtained per unit area is surprisingly large.

Plan. Plan your garden on paper. Let the plan be simple. Elaborate systems of paths, cute little edgings and the like are out of place in this type of development. Let functionalism prevail. After all nothing looks better in a vegetable garden than straight rows of healthy vegetables. They are beautiful in themselves. This does not mean that you should not set aside a corner for a few flowers. Just don't mess up the whole area with them.

Your first year's plan will not work out entirely right. Keep careful records and notes of the garden and amend the plan the following year. Do this annually.

Among the chief matters of concern in planning are rotations (do not plant the same kind of crops in the same place each year), successions (how to space sowings so that a continuous supply of vegetables results and what to plant to follow crops harvested early), amounts (the beginner almost always plants too much of some crops and too little of others), and grouping (arranging the crops so that definite areas of the garden become vacant at one time and can be conditioned and replanted more or less together, and so that crops that occupy the ground through almost the entire season such as pole-beans, corn, tomatoes, eggplants and peppers are together, as also are the few perennial crops you grow).

Frequent surface cultivation keeps down weeds and saves moisture, promoting healthy growth.

Here are the tools required for successful growing of vegetables. Canister in foreground is sprayer.

GARDENING

Grow These Vegetables From Seed

	Sow, and Th'n Out Seedlings if Necessary	Sow, and Transplant Seedlings	Sow Early Indoors or in Frame	Sow Early Outdoors	Sow After Ground is Warm and Weather is Settled	Make Successional Sowings	Approximate Number of Days From Sowing to Harvesting	Distance Apart Between Rows, In Inches	Distance in Inches Between Plants or Between Hills in Rows	Depth to Sow in Inches	Amount of Seed Per 100 Feet in Ounces	Comments
Beans, Dwarf or Bush					✓	✓	45 55	24	3	1	8	Do not work among when wet.
Beans, Pole					✓		65	48	36	1	4	Do not work among when wet. Plant hills.
Beans, Bush Lima					✓		75	27	3	1	10	Tender, don't plant too early.
Beans, Pole Lima					✓		85	48	36	1	8	Plant in hills. Tender, don't plant too earl
Beets				✓		✓	55–70	12–14	3	3/4	1	Will not thrive if soil is acid. Sow think each "seed" is really several see stuck together and produces sever plants.
Broccoli		✓	✓	✓		✓	60–100	36	20	1/2	1/4	Provides picking over long periods.
Brussels Sprouts		✓			✓		90–120	36	20	1/2	1/4	Select sowing date so that crop mature after killing frost.
Cabbage, Early and Mid-Season		✓	✓			✓	80–90	24	15–20	1/2	1/4	Do not plant too many of any one kin All plants of a variety mature togethe
Cabbage, Late		✓		✓	✓		100–120	30–36	20–24	1/2	1/4	Select sowing date so crop matures end of summer.
Carrots	✓			✓		✓	65–80	12	2–3	1/2	1/4	Thrive only in well worked, mellow soi free of clods and roughage.
Cauliflower		✓	✓	✓			80–110	24–30	18–24	1/2	1/4	A difficult crop to grow except whe cool summers prevail.
Celery		✓	✓			✓	110–140	24	6	1/16	1 pkt.	Needs rich soil and abundant moisture.
Celeriac	✓			✓			120	18	6	1/4	1 pkt.	Easier to grow than celery, requires mois soil.
Chinese Cabbage	✓	✓				✓	80–100	15–18	8–10	1/2	1/4	In north is best grown as fall crop; i south as a winter crop. Needs coo weather.
Collards	✓		✓	✓		✓	65–70	24–30	15–18	1/2	1/4	Very hardy and easy to grow. Stand h weather well.
Corn	✓				✓	✓	65–100	30–36	9–12	1	4	Better in rows than in hills.
Cucumber	✓		✓		✓		60–72	48	18	1	1/2	Will not thrive if soil is acid. Needs plent of moisture.
Eggplant		✓	✓				125–135	30–36	24	1/2	1 pkt.	Heavy feeder, needs rich, moist ground.
Endive	✓	✓	✓	✓		✓	45	18	9–12	1/2	1/4	Sow also in late summer for fall use.
Florence Fennel	✓					✓	85	18	4	1/2	1/4	Draw soil up about bases of plants whe they are about as big as eggs.
Kale		✓			✓		50–65	20–24	12	1/2	1 pkt.	Very hardy. Light fall frost improves i flavor.
Kohlrabi	✓			✓			65	15	3–4	1/2	1/4	If not grown quickly the roots are toug and woody.
Leeks		✓	✓				130	18–24	4–6	1/3	1/4	Plant in trenches or deep drills so tha plants can be "earthed up" with soil t blanch them. Do not earth up early i season or plants may rot.
Lettuce, Head	✓	✓	✓	✓	✓	✓	50	15	9–12	1/4	1 pkt.	Make frequent sowings to insure succes sion. Select special varieties for h weather sowing.
Lettuce, Leaf	✓		✓	✓	✓	✓	45	15	3–6	1/4	1 pkt.	Make frequent sowings to insure succes sion. Select special varieties for h weather sowing.
Muskmelon or Cantaloupe	✓				✓		75–80	60	48	1/2	1/2	Sow in hills, 8 to 10 seeds to each. Thi to 3 or 4.
Okra	✓				✓		65–70	30–36	15–20	1/2	1/2	Pick pods while they are young and ten der and use them promptly.
Onions	✓		✓	✓		✓	120	12–15	2–4	1/2	1/4	Onions raised from seeds keep bette through the winter than those raise from sets. Be sure that onions to b stored ripen thoroughly before storing
Parsley	✓			✓			90–95	15	4–6	1/3	1/4	Likes firm soil. Apply light dressings o fertilizer through growing season.
Parsnip	✓			✓			120	18	3–4	1/2	1/2	Are improved by frost, do not dig to early.
Peas				✓		✓	50–60	36–60	1	1	16	Distinctly a cool weather crop. Sow earl as possible. Varieties that grow mor than 2½ feet tall need supporting wit brush wood or chicken wire. Sowing made late in summer yield fall crops.
Peppers		✓	✓				115	30–36	18–20	1/2	1 pkt.	Excessive amounts of nitrogen in the so may prevent the flowers from settin fruits.

GARDENING

Pumpkins	✓			✓		60–75	60	60	1	1/2	Sow in hills, 6 or 8 seeds to each, later thin the plants out 3 to a hill.
Radishes	✓		✓		✓	30–35	12	1–2	1/2	1/2	Sow every two or three weeks for succession. Thrive best in cool weather.
Rutabaga	✓					90	18	6–10	1/4	1/4	Sow so that crop reaches maturity after fall frost. Avoid sowing too early.
Soy Beans	✓			✓	✓	90–120	24–36	3–4	1	8–16	Well suited for warmer parts of the country.
Spinach	✓		✓		✓	50–60	12–14	3–4	1/2	1/2	Sow every two weeks for succession. Succeeds best in cool weather.
Spinach, New Zealand	✓			✓		35–45	12–18	12–18	1	1	Produces all summer if main shoot is not picked.
Squash	✓			✓		55–95	48	48	3/4	1/2	Needs rich, warm, well drained soil. Sow in hills, 6 or 8 seeds to each; later thin plants to 3 to a hill.
Swiss Chard	✓		✓			50	18–20	6	1/2	1	Stands summer heat well. Apply light applications of fertilizer during the growing season. Pick leaves that are young.
Tomato		✓	✓			115	36–48	30–48	1/4	1 pkt.	Best for garden purposes when staked and trained to one or two stems, or grown on trellis and pruned.
Turnip	✓		✓		✓	60–70	14–16	3–4	1/2	1/2	Distinctly a cool weather crop. Sow in late summer for fall crops.
Watermelon	✓			✓		85–90	96	96	1/2	1/2	Plant wilt-resisting kinds only. Plant in hills.
Witloof Chicory	✓			✓		95	24	3	1/2	1	After freezing "force" roots indoors, for winter vegetable or salad.

PLANTING ASPARAGUS

In ground preparation, make trenches yard apart, a foot wide. Spade manure or compost into bottom.

Place year-old plants atop soil ridges with roots hanging over sides. Cover with humus to 3 inches.

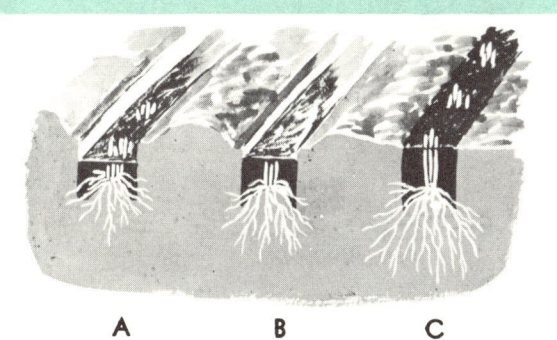

A   B   C

As the shoots grow up fill in more and more soil gradually, as in A, B, C. Note growth of the roots.

After killing frost, cut down the tops and mulch the beds with manure. Leave this way until spring.

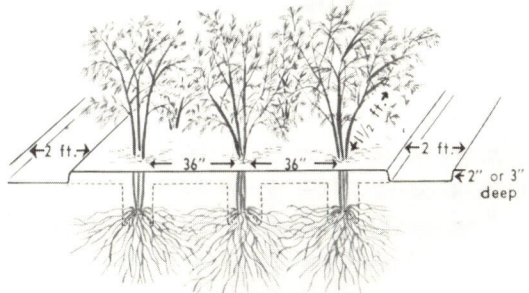

Do not cut away shoots the first summer, but allow healthy growth. Make shallow paths between beds.

In second spring cut a few of the stubs that show but make no regular cutting until the third year.

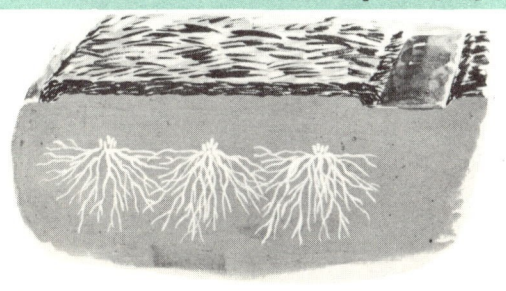

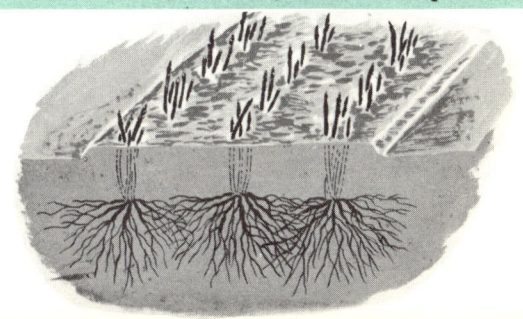

GARDENING

PLANTING PLAN

Left Plot (50 feet × ~20 feet)

Size	Bed
9'	COMPOST PILE / HOTBED / COLD-FRAME (6')
4'	RHUBARB BED
2'	(empty strip)
8'	ASPARAGUS BED
2'	ONION SETS
1'	ONION SEEDS
1'	ONION SEEDS
2'	PARSNIPS
2'	PEPPERS
2½'	EGG PLANT
2½'	TOMATOES
3½'	LETTUCE (catch crop) / TOMATOES
3½'	RADISHES (catch crop) / CORN
3½'	SPINACH (catch crop) / CORN
3½'	EARLY PEAS followed by CORN

GARDEN PATH

Right Plot

Bed	Size
BED for raising seedlings CABBAGE, etc. / HERBS	4'
CARROTS—1st sowing—followed by CHINESE CABBAGE	2'
BEETS—1st sowing—followed by ENDIVE	1'
TURNIPS—1st sowing—followed by BEETS	1'
CABBAGE—1st planting—followed by BEETS	2'
BROCCOLI—1st planting—followed by CARROTS	2'
BROCCOLI—1st planting—followed by CARROTS	2'
STRING BEANS—1st sowing—followed by LATE CABBAGE	2'
STRING BEANS—1st sowing—followed by LETTUCE	1½'
STRING BEANS—1st sowing—followed by BROCCOLI	1½'
BUSH LIMAS—1st sowing—followed by BROCCOLI	1½'
BUSH LIMAS—2nd sowing—followed by LETTUCE	1½'
BEETS—2nd sowing—followed by SWISS CHARD	1½'
CARROTS—2nd sowing—followed by SPINACH	1'
CABBAGE—2nd planting	1½'
BROCCOLI—2nd planting	2'
BUSH LIMAS—3rd planting	2'
KALE	2'
FENNEL / SWISS CHARD	2½'
CELERIAC	2'
NEW ZEALAND SPINACH	2'
SPINACH (catch crop) / 3 hills CUCUMBERS 3 hills SQUASH	3'
KOHLRABI (catch crop) / POLE BEANS	3'
POLE BEANS	4'

50 feet × 40 feet

Suggested for a Vegetable Garden 50 feet by 40 feet

GARDENING

Roots are bending (A) because dibble hole is not deep enough. Don't leave roots in a hole (B).

Holding plant, thrust dibble at slight angle, then lever it over toward plant, after which remove.

Fill hole with water, washing in sides so that soil is settled around newly set out plant.

In planting with a trowel, make hole big enough to hold roots. Here cabbage plants are set out.

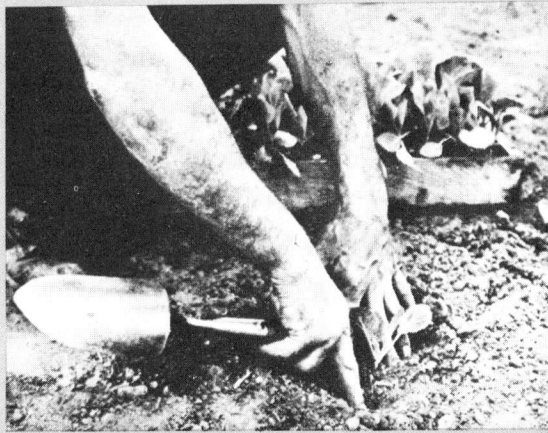

The second step is to make the soil well firmed around the roots of the young cabbage plants.

You must decide for yourself what crops you will grow. Each family has its own likes and dislikes. Unless the garden is large leave out potatoes, asparagus and other crops that need considerable space. Even corn is doubtfully worthwhile in the small garden yet nearly everyone will want to include at least a few hills or rows. Unless you are exceptionally skilled omit or try in small amounts only crops that are known to be difficult in your locality.

Summer Care. Give your vegetable patch attention. Neglect is the real enemy of success. You may not spend much time on each occasion, but be prompt and frequent.

Keep the garden shallowly cultivated (not more than an inch deep). But stir the soil often. Never let its surface cake and crack. Between widely spaced crops like tomatoes and pole beans you may mulch the surface to reduce the need for cultivating but among lower crops, such as carrots, spaced closely together, repeated use of the cultivator or scuffle hoe is better.

In dry weather water copiously. Don't give daily sprinkles. When a crop needs water soak the soil to a depth of at least six inches (more is better). A few hours later cultivate and then give no more water for five, six, seven days or more depending upon the needs of the plants. Don't worry if the surface inch of soil dries. It's what's underneath that counts. •

GARDENING

Photos courtesy, Stark Bros. Nurseries

Hardy Fruits

It isn't enough merely to let nature take its course. If you want your labor to bear fruit, plant properly and care for your trees.

IF you want good home-grown fruit you must care for the plants that are to produce it. It's not enough to plant a couple of apple trees, a few grape vines or a strawberry patch and then sit back and let nature take its course. Even more than in the vegetable garden is it necessary to know *what* needs doing, and to do it *at the right time*. With most vegetables, mistakes, no matter how serious, affect one year's crop only. The following year you make a clean start. But neglect or mistakes made in the fruit garden may result in poorer crops for several future years, possibly more.

Become informed *before* you plant fruits. Your best source of information is your state agricultural experiment station. The authorities there will be glad to advise you of varieties best adapted to your particular locality, of special spray schedules to follow, and of other details of local application.

The larger tree fruits need considerable space. They are doubtfully worthwhile for the really small garden. This is especially true of many varieties of apples, pears,

GARDENING

sweet cherries and plums which do not bear satisfactorily unless another compatible variety of apple, pear, sweet cherry or plum is growing nearby (which means that at least two trees of a kind must be planted). Another thing: spraying equipment capable of reaching the tops of the trees is necessary. It does not pay to purchase this for two or three trees and it is often difficult or expensive to hire it just when it is needed. Standard trees are fine, of course, if you have the space and can give them all the attention they need.

Much has been written about the promise of apples, pears and other fruits grown on dwarfing stocks. For the vast majority of home gardeners these are more practicable as decorative items than as fruit producers. To keep them in fruiting condition calls for high skill. It is improbable that you will acquire the knowledge and judgment to exercise this or would find time to attend to the minute details necessary to their successful cultivation. Use dwarf fruits as espaliers to decorate the garden. Don't expect too much in the way of fruits from them, although such fruits, when properly grown, are as large and as tasty as fruit grown on regular-sized trees.

Small fruits—berry bushes, strawberries and grapes—are quite another thing. These are quite practicable for even the very small garden. They do not take up much room and can be managed without expensive equipment.

Almost all fruits grow well on fertile loamy soil that is well drained. (Blueberries, however, need very acid conditions!) All need plenty of sunlight, so do not plant where the sun is likely to be obstructed. For blackberries, place a netting around the bushes to prevent birds from taking the fruit.

Elevation is important. A variation of fifty or seventy-five feet often makes considerable difference. Avoid low-lying frost pockets.

Make sure you get vigorous, healthy, planting stock of normal planting age. Don't buy older stock, so-called bearing-age trees. It doesn't pay.

Unpack shipments as soon as they come from the nursery. If at all dried soak the roots in water for a few hours before planting. If you cannot plant immediately heel in the plants (plant them temporarily closely together in soil, allowing their tops to lean at a forty-five degree angle or more). Never let the roots dry.

Fruits are long-time crops. Prepare the ground thoroughly for them. When planting make holes of ample size to permit spreading the roots without crowding. Take care that the plants are set at the correct depth (ordinarily very slightly deeper than they have been in the nursery). Work good soil between the roots and pack it firmly. Drive stakes for fruit trees before planting, secure the trees to them immediately after the planting is finished. •

Buy young fruit trees only. This apple tree is ready for soil.

A good, healthy root network is vital. Don't let roots dry out.

Before planting, cut off broken roots cleanly with a knife.

GARDENING

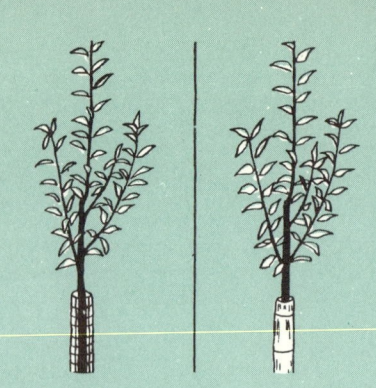

Wire or paper protectors are the best defense against rabbits and field mice.

Pruning trees is a simple but important operation. Above is an apple or a pear tree before and after pruning. Below is a peach tree before and after pruning.

The dwarf apple tree is ideal for small gardens as they are bush-sized, yet yield the same fruit that larger trees do. Plant them 8 to 10 feet apart. As shown below, they are highly decorative when they are in bloom and can be used for borders and such.

The Fruits

APPLE. Any ordinary soil except that which is extremely dry. Space standard trees 40 feet apart. Keep soil cultivated or mulched while trees are young, cultivated, mulched or in sod at maturity. Reasonably good soils need no additional fertilizer until trees begin to bear. Then fertilize yearly according to need. Five or six spray applications needed. Fruits on spurs, prune accordingly. Thin fruits to 6 or 7 inches apart.

APRICOT. Soil deep, rich, with good subsurface drainage. Space 16 to 20 feet apart. Select northern or western exposures. Cultivate or mulch. Thin fruit severely. Three spray applications needed.

BLACKBERRY. Any ordinary soil not too dry. Plant one-year plants 5 feet apart in rows 8 feet apart. Cultivate shallowly or mulch. Cut out second-year canes after fruiting. Allow three or four new canes to develop each year. Pinch these when 2 feet tall. The following spring shorten their branches to 18 inches. Avoid overfertilizing with nitrogen. Where necessary protect in winter by laying canes down and covering them with soil.

BLUEBERRY. Suitable only for sandy, very acid soils that are not dry. Set plants 8 by 8 feet apart. Cultivate frequently but shallowly or mulch with peat-moss. Plant two compatible varieties together to ensure fruit. Use acid fertilizer only. Prune out old, unproductive wood.

CHERRY, SWEET. Prefer light soils. Obtain trees on Mazzard roots. Set 25 to 30 feet apart. Does not like hot summers. Susceptible to severe winter cold. Keep ground cultivated or mulched. Little fertilizing needed. Mature trees need no pruning other than removal of dead, injured and occasional unwanted branches. Three spray applications required.

CHERRY, SOUR AND DUKE. Any good soil. Stand much more cold and heat than sweet cherry, and in most places are easier to grow, particularly the sours. Obtain trees on Mazzard roots. Set sours 18 feet, dukes 22 feet apart. General care same as for sweet cherries.

CURRANTS, RED AND WHITE. Rich, heavy, fairly moist soil is best. Likes cool climate. Fertilize freely. Mulch. Set one- or two-year old plants 4 to 5 feet apart in rows 6 feet apart. Prune out all branches when they become three or four years old. Each year allow two or three of the strongest new shoots to mature. Remove others early. Four or five spray applications needed.

FIG. Moist heavy loams, well limed, are best. Plant 10 to 30 feet apart—the greater distance in mild climates. Prune to encourage development of many new shoots each year. Mulch or cultivate shallowly. Fertilize freely. In north protect trees in winter by wrapping them in heavy burlap, or some similar material, and by applying a heavy mulch over their roots.

GOOSEBERRY. Cultivate as advised for currants. Appreciates very light shade.

GRAPE. Any ordinary soil well supplied with humus and not excessively rich. Plant one-year vines 8 or 9 feet apart each way. Self-sterile varieties must be interplanted with pollinator varieties to ensure fruit. Train to wires, trellis or other supports. Cultivate shallowly, or mulch. Fruit is borne on new wood. Prune with this in mind. Six or seven spray applications normally required.

NECTARINE. Cultivation same as for peach.

PEACH. Light, well-drained, warm soil. Sheltered position on fairly high ground, preferably sloping to west or north. Set 18 feet apart each way. Keep ground cultivated or mulched, never in sod. Avoid excessive fertilization. Prune freely to encourage strong young fruiting wood. Thin fruits to 4 or 5 inches apart about four weeks after they set. Most varieties are self-fertile; a few need other varieties nearby as pollinators. Three to five spray applications needed.

PEAR. Prefers heavy, but will grow in any ordinary soil if not extremely dry. Plant in fall or very early spring. Set 20 to 25 feet apart. Pears are subject to fire-blight, particularly during their youth. To minimize the possibility of this avoid over-fertilization with nitrogen and do minimum amount of pruning until trees begin to bear. Excessive growth encourages the disease. Growing in sod rather than in mulched or cultivated soil is advisable. Fruits on spurs, prune accordingly. Five or six spray applications needed.

PLUM. European varieties prefer rich heavy soils; Japanese and American varieties like lighter soils. Set trees 15 to 20 feet apart. Cultivate shallowly or mulch. Avoid overstimulation with nitrogen. Don't do more pruning than absolutely necessary. Thin fruits by removing 20 to 50 per cent immediately following the natural June drop. Three spray applications needed.

QUINCE. Soil warm, well drained, deep, moderately fertile. Plant 15 feet apart. Plant only stock propagated by layering. Train as bushes rather than as trees. This permits removal of branches affected with fire-blight without total loss. Prune to keep top open with branches well spread out. Cultivate shallowly. Avoid overstimulation with nitrogen.

RASPBERRY. Soil deep, well drained, fairly heavy. Good air drainage is necessary. Avoid low lying frost pockets. Plant disease-free plants in spring. Plant reds and others that produce suckers 3 feet apart in rows 6 feet apart, blacks and other non-suckering kinds in hills 5 feet apart. Cut to within 6 inches of the ground at planting time. Prune blacks like blackberries. Prune reds, purples and other suckering kinds by cutting out old canes after fruiting. Thin others to retain three or four to each foot of row. Tie to wires. Two or three spray applications needed in addition to other control measures for particular insects and diseases.

STRAWBERRY. Soil rich, fairly moist, well prepared. Thrives best where cool seasons prevail. Plant self-fertile varieties and on cultivated land only, where sod has not been for two or three years. Plant runners in spring, potted plants in July or August, 2 feet apart in rows 3 feet apart with crowns just level with surface. Allow two runners from each plant (one on each side) to root into row so that plants are finally 8 inches apart. Remove all other runners. Alternatively plant 18 inches apart in rows 2 feet apart and keep all runners off. Mulch 2 or 3 inches deep with salt hay or leaves after ground has frozen. Remove mulch from plants in spring, but leave between rows and under plants. After fruiting cut foliage close to ground and rake off old mulch material. Fertilize and cultivate shallowly, and rake half an inch of soil over old crowns. Replant every year or second year in new location. Three or four spray applications needed.

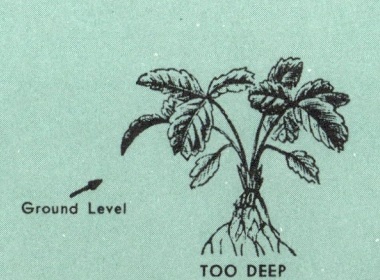

Ground Level

TOO DEEP   JUST RIGHT   TOO SHALLOW

In planting strawberries, care should be taken to set them in at the proper depth.

Photo courtesy, Mrs. Bernhard Hoffmann

HERBS—for Flavor and Fragrance

If you've got a patch of ground where nothing seems to thrive, try planting herbs. You'll be pleased with the flavory, savory results.

HERBS grow well in places where most garden plants would not be particularly happy. Nearly all flourish in gravelly or sandy soils too lean to nourish a worthwhile cabbage or to support a respectable delphinium. Almost all need full sun. Many stand drought well.

Not only do herbs thrive, but their products are superior when they develop under these conditions. The fragrant ones smell better, the savory ones taste better than if they are grown on fat, fertile land.

Although the soil for herbs should be sparingly fertile see that it is prepared deeply. Have the sub-surface drainage sharp except perhaps for mints, sweet-flag, sweet ciceley, angelica and lovage, which prefer fairly moist root runs. Fertilize freely with bone-meal and unleached wood ashes. Apply lime generously. Very few herbs like acid soils.

Choose a sheltered location for your herb garden so that breezes do not easily dissipate the perfumes, and so that such lovers of cozy warmth as rosemary, borage and southernwood will flourish.

Because people through the ages have used a vast number of different plants for

APPLE MINT   DILL   SWEET BASIL

flavor, fragrance and as cures or supposed cures for their ills, enthusiastic herb gardeners admit a great array into their collections. We shall limit ourselves to the more important.

Perennial Herbs. Notable among herbs that persist from year to year are different kinds of mints and thymes, sage, tarragon, pot marjoram, costmary, horehound, hyssop, chamomile, lavender, southernwood, wormwood, rue, chives, tansy, angelica, garlic, rosemary, balm, horseradish, winter savory and a number of artemisias.

Some (ordinary sage and common thyme for example), are easily raised from seeds, but tarragon, garlic and certain others can not be so propagated. All can be increased vegetatively by division or cuttings. If you intend to raise slow-growing perennials such as lavender, from seeds, sow them indoors eight or ten weeks before the plants you raise can be set outdoors.

Biennial Herbs. Caraway, parsley, and clary, are the chief biennial herbs; the kinds that die during their second summer. Raise new crops each year. Sow the seeds of parsley early, but do not plant caraway or clary until June, otherwise they run to poor flower and die the first year.

Annual Herbs. Grow anise, dill, borage, pot marigold, chervil, coriander, cumin, sweet fennel, sweet basil, bush basil, summer savory, sesame and nasturtium from seeds sown in the open garden in spring. Certain perennials including sage and thyme can be treated as annuals if desired. In practically all cases sowing outdoors *early* is to be preferred to raising young plants inside and transplanting, although you may find this latter advantageous if spring comes very late in your locality. Of most annuals make more than one sowing during spring and early summer so that you will have other plants when the earliest sown are harvested.

Chives and parsley, dug from soil in early fall and planted in pots grow through winter indoors.

Florence Fennel, an anise-scented herb, is easily grown and is cooked and eaten as a vegetable.

Care Of The Garden. The herb garden calls for little hard work, mostly just day to day attention, good housekeeping as it were. Weeding and shallow cultivation, pinching, sheering back, and harvesting as the needs of the plants demand; in addition, the collection of seeds for sowing at once or in the future will keep you busy.

Take Some Indoors. In early fall, well before killing frost, carefully transplant some chives, parsley, basil, chervil, tarragon, balm and mint to pots. Use a well drained soil and keep the plants in the shade for a week or ten days before you bring them in. During winter keep them in a sunny window in a fairly cool room. They will provide you with useful pickings. Do not bring the mint indoors until frozen.

CORIANDER   ANGELICA   CRISP-LEAVED TANSY

The Shady Garden

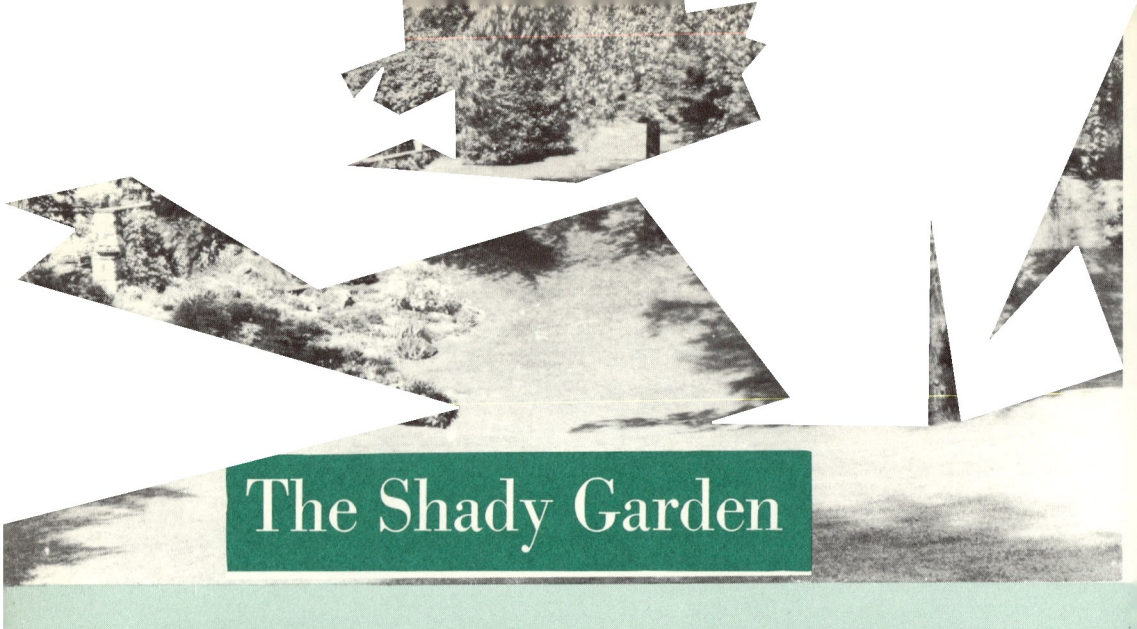

A cool, restful scene is often preferred to gay brilliance, but the problems of gardening in shade must be understood.

GARDENING in shade is quite different from gardening in sun. Its problems are different; the effects attained are different, and the plants used are mostly different, too.

In heavy or moderate shade, rely mostly upon form, texture, and varying tones of green to create summer pictures—the bright colors of the sunny garden are not available to you. The shady garden in summer is cool and restful rather than gay and brilliant.

In spring it is different. You may then have a variety of colorful flowers.

To garden well in shade you must adjust your plantings to the environment, which is very different from that of the sunny garden. The differences are not those of light intensity alone. Temperature, atmospheric humidity, soil moisture, root competition, and other factors play their parts.

Kinds of Shade. There are different kinds of shade. Under dense evergreens where the ground is darkened the year 'round little or nothing will grow. Deciduous trees that cast heavy shade in summer may admit of the cultivation beneath them of plants that grow in the spring only.

Trees that carry not-too-dense foliage such as the pin oak and birches, and those that admit plenty of side light because their lowest branches are fairly high give opportunity to grow a greater variety beneath them.

That charming shade that results from sunshine filtering through a light overhead canopy makes possible the most lovely of all shady gardens.

Also to be considered are situations that are in full sun for part of each day and are shaded for the remainder. They give ample scope for interesting plantings.

Causes of Shade. Consider, too, the cause of the shade. Buildings, walls, and non-living fences make no demands upon the soil. Trees, shrubs and hedges do.

It is often this root competition rather than actual shade that may make it just about impossible to grow anything underneath Norway maples and beech trees. Deep rooting trees that cast the same amount of shade as the maples or beeches present much more favorable planting opportunities. Distant trees may cast shade beyond the influence of their roots. This type of shade is favorable.

The Soil. The principles of soil improvement and management discussed in the chapter "Garden Soils" apply to the shady as well as to the sunny garden. Deep preparation, adequate sub-surface drainage and the desirability of a fairly high humus content are important.

The majority of shade-loving plants appreciate more humus in the soil than is normally provided in the sunny garden. They are woodlanders accustomed to benefiting from an annual leaf fall. The liberal admixture of old rotted manure, leaf-mold, compost and peat-moss with the soil helps them tremendously and so do mulches of

GARDENING

these or similar materials. Give this your attention. Another advantage of mulching is that it prevents the soil from being compacted by drip from overhead trees.

In general, woodlanders prefer organic fertilizers to those of purely chemical origin. Use, therefore, bone-meal and dried blood, tankage, cotton-seed meal and the like rather than commercial fertilizers made for vegetable and flower gardens.

Among woodland plants are a number that are exceedingly finicky about the exact degree of the acidity of the soil—the mayflower and many wild orchids, for example. If you want to grow these you must study their particular needs.

The Plants. In addition to shade loving plants—those kinds that really need shade—there are many plants that are shade tolerant. These grow well in sun but will stand more or less shade if the soil and situation are otherwise favorable. Such plants are excellent for places that get full sun for part of the day and shade for the remainder and spots that get filtered sun.

Allow more distance between plants set out in the shade than you do when planting sunny gardens. That is how nature does it. If you follow her lead your planting in the shade will look more convincing and be more satisfying. Well spaced plants benefit from more side light and more reflected light than do crowded specimens. They can spread their foliage wider to collect the fullest amount of light from above.

Plants For Shade

DECIDUOUS SHRUBS AND SMALL TREES

	For light shade	For medium shade	For heavy shade
Azaleas	✓		
Chokeberry	✓	✓	
Five-leaved Aralia	✓	✓	
Jetbead	✓		
Kerria japonica	✓		
Privet	✓		
Shadbush	✓		
Snowberry	✓	✓	
Spicebush	✓		
Sweet Pepperbush	✓	✓	
Viburnum, Maple-leaved	✓	✓	✓
Viburnum tomentosum	✓	✓	
Xanthorhiza	✓	✓	

EVERGREEN SHRUBS AND TREES

	For light shade	For medium shade	For heavy shade
Evergreen Euonymus	✓	✓	✓
Hemlock	✓	✓	✓
Inkberry	✓	✓	
Leucothoe	✓	✓	✓
Mountain Laurel	✓	✓	✓
Pieris (Andromeda)	✓		
Rhododendron, Catawba	✓	✓	
Rhododendron Maximum	✓	✓	✓
Yew, Canadian	✓	✓	✓
Yew, Japanese	✓	✓	

BULBS

	For light shade	For medium shade	For heavy shade
Bloodroot	✓	✓	
Bluebells (Spanish and English)	✓	✓	
Camassia	✓	✓	
Colchicums	✓		
Dogtooth-violets	✓		
Grape Hyacinth	✓		
Jack-in-the-Pulpit	✓	✓	✓
Lilies (many kinds)	✓		
Narcissi (including daffodils)	✓		
Snowdrops	✓		
Trilliums	✓	✓	✓
Virginia Bluebell	✓		
Winter Aconite	✓		

VINES

	For light shade	For medium shade	For heavy shade
Boston Ivy	✓	✓	
Climbing Hydrangea	✓	✓	
Dutchmans Pipe	✓	✓	✓
English Ivy	✓	✓	✓
Virginia Creeper	✓	✓	

PERENNIALS AND BIENNIALS

	For light shade	For medium shade	For heavy shade
Ajuga	✓	✓	✓
Astilbe	✓		
Baneberry	✓	✓	
Christmas Rose	✓	✓	
Chrysogonum	✓		
Cimicifuga	✓		
Clintonia	✓		
Creeping Jenny	✓	✓	✓
Daylilies	✓		
Dicentra Eximia	✓	✓	
Epimediums	✓	✓	
Ferns (many kinds)	✓	✓	
False Solomons Seal	✓		
Foam Flower	✓		
Forget-Me-Not	✓		
Foxglove	✓	✓	
Galax	✓	✓	✓
Gill-Over-The-Ground	✓	✓	✓
Goatsbeard	✓	✓	
Hostas (Funkias)	✓	✓	✓
Iris Cristata	✓		
Iris Verna	✓	✓	
Lily-of-the-valley	✓	✓	
Lily-turf	✓	✓	✓
May-apple	✓		
Pachysandra	✓	✓	✓
Phlox Divaricata	✓		
Primroses	✓		
Shooting Stars	✓	✓	
Violets	✓	✓	
Vinca	✓	✓	

ANNUALS AND TENDER PERENNIALS

	For light shade	For medium shade	For heavy shade
Balsams	✓		
Begonias	✓		
Caladiums	✓	✓	
Fuchsias	✓		
Flowering Tobacco	✓		
Impatiens	✓		
Lobelia	✓		
Torenia	✓		

Photos courtesy, Lord & Burnham Co.

Hotbeds and Cold-Frames

Vegetables and flowers that make an early start need preservation through winter and protection in spring.

INSTALL a cold-frame and, if possible, some form of heated glass structure in your garden. You can then raise many of the plants you need both economically and easily. The heated structure may be a greenhouse, a frame warmed by hot water, steam, electricity or a vent from the cellar, or it may be a frame containing a bed of soil called a hotbed warmed by electricity or fermenting manure.

In a greenhouse you can grow a great variety of plants throughout the entire year. A heated frame is grand for preserving such plants as geraniums, lantanas, and heliotropes through the winter and for raising young vegetables and flower-garden plants in the spring. Hotbeds and cold-frames are most useful for the spring protection of vegetables and flowers that need an early start—tomatoes, snapdragons, and petunias for example, and for preserving through the winter many other plants.

Biennials such as canterbury bells and English wallflowers are wintered in cold-frames in the North and so are newly propagated shrubs, evergreens and rock garden plants. Any of these glass structures gives you an opportunity to propagate a great many plants by means of cuttings.

Under special circumstances, for instance, when cool summer conditions are sought for violets or primroses, cold-frames are faced to the north but nearly always they, like hot beds, are faced as nearly due south as possible. Choose a sheltered place for both frames and hotbeds. Cold, sweeping winds are harmful

Correct ventilating is most important with all glass structures. Take care that the temperatures inside do not build up rapidly so that the plants are harmed. On the other hand, the sudden admission of any considerable volume of cold air to a frame containing tender plants is highly dangerous. In cold weather ventilate gradually. Open the sash just a tiny crack to begin with, more as the day warms up. Close down gradually in the afternoon or evening. In mild weather ventilation may be left on all night.

Do not keep frames that contain hardy plants too warm during the day, even in winter. Plenty of ventilation whenever the temperature is above freezing should be the rule. On very cold nights cover the sash with wooden shutters, blanket-like covers, or mats made of straw or reeds. These are important over hotbeds.

Choose sheltered yet sunny position for the hot-bed or cold-frame. Plan layouts well in advance.

Ventilation is important in cold-frame. Let fresh air in from the side opposite to wind-direction.

In making electrically heated hotbed place stout wire mesh on the soil-heating cable to protect it.

About six inches of good soil is placed over mesh and the glass-paneled frames are put in position.

On cold nights mats and wooden shutters are used to provide additional insulation for the hotbed.

Hotbed drawn in plan and section shows how cable is installed and where thermostat may be located.

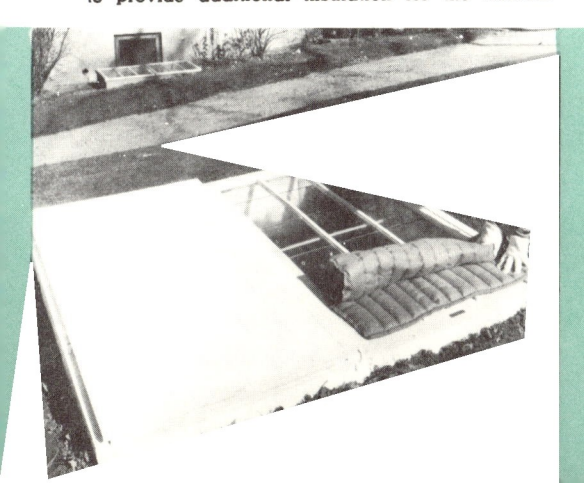

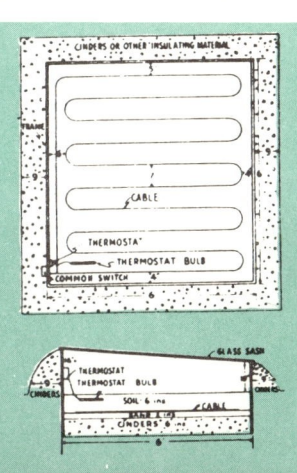

GARDENING

Indoor sowing requires piece of crockery over hole for drainage.

Next, cover crockery with rough leaves to stop soil washing down.

Fill with soil, make as level as possible, press down the surface.

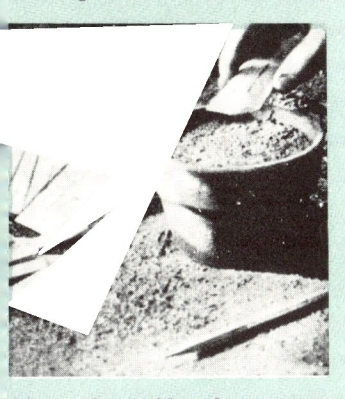

Water thoroughly, then scatter seeds and press under lightly.

Label, then cover with a sheet of glass and layers of brown paper.

Remove glass when growth begins but keep in shade a few days.

How to Sow Seeds

When, where and how you sow may be a matter of life or death to the plants you wish to raise.

TO grow, seeds must have moisture, warmth and air. In addition, they must be alive. Some lose their vitality within a few weeks of ripening, others are good for many years. Most are reliable for twelve months from the time they are gathered, then gradually deteriorate.

Seeds of bog plants and water plants usually die if they become really dry. Store them in moist moss or in water. These are capable of obtaining the oxygen they need from water. Other seeds are not. Therefore, it is fatal to sow those of ordinary land-plants in waterlogged soil. Good drainage is essential. Each soil particle should be surrounded by a film of moisture. The spaces between should contain air. This necessitates good subsurface drainage and watering as often as is necessary to replenish moisture lost by evaporation. It is fatal to let the soil dry just at the time the seeds are sprouting. Desiccation is rapidly followed by death.

Timeliness. Choose the times of sowing your seeds carefully. Consider especially temperatures and the number of growing days available. It is useless to sow certain crops (lima beans and cucumbers for example) while the soil is yet cold; it is difficult or impossible to persuade seeds of many perennials to germinate during extreme summer heat. Those annuals that die in hot, humid weather must be sown early so that they will bloom before this comes along. Biennials sown too late will not produce plants large enough to be satisfactory. Adjust the sowing dates of plants raised early indoors so that they are the right size for planting outdoors when planting time comes along. Timeliness is of the first importance to successful seed sowing.

Soils. In order that seeds may be assured sufficient air, prepare the soil so that it is crumbly and porous. Clayey soils cake

1513

To sow pole beans in hills, drive the pole well into the ground and mound around it with a hoe.

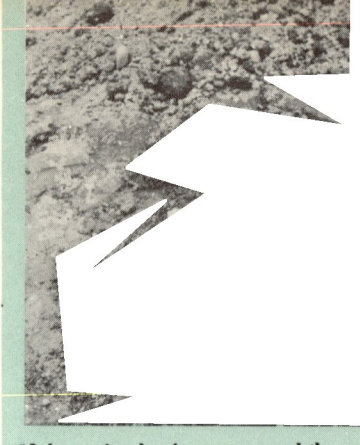

Make a circular furrow around the pole, space the beans with eyes downward, then cover with soil.

at the surface and seal off the air.

For indoor sowing use soil consisting of about equal parts of medium-heavy top soil, coarse sand and peat-moss or leaf-mold. If the topsoil is heavy increase the proportions of sand and humus, if distinctly sandy reduce the amount of sand added.

Let the soil be reasonably fine but not excessively so. Its fineness should be in relation to the size of the seeds. Large seeds such as sweet peas and beans may be sown in coarser soil than radishes and stocks, and for these latter the earth may be less fine than for extremely small seeds such as lobelias and begonias.

When sowing indoors, sift the soil through a three quarter inch mesh. Use this for filling the body of the pots or flats. For small seeds, top off the flats or pots with a half inch layer passed through a half inch mesh. For very fine seeds pass the surface soil through a quarter inch mesh, or even through mosquito screening.

Prepare outdoor seed beds by forking them and making the surface reasonably fine and quite level. Then, when the soil is moderately moist (never when it is wet and sticky) compact it moderately by treading it. With a rake work the upper two or three inches of soil back and forth until it is really fine.

It is very important to catch the soil in just the right condition for early sowings. Often, following a sunny or breezy period it will be in just the right condition and then rain will change matters entirely and seed sowing may not be possible for another week or two. Take advantage of every opportunity the weather affords.

Seed Sowing Indoors. Seeds sown indoors are accommodated in flats (shallow boxes), pots, or pans (shallow flower pots). These should be clean. They must be provided with drainage holes. Place an inch or so of coarse cinders or broken pieces of flower pots over the drainage holes. On top of this spread a thin layer of coarse leaves or moss. Then fill nearly to the top with the prepared soil, pressed moderately firmly with the finger tips. Let the finished surface be slightly lower than the rim of the container and perfectly level. Before scattering the seed, water the soil thoroughly. Use boiling water if possible. Apply it in the form of a fine spray. Let it drain for ten or fifteen minutes before sowing.

Scatter the seeds evenly (the distance between seeds should be about four times their average diameter). Press them lightly into the surface. Sift fine soil over them to a depth of once or twice their diameters. Extremely fine seeds such as lobelias and begonias need no soil covering. Label the receptacles. Cover them with sheets of glass over which paper is laid, and place where they are to germinate. The temperature needed varies somewhat according to kind, but the majority of commonly grown plants succeed between fifty-five and sixty-five degrees.

Examine daily until the plants appear. Quick germinating seeds will need no watering during this period. Those that come up slower will probably require attention. Never permit the soil to dry. As soon as you can see the young plants, remove the glass and paper. Protect from bright sunlight with paper or cheesecloth. Use a fine syringe to keep the surface soil moist. Water thoroughly whenever necessary by immersion or by spray.

As the plants develop they push their roots deeper into the soil. Maintaining the surface in a constantly moist condition is then of less importance—in fact it is rather advantageous to have it somewhat on the dry side during spells of dull weather. Do not, however, let the entire body of soil dry out.

When several flats of seeds are sown together they may be piled one on the other until they sprout.

Seed Sowing Outdoors and In Frames.

Outdoors, seeds are sown either where the plants are to mature or in beds or frames from which the young plants are later transplanted. When sowing where the plants are to remain, incorporate manure and fertilizer. Do not do this when making a nursery-bed.

Seeds are broadcast by scattering them evenly over the entire area, or are planted in drills (rows) or in hills (groups). The broadcast method is used for lawns and for some annuals. It is more wasteful of seed than the other methods and it adds to the difficulty of weeding and cultivating. Seeds which are broadcast are worked into the soil by lightly raking the surface back and forth. Following this, the surface is firmed either by pressing it with a board, tamping it lightly with flat side of the head of a hoe, or by using the garden roller.

The drill method involves making shallow furrows. Let their depth vary according to the soil (on light soils sow more deeply than on heavy soils) and according to the type of seed being sown. It is usual to sow seeds at from two to four times their own diameter. When sowings are made early in the year while the soil is cold, sow somewhat more shallowly than for later sowings. Soak the drills before sowing with a slowly flowing stream from a hose or watering can. This pre-watering is a much better method than the more common practice of sowing first and watering afterwards, which may cake the surface. Scatter the seeds thinly and evenly along the bottoms of the drills. Cover by pulling over them with the rake some of the soil from along the sides of the drill. Then firm lightly with the back of the rake or hoe and rake the whole surface very lightly and in the same direction as the drills. Do not disturb the seeds.

When sowing in hills, it is usual to make a low mound at each station by pulling together the surface soil with a hoe. Into the top of each of these "hills" a shallow depression is made and several seeds are sown in this and are then covered with soil. Sometimes mounds are dispensed with and a shallow depression is drawn with a hoe at each plant station. Several seeds are scattered in each depression and are covered with soil. Seeds sown out-of-doors or in frames should be labeled in the same manner as those sown indoors.

For sowing in drills, rake the soil until it is as fine as possible.

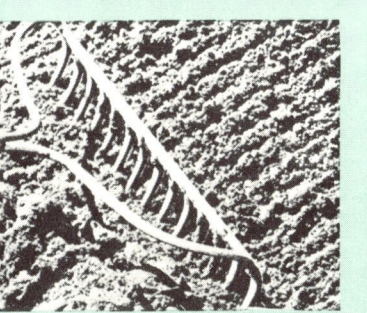

Use a yardstick to measure the distance needed between drills.

Guide-cord helps make furrows straight. Pull hoe toward you.

For small or medium-sized seeds draw drills with handle of hoe.

Soak drill-bottoms with water, then scatter the seeds thinly.

After covering seeds with soil press down, then rough lightly.

GARDENING

Typical leafy cuttings including geranium, begonia, English ivy, wandering Jew.

Raising Plants from Cuttings

Sometimes a bit of stem lying around on soil will root—
but propagation by cuttings isn't usually as easy as all that.

It is a simple matter to propagate many kinds of plants from cuttings or slips. Some, such as sedums, are so easy that scraps which lie on the ground root spontaneously. A few, such as lilacs, are difficult even for professional propagators. Between are the geraniums, begonias, red currants, privets and hundreds of others that are easy to root if given just a little care.

The kinds of cuttings most commonly used are leafy stem-cuttings, hardwood-cuttings, and root-cuttings.

Leafy Stem Cuttings. The housewife who keeps a shoot of English ivy in a glass of water or who plants a rose "slip" in summer under a Mason jar and in this way raises new plants is propagating by means of leafy stem cuttings.

The techniques she employs or modifications of them are used to secure increase of thousands of kinds of popular plants—geraniums, begonias, lantanas, heliotropes, fuchsias, carnations and chrysanthemums among flower garden favorites, numerous kinds of shrubs, evergreens and vines, and such groundcovers as vinca, pachysandra, and trailing roses.

Leafy stems of most (but not all) garden plants can be induced to root if they are taken at the right season and are kept under suitable conditions. Some, such as begonias, root readily anytime. Others, including most shrubs and evergreens, only when the wood is just right.

When you remove a leafy shoot from its parent you immediately cut it off from its supply of water (its roots). Yet its leaves continue to give out moisture. If this loss is not replaced the shoot dies. Your first concern then must be to check excessive water loss from your cuttings, your second to make it possible for the cuttings to obtain moisture.

To avoid excessive loss, keep cuttings which cannot be planted immediately wrapped in moist newspaper. Also, remove the leaves from the part of the cutting that will be buried when it is planted. If the cuttings are decidedly leafy cut off some of their upper foliage, remove some entire leaves and, if they are big like hydrangeas, cut off part of each large leaf that is left. Maintain a moist atmosphere. To do this set the cuttings in a greenhouse, cold-frame, or terrarium or under a belljar, Mason jar or similar device. Avoid drafts. Give a little ventilation—at first only just enough to keep the air from being dripping wet—somewhat more as the cuttings establish themselves, but never enough to cause the foliage to wilt. After roots have formed, gradually accustom the young plants to normal air conditions. Sprinkle the cuttings lightly with a very fine spray of water once, twice or more times a day, but never so late that they are wet when night falls. Shade lightly from direct sunshine.

To encourage and make it possible for the cuttings to absorb moisture, plant them in a medium such as coarse sand, sand and peat-moss, powdered pumice or vermiculite that insures a supply of air to the roots as well as moisture. Many cuttings will root

GARDENING

in water but in almost all cases water is not to be preferred. Keep the medium always evenly moist, not constantly saturated. This necessitates good drainage underneath. Except in the case of vermiculite make the medium firm before planting, and firm it well about the newly set cuttings, particularly about their bases. Leave vermiculite loose. Make sure that the base of each cutting rests on the bottom of the hole in which it is placed for rooting.

Your cuttings will root better if you cut their bases just beneath a node (joint). Slice across the stem horizontally with a keen knife.

Most cuttings root quicker if the rooting medium is kept five or ten degrees warmer than the average air temperature. This is not *necessary*, however, except with a few distinctly finicky kinds.

First step in the insertion of leafy cuttings in the flat is to place drainage material in bottom, then fill with rooting medium such as clean sand.

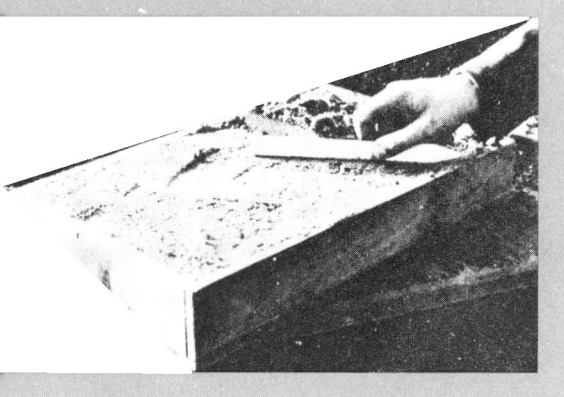

Unless vermiculite is used as the rooting medium the sand should be well packed down into the flat as shown below before leafy cuttings are put in.

A sharp knife and a dibble are all the tools you need for inserting plants. Sharp dibble in the center is not a good type, blunt one is better.

After making a hole with the blunt dibble just deep enough to receive the base of the cutting, put plant in place with its leaves above ground.

With the base of the cutting resting in bottom of hole, firm the sand against the stem of the plant by stabbing at it with end of the dibble.

After the cuttings have been put in, water them well with a fine spray and then keep them in a moist atmosphere to prevent them from wilting.

GARDENING

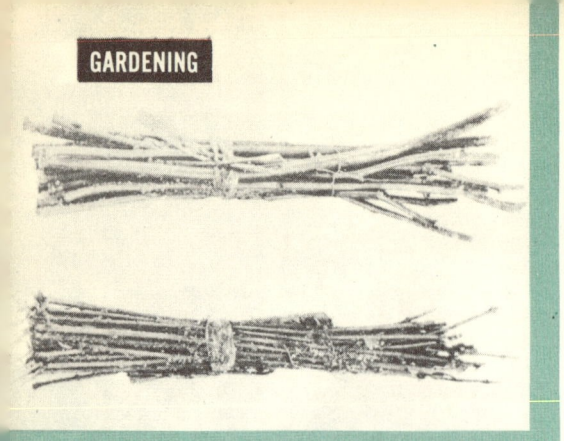

When taken up in early spring the cuttings have already calloused and in some cases have formed small roots. They are then planted in nursery rows with their tips just sticking above level of soil. They grow quickly and inside of a year mature into sturdy, well-developed young shrubs.

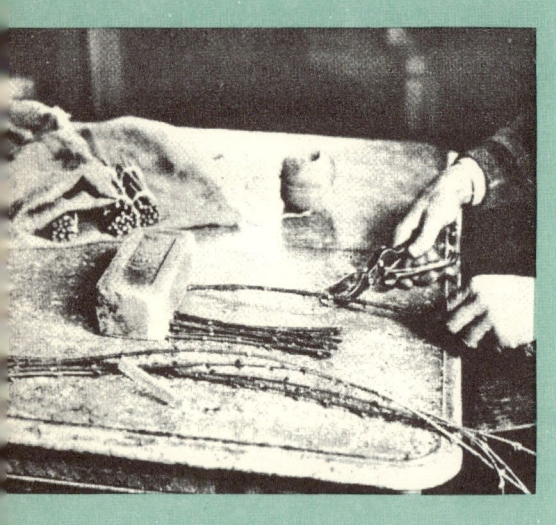

To make hardwood cuttings, shoots of the current season's growth are taken after leaf-fall and cut into pieces of approximately 8 or 9 inches long.

These are then tied into bundles and are labeled with care, then are buried in frames or are put outdoors in sand below the level of soil-freeze.

When inserting cuttings space them so that they scarcely touch each other. After planting remove promptly any decayed leaves or parts or leaves that develop.

Hardwood Cuttings. If you cut a twig from a privet in the fall and leave it on the ground it will dry and die. If you prevent it from drying it will live and, under suitable conditions will, in spring, develop roots and shoots and form a new plant. So will many other deciduous shrubs. That is the basis of propagation by hardwood cuttings.

Make hardwood cuttings in fall after the leaves have dropped. Select firm, strong shoots that developed during the current year—that is, that grew during the summer just closed. Cut these into pieces each six to ten inches long. Slice the base of each across horizontally just beneath a node and cut its top slantwise just above a node.

Tie the prepared cuttings in bundles with soft string, with their bases all at one end. Let each bundle contain up to fifty cuttings. Label them.

Bury the bundles in sand in a cold-frame or out-of-doors letting them rest either horizontally or with their bases upwards. Cover with sand to a depth of six or eight inches and later, after the surface has frozen, throw a layer of hay or leaves over it. The idea is to prevent the cuttings from actually freezing. In spring, well before the trees open their buds, dig the cuttings up and plant them individually in rows in a nicely prepared nursery bed.

At the time you lift the cuttings their bases will be well calloused and in many cases they will have developed promising young roots. Don't let them dry.

With a spade, open a narrow trench that has one side nearly vertical and is of such a depth that when the base of a cutting rests on its bottom its upper end protrudes not more than an inch above the surface.

Set the cuttings in the trench, leaning them against the nearly vertical side and space them three to four inches apart. Fill the trench with sandy soil and tread it firmly. In heavy soils an inch of coarse sand on the bottom of the trench is helpful.

If you are setting more than one row of cuttings, allow sufficient space between to permit you to cultivate. Don't allow the soil to become really dry at any time. Water thoroughly when necessary.

During the summer hardwood cuttings make substantial growth. The following spring dig the young plants up, prune them back fairly severely and transplant them to a nursery bed where they can develop further. In the nursery allow them more

GARDENING

room than they had in the cutting bed.

Among popular plants that are easily propagated by hardwood cuttings are: deutzia, weigelia, mock-orange, snowberry, coralberry, forsythia, euonymus, viburnum, spirea, shrubby dogwoods, firethorn, franklinia, bladder-nut, willows, poplars, honeysuckles, climbing roses, beautyberry, vitex, rose of Sharon, grapes, gooseberry, currants, and mulberry.

Root Cuttings. Some plants can be easily increased by using pieces of root as cuttings. Horseradish for example and pachysandra, trumpet creeper, Japanese anemones and blackberries.

Select fat roots, cut them into pieces each two to four inches long and plant them outdoors in sandy soil, in cold-frames or in beds of peat-moss and sand indoors.

Make root cuttings fairly late in the fall. If they are to be raised indoors plant them immediately in the propagating bed. Keep them cool at first, somewhat warmer after a month or six weeks. If they are to be planted outside store them until spring in peat-moss and sand in a temperature of about 40 degrees and then plant them in frames or in the garden. You may winter root cuttings by burying them in sand outdoors provided they are protected from hard freezing. If planted indoors pot the young plants when they have developed sufficiently, if outdoors transplant the following spring.

Cuttings of many plants root more quickly and certainly if you treat them with a root-inducing hormone before planting. Follow the manufacturers' directions when using these preparations. •

Here is a leafy cutting of hydrangea all ready for insertion. Note that lower leaves have been removed and some upper leaves cut back in size.

When a good mess of new roots have formed about two inches long, set the young plants one by one in pots that have been filled with sandy soil.

When the shrubs have reached a stage of relative growth, such as this half-ripened plant, it will be possible to take additional cuttings from it.

Evergreen cuttings are usually inserted indoors in the fall. Here are cuttings of an arborvitae and a yew that have rooted enough for potting.

How To Divide Plants

By splitting a plant into two or more smaller ones you can increase your garden yet keep it from becoming too crowded.

DIVIDING or "separating" is the simplest of all vegetative propagation. It's just a matter of splitting one large plant into two or more smaller ones. Each division or separation, if planted under conditions suitable to its kind, grows.

Divide plants not only to obtain increase but also to reduce the size of those that have become too large; also to prevent crowding and consequent weakening of the stems within the clumps themselves.

Some fast-growing perennials need dividing every year or two. Others thrive for many years undisturbed. So with bulbs. The best rule to follow is to dig them up, separate them, grade and replant them when they begin to show signs of deteriorating.

Basic points about dividing plants are (1) Discard those affected with viruses or other incurable or difficult-to-cure conditions. (2) Separate bulbs that are to be stored for the summer, such as tulips, at lifting time; all other plants at the beginning of a period of active root growth. Thus you will divide most hardy perennials and certain shrubs in early fall or in spring. Irises, oriental poppies and some

To divide an iris, dig up the plant and pull the large clumps of leaves and roots apart with hands.

Cut back the foliage fully half way, as shown at right. These divisions are ready for re-planting.

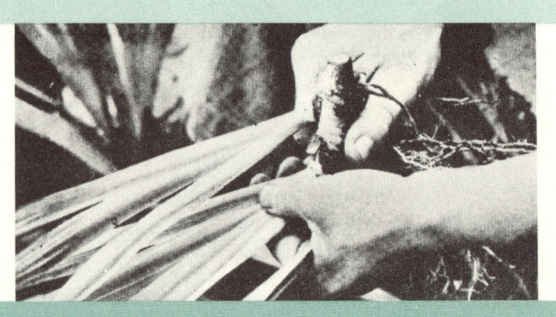

Cut into smaller pieces with a sharp knife. Make sure that you discard any weak or diseased leaves.

Plant irises with rhizomes level with the ground. With foliage cut this way less moisture is lost.

others that begin a new cycle of root growth in summer at that time. Primroses and a good many other spring-blooming perennials may be successfully divided immediately after they have bloomed. Divide dahlias, cannas and plants that are wintered in storage just before they are started into new growth in spring.

When dividing perennials or shrubs see that each division has a generous amount of roots as well as some plump buds or top growth. Usually the most vigorous parts of shrubs and perennials are the younger portions that form the outsides of the old clumps. Save these parts and discard the centers unless you want rapid increase.

A good sharp spade or a hatchet are satisfactory tools with which to split shrubs. Some of the more vigorous perennials can be divided in like manner but I prefer to cut most into pieces with a heavy, sharp knife or to pull them apart either with the hands or by thrusting a pair of forks back to back closely together well down into their roots and then prying apart.

With a little practice you will be able to separate even the more difficult kinds such as peonies, Christmas roses and coralbells without much trouble. Do not let the divisions dry out. Plant them promptly.

There is little danger that herbaceous plants divided when they are without leaves or when their new growth is only just beginning will, after planting, lose moisture faster than their roots can replace it. But this is not true of plants divided when in leaf, as evergreens must be, and some other plants are. These face a real danger of death by desiccation.

To prevent this employ the following practices. (1) When you prepare the divisions for planting cut back the foliage, thus reducing the leaf area from which moisture is lost. Leafage may be reduced from one third to two thirds in most cases. (2) Retain the maximum amount of roots possible with each division. (3) If possible select moist, dull weather for planting. (4) Shade from bright sunshine and protect from drying winds for a few days or a week or two after planting. (5) Water the foliage lightly several times daily.

In special cases it is greatly advantageous to plant leafy divisions in a shaded coldframe and to keep this closed or sparsely ventilated until the young plants have recovered from the shock of dividing. This prevents excessive loss of moisture from the leaves.

Deciduous shrubs, even if divided when dormant, may soon produce more leafage than their roots can support. It is a good plan to cut the stems of such divisions severely back before they are planted, or to thin the stems out thoroughly.

Keep the soil in which newly planted divisions are planted moist but not constantly saturated. Remember, roots need air as well as moisture.

Some plants, such as red raspberries, send up sucker growths some little distance away from the main clump. The digging up and transplanting of these is a form of division. •

In dividing perennials, every little rooted shoot can be cut and used if rapid increase is desired.

Make the soil firm and well tamped around roots. If well placed plant will thrive for many years.

Plant the divisions before they have a chance to dry out. Ground should be in fertile condition.

As a final step, level off the soil and roughen the surface shallowly to give finished appearance.

GARDENING

Increase Plants by Layering

IF you snip a piece off a plant and induce it to form roots you are propagating by cuttings. If you cause roots to form on the piece first and then snip it off you are propagating by layering. Some plants layer themselves. Branches of forsythias and blackberries, for example, take root and give rise to new plants. Strawberries send out runners which bear plantlets that root into the ground.

You can increase many kinds of plants by layering, lilacs, rhododendrons, wisterias, magnolias, hollies, junipers, yews, quinces, hydrangeas and many roses, for instance.

To layer strawberries and other plants that produce runners fill three-inch pots with good, sandy soil. Remove all but four or five strong runners from each vigorous plant. Cut the ends off these just beyond the first young plantlet. Sink the pots to their rims in the soil. Place a plantlet on top of each pot and peg it down with a wire peg or staple. Keep the soil moist. When the plantlets have rooted freely into their pots cut the runners between them and their parents. About a week later transplant them from their pots to permanent beds. That is the simplest type of layering.

The next easiest is tip-layering. This is used for blackberries, black raspberries, loganberries and similar plants. Bend a cane over in summer and bury its tip to a depth of about three inches in the soil, pegging or weighting it so that it cannot spring out. Keep the soil moist. A new plant soon forms. In late fall or in spring cut the young plant free from its parent. Transplant it in spring.

Ordinary layering consists of burying a portion of a stem some little way behind its tip in soil. The end of the shoot itself sticks out and develops into a new plant when the buried portion forms roots. This is how to do it:

In spring or early summer select one year old branches of healthy rhododendrons, magnolias, hollies or almost any kind of tree or shrub that has branches that will bend to the ground. Loosen the soil and mix with peat-moss. If it is heavy, mix in some coarse sand. If very poor, dig out two or three shovelsful and replace it with a mixture of good topsoil, peat-moss and sand.

GARDENING

At the end of two years a rhododendron that has been layered has developed a fine mass of roots and is ready to be snipped from its parent plant and transplanted. Many species can be cut from parents in a year, but rhododendrons are slow.

To layer strawberry runners remove all but three or four runners from each plant (1) and cut as at X. Fill pots with soil, sink them in the ground and staple runner as in 2. In about a month you will have a fairly well established young plant.

Plant a branch, let it root, cut it off, nurse the shoot. That's layering—here's how.

Before you put the branch out into the soil injure it in some way at the point that will be underground. This partly checks the sap flow and aids root development.

The needed injure can be done in one of various ways. You may grasp the stem in both hands and give it a sturdy half twist so that the bark loosens or breaks from the underlying wood. Or take a sharp knife and cut the stem a little below a node. Cut upwards toward the tip. Make the cut an inch or so long, and let it extend to a depth of one third the thickness of the branch. Yet another method is to split the branch with a chisel and then peg the slit open with a small wooden wedge.

Bury the injured part of the stem in sandy, peaty soil—to a depth of four or six inches if it is a branch of a sturdy shrub, not more than an inch or two if it is a smaller plant such as an evergreen candytuft. Peg it in place with forked twigs or long wire staples and, if needed, drive a stake into the ground and tie the end of the branch that sticks out of the soil to it. Make sure that the layer is firmly anchored. It must not be loose. Keep soil moist. •

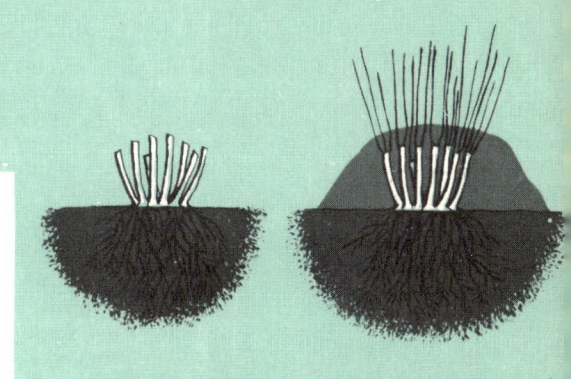

In mound layering, cut back shrubs in the spring and mound sandy soil over old stubs as above. New shoots will root into mound (below) can be cut off as individual shrubs.

How to Bud

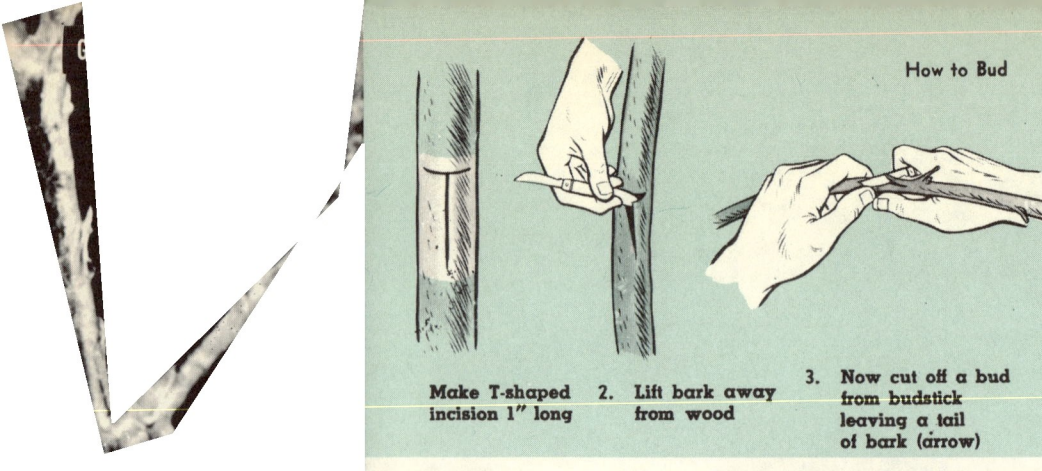

1. Make T-shaped incision 1" long
2. Lift bark away from wood
3. Now cut off a bud from budstick leaving a tail of bark (arrow)

how to GRAFT and BUD

In order to form a more permanent union you may join two living plants together —once you master the simple principles.

GRAFTING is the joining together of two living plant parts to form a permanent union. The part that includes the roots is called the stock. The part grafted on to the stock is the scion. Budding is a form of grafting in which the scion consists of a single bud.

There is nothing mysterious about grafting. You may do it yourself in your own garden once you master the simple principles. These are: (1) Stock and scion must be closely related botanically. You can graft a garden rose on to a wild rose or a Delicious apple on to a seedling apple. Stock and scion in each case belong to the same genus. You can even graft a pear tree on to a quince or a lilac on to a

Whip Grafting Step by Step

Bottom part — Top part — Fit and bind with raffia — Enclose with grafting wax

Saddle Grafting by Steps

Bottom part — Top part — Fit and bind — Seal over

GARDENING

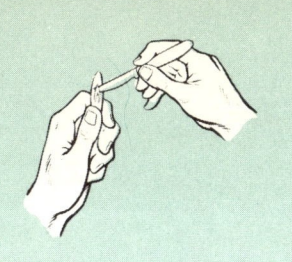

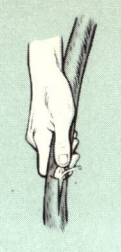

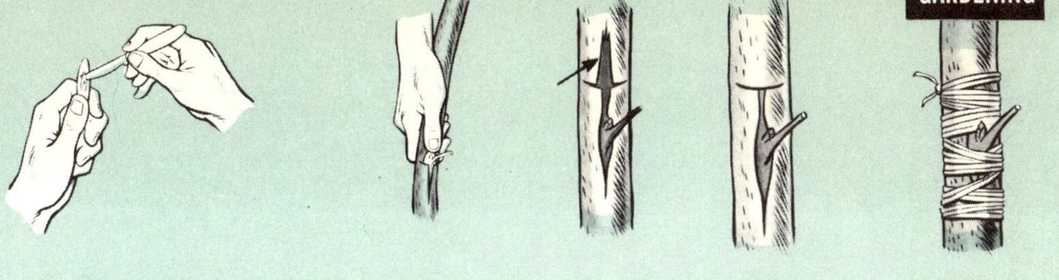

4. Pick out wood clinging to bud
5. Slide bud into incision
   Tail should protrude (arrow)
6. Cut tail flush
7. Tie with raffia or cotton tape

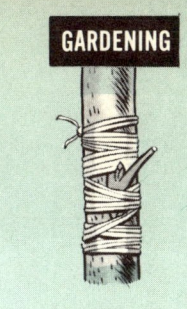

privet. Here stocks and scions belong to the same botanical families. But you cannot graft a lilac onto a quince, an apple onto a privet, or a cherry onto an oak because in these cases stocks and scions are not related closely enough.

(2) The cambium layers of stock and scion must be brought into close contact. The cambium is a thin layer of actively growing tissue between wood and bark.

(3) Stock and scion must be bound together to prevent movement and be prevented from drying at point of graft.

(4) Grafting is done in spring just before active growth begins. Bud in summer.

There are numerous kinds of grafting. We are concerned with the most useful.

Suppose you want to propagate young trees of a particularly good variety of apple. Seeds will not produce trees that have fruit the same as that of the parent. Cuttings will not root. You can't divide an apple tree. Grafting is the way to raise the plants you want.

Obtain one-year-old seedling apple trees. Plant them in a nursery bed in the early fall. In spring, two or three weeks before grafting time, cut from the tree you want to propagate strong one-year-old shoots to use as scions. Tie these in bundles and bury them in sand on the north side of a building. This will keep them dormant.

Just before the buds on the stock begin to grow take up the scions. Cut the top off each stock about two inches above the ground. Then with clean slicing cuts of a sharp knife cut stock and scion to fit accurately together as shown in the illustrations. Also cut the top off the scion, leaving it three or four inches long.

As stock and scion are of approximately the same diameter, make use of the whip graft method. Make sure the cambiums are in contact at least on one side. Tie securely together with raffia or thin cotton strips. Cover the graft immediately with grafting wax to exclude air and insects.

Old apples and some other trees that are not of a satisfactory variety can be changed over to another by "top working" them—cutting them back and grafting on to the stubs scions of desired varieties. Cleft grafting or rind grafting is used here.

Peaches and other "stone" fruits and roses are usually propagated by budding.

For scions or budwood use strong shoots of the current season's growth that have well-developed buds. Cut off the leaves. To insert a bud, follow the steps shown in drawings at the top of these pages. •

Rind Grafting

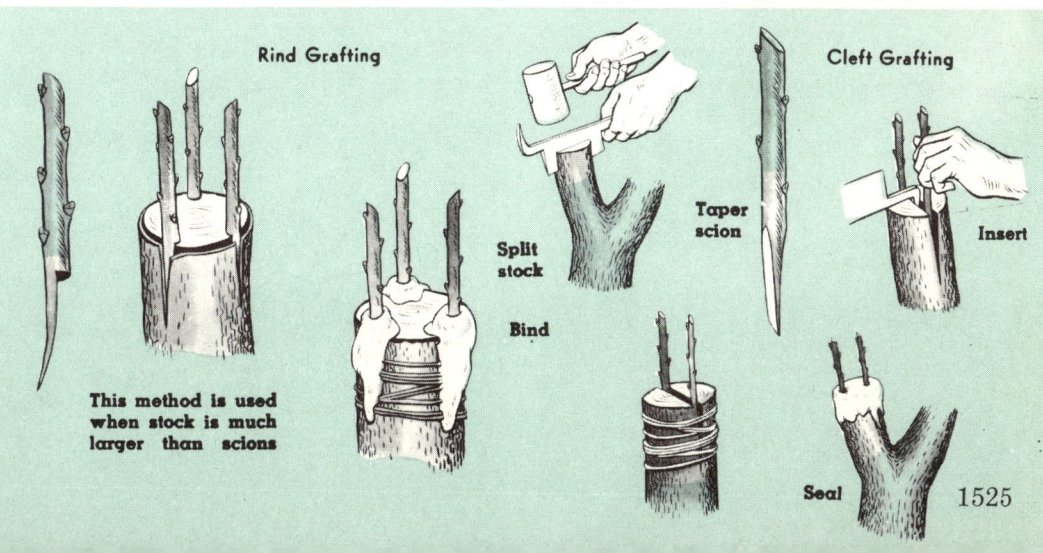

This method is used when stock is much larger than scions

Cleft Grafting

Split stock
Taper scion
Bind
Insert
Seal

1525

GARDENING

Give Your Plants Winter Protection

It isn't the cold, it's the duplicity of winter weather— its alternate freeze and thaw—that you need guard against.

First step in preparing hybrid tea and hybrid perpetual roses for winter: in late fall shorten long shoots enough to prevent damage from storms.

After trimming shoots use a hoe to draw surrounding soil from the rose bed and heap carefully around the base of individual plants as shown.

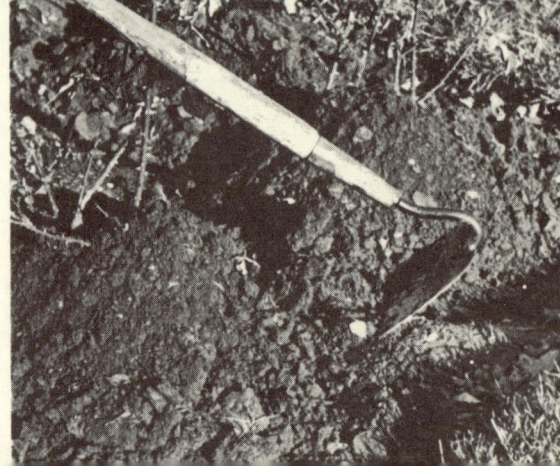

GARDENING

DON'T think of winter protection merely as a matter of keeping plants warm. It's not that simple. Temperatures are important but other factors are, too.

Alternating thawing and freezing may do far more harm than steady cold. Winds and strong sun late in winter may be more disastrous than winter cold. Snow lying for long periods often counterbalances low temperatures. Plants on poorly drained or heavy soils are more likely to suffer than are those on lighter or porous soils. Very rich soil may bring lush, poorly ripened growth more likely to winter-kill than the firmer growth made on rather leaner soils. Attacks by insects or diseases, improper pruning and other cultural faults can all increase susceptibility to winter-injury.

Well, what to do about it? Take really tender plants such as geraniums and begonias indoors, also such summer bulbs as cannas and gladioli.

Slightly tender plants that are small may be wintered in cold-frames. In cold-frames, too, you may carry over young potted trees and shrubs, perennials and rock garden plants. "Slightly tender" covers different plants in different localities. Local experience is your best guide. At New York pansies and Canterbury bells are in this category. But what about plants that must be left outdoors?

We can protect their roots with mulches and we can protect the tops.

Mulching the soil surface reduces the depth to which frost penetrates and minimizes the bad effects of alternate freezing and thawing. In a way it is a substitute for a winter-long snow covering.

Use almost any loose organic material, littery manure, leaves, salt hay, peat-moss, corn stalks, straw, pine needles, or the like. Let the mulch be two to six inches deep. Do not apply it until the upper inch or two of the soil has frozen and winter has definitely arrived.

Be particularly careful not to cover the tops of plants that stay green all winter, such as foxgloves, evergreen candytuft and pinks, with a heavy layer. Mulch the soil about them and cover their tops very lightly with something that admits air but does not mat down. Branches of evergreens such as pine and fir are suitable. So are salt hay, straw and corn stalks. Place a few pieces of brushwood over the plants before you spread these last mentioned coverings.

Protect evergreens likely to suffer from "winter-burn" by mulching heavily, by erecting windbreaks on the north, northeast and northwest, and by shading from strong sun. Windbreaks and shading may be made of laths nailed closely together on a framework or by burlap screens. Invert bushel baskets over small specimens. Another good way with evergreens is to stick branches of evergreens that retain their needles when cut (pine and fir) into the ground around them or to stand evergreen branches against the plant to be protected and tie them into place.

Do something about deciduous woody plants tender enough to be harmed by severe cold. Roses and French hydrangeas are in this category in many sections. So are figs in climates like New York City. The problem is to keep the branches from exposure to excessively low temperatures.

As an alternate plan to the second step where the ground level of bed is to remain unchanged, bring soil from outside source to cover bushes.

Concluding photo shows bed of hybrid tea roses with tops somewhat shortened back and soil piled to a height of eight inches around each base.

GARDENING

Deciduous trees and shrubs inclined to be tender, such as fig trees in the New York area, can be adequately overwintered by wrapping them in burlap, straw or waterproof paper.

You can do this by burying them in the soil. Climbing roses, tree roses and figs that have their branches trained close to the ground may be laid down and covered. After the soil has frozen mulch with straw or leaves. Draw mounds of soil to a height of eight inches about hybrid tea roses. Mulch after it has frozen. It does not matter if the upper parts of the canes of these are killed because they are pruned away in spring.

Another way of protecting stems susceptible to cold is to wrap them in layers of straw, corn stalks, burlap or heavy waterproof paper.

If you drain your water-lily pool move the tubs together and cover with straw or leaves to prevent freezing. Small pools may be left undrained if bridged across with boards

A light covering of salt hay or straw interspersed with slender branches to hold the ingredients firmly in place will form a satisfactory protective mat for your rock garden in winter as at right.

For young or particularly choice rock garden plants winter protection is assured by burying them in small pots to the depth of the pot rims. Set the pots in ashes enclosed by a cold-frame.

GARDENING

Even covering of littery manure, leaves, straw or salt hay offers good winter protection for tulip, hyacinth and daffodil beds. Remember to remove the covering gradually in early spring.

Certain plants should not be exposed to rigorous winter climate. As an example, in the case of dahlias and other tender bulbs, carefully dig them up and store indoors for remainder of the winter.

and well covered with mulch. Hardy aquatics may then be left in place. Hardy water-lilies may be left in pools if they are deep enough so that their roots will not freeze. Float a few logs or empty barrels on the water to take up the expansion as it freezes

Save evergreens and any deciduous trees and shrubs that are in danger of breakage by accumulations of snow, particularly of snow that is wet and heavy and is likely to freeze. With a wooden rake shake the branches gently. Watch out for snow slides from roofs on to foundation planting.

Don't remove winter protection too early in spring. Wait until the buds are ready to grow. Uncover gradually and during dull, moist weather if possible. •

In cold or exposed areas build a burlap screen over a wood frame around choice evergreens to protect them from winter winds and sunshine. Open side shown in the photo will be closed.

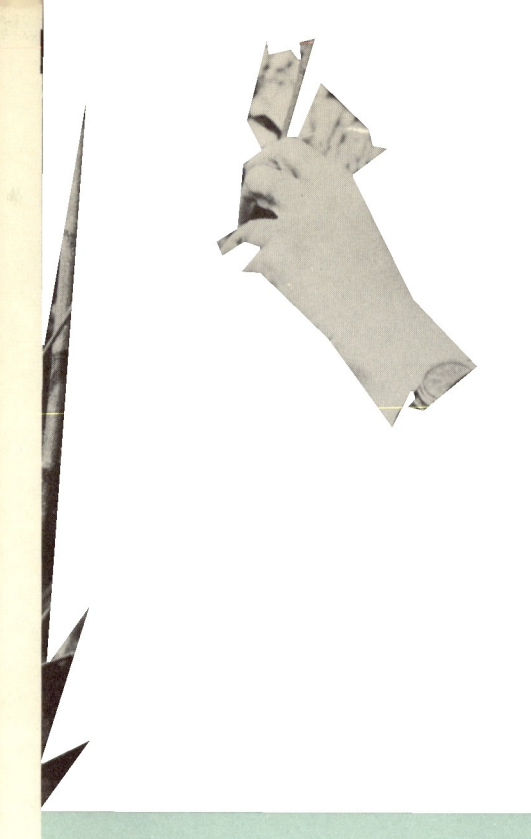

How to Prune

Don't commit butchery on trees and shrubs. On the other hand, don't be too tender-hearted, either. Learn to prune properly.

Sucker shoots that grow from branches of fruit trees should not be permitted to crowd the center part of the tree.

PRUNING is an acquired art. Without adequate understanding, men are apt to commit a kind of tree and shrub butchery in its name while ladies are likely to approach their victims with such tender hearts that the few pathetic snips they make are ineffective.

Pruning needs intelligent understanding. Never cut off a limb or branch without having an entirely good reason for doing so. Prune out dead branches without hesitation. Remove also those infected with diseases that call for this treatment as well as branches severely infested with scale insects. But beyond that consider carefully before you cut. Always use sharp tools.

The kind of pruning needed may vary at different periods in the life of a plant. Many shrubs and trees benefit from being cut back rather severely at planting time. During their early years trees, vines, and shrubs trained to particular habits require formative pruning. Most fruits and some ornamental trees and shrubs need pruning as part of the annual routine.

Rejuvenation Pruning. This is a drastic, but effective, way of restoring neglected shrubs of many kinds which are tall, straggly and bare-bottomed. Simply cut the specimen down to within a few inches of the ground in early spring. Then feed it liberally with manure and bone-meal or with a balanced commercial fertilizer. Water thoroughly and repeatedly if the weather is dry. At the end of the first season you will have a very respectable and shapely young shrub.

Not all kinds respond to this treatment. Among those that do are spireas, mock-oranges, deutzias, weigelias, viburnums, snowberry, Indian currant, lilacs, privets, honeysuckles, shrubby dogwoods, tamarix and barberries. If you cut down grafted lilacs or other shrubs propagated in this way be careful that the shoots that grow and are allowed to remain do not arise from the worthless understock.

Most broad leaved evergreens respond to rejuvenation pruning. Rhododendrons, mountain laurel, true laurel, hollies, and aucuba are examples. Yews may be cut back severely too.

Shade Trees. Prune young shade trees to encourage them to develop strong adequate frameworks not subject to storm-damage and branched rather high up. Remove unwanted branches before they thicken.

Eliminate weak crotches. These occur when the central shoot of a young tree divides into two shoots of about equal thickness or when a strong side shoot develops and grows upwards almost parallel with

1530

In pruning a climbing rose, cut out old flowering canes, retain strong new ones that develop.

If the bush does not produce enough new canes, retain some of old, but prune side branches off.

With new flowering canes cut out, tie young ones into place. These will bloom the following year.

Here is an old cane with all its side branches pruned off ready to be tied into place on bush.

the central shoot. If these equal leaders are allowed to develop the tree is very likely to eventually tear apart at the point where the two branches meet. In old trees this danger can be greatly lessened by bolting or cabling the limbs together. It is better to avoid this necessity by preventing the development of such danger points. Do this by cutting out one branch of the crotch before it exceeds pencil thickness.

Cut out the least important of each pair of crossing branches. If one branch grows much faster than the others shorten it while yet young to preserve the general shapliness of the tree.

When it comes to pruning large trees—work that involves climbing and perhaps the removal of heavy branches—hire a qualified expert on a contract basis. Don't do it yourself and don't let anyone unskilled in tree surgery do it. Slips and mistakes may result in serious injury or may be fatal.

Contrary to common belief it doesn't matter what time of the year shade trees are pruned provided the temperature is not so low that the wood is frozen and brittle. Maples, birches, mulberries and some others "bleed" profusely if pruned in spring. This looks alarming. It does no appreciable harm. To avoid bleeding prune in summer.

Stubs should never be left when pruning. Cut branches flush with the trunk or branch from which they originate. Take off heavy limbs by first making an undercut a few inches away from the main trunk or branch. Then overcut a couple of inches outward from the undercut until the branch is off. Then saw off flush the short stump that remains. Cover all wounds with tree-wound paint.

Deciduous Flowering Shrubs and Trees. These fall into two classes. (1) Those that bloom on branches a year or more old. (2) Those that bloom on current season's wood. Forsythia is a good example of (1), rose of Sharon of (2).

Rose of Sharon cut severely back in winter or spring flowers the same year, forsythia does not. Learn precisely which shrubs belong to which class before you prune. You can not generalize. French hydrangeas belong to (1), peegee hydrangea to (2); bridal wreath spirea to (1), Anthony Waterer spirea to (2); alternate-leaved butterfly bush to (1), common butterfly bush to (2); rambler roses to (1), hybrid tea roses to (2) and so on.

Most shrubs that flower on previous year's wood do so in spring or early summer. You may prune them immediately after they have bloomed by cutting out all thin, weak shoots, ill-placed branches, and

Here is a hybrid tea rosebush before pruning. **Proper way to cut off all weak and dead wood.**

as many old flowering stems as necessary to assure the new growths light and air to develop into strong flowering branches for the following season.

Pruning these immediately after blooming is ideal but pressure of other work is great at that time so that it is often more practical to prune in fall, winter, or spring. This sacrifices some flowers but there is no great loss if the work is intelligently done. With some, forsythia for example, the prunings can be brought indoors and forced for winter bloom in vases of water.

If you prune shrubs that flower on old wood in winter or spring cut out only weak and ill-placed branches and a few older branches to admit some light and air. Do not trim the ends off all the branches. Do not cut the shrubs hard back (unless you are purposely sacrificing a season's bloom to effect a complete rejuvenation). Just thin the bush somewhat.

Prune shrubs that flower on current season's wood in winter or early spring. Cut them back as far as you wish—almost to ground level if you want to keep the bushes as low as possible. Once the frame work of the bush is established at its required height cut the previous year's growths back to within about one half inch of their bases. Thin out the weaker shoots that develop so that those retained are not crowded.

Most flowering trees and many deciduous shrubs need no considerable pruning every year. Magnolias, cherries, crab apples, dogwoods, azaleas and gordonias for example.

Three wrong ways to prune and one right way. A is too far above bud. B is started too low and C has low side of cut on side of branch bearing bud. D shows proper relationship of cut and bud.   **When cutting branches of shrubs be sure to make a clean sloping cut just above the base of the side branch. Cut-off branch is held to show how cut is angled. Always use tools that are sharp.**

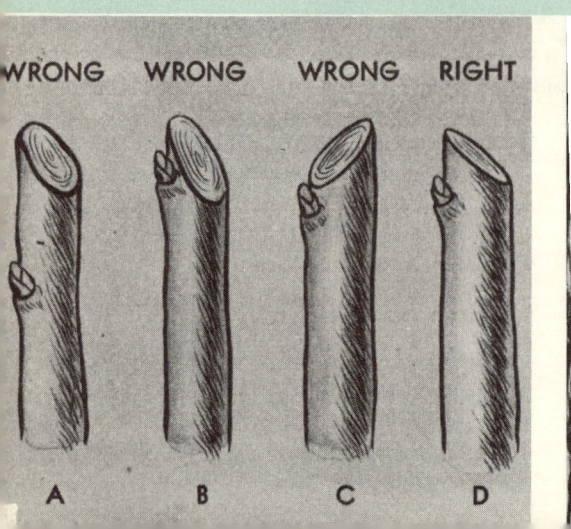

GARDENING

Rosebush pruned. Use approved pruning shears.

Berried Shrubs. Do not prune shrubs grown for their ornamental fruits—barberries, viburnums, firethorns, etc.—more than absolutely necessary. Remove dead or badly placed branches and do a little judicious thinning out in early spring.

Evergreen Shrubs. Broad-leaved evergreens such as boxwood, mountain laurel, rhododendrons, azaleas, pieris, hollies and barberries normally need no pruning other that the shortening of an occasional over-ambitious branch. Yews may be kept compact by shortening their annual growths in summer or spring.

Vines. Evergreen vines should be pruned to keep them from becoming too dense or heavy and to contain them within their allotted space. Prune just before new growth begins. Flowering vines should be pruned in spring if they bloom on current season's wood, immediately after flowering if they bloom on older wood. Summer pruning, which consists of shortening the young growths (when they become eighteen inches or so long) back to a length that includes only six or seven leaves from the base is greatly helpful in inducing wistarias to bloom. Cut the shortened growths back to a length of six inches in winter and to within half an inch of their bases after they flower (or if they don't flower after new leaf growth begins).

Roses. Climbing roses and species roses are pruned in summer immediately after they bloom, all others in spring just as growth begins.

Prune hybrid teas by cutting out all dead, weak, diseased and crowded stems and by shortening back others to from four to eight inches. The rule is, the stronger the shoot the longer you leave it. Do the same with hybrid perpetuals but leave the shoots three or four times as long. Dwarf polyanthas and floribundas need little pruning other than cutting out of dead, diseased and weak wood.

Climbing hybrid tea roses are pruned by removing in spring or summer an occasional old cane (provided new shoots are available to replace it) and by cutting off short flowering shoots after the blooms have withered.

Prune climbers of the rambler and pillar types immediately after they bloom. Retain as many strong new canes as possible and

When shrubs become overcrowded it is necessary to thin them out at the base. Hold stalk firmly in one hand and cut with the other as low down as possible. Many shrubs find this beneficial.

Here is a shrub that was thinned out after it bloomed in spring. Its new growth has had a lot of sun and air and it will bloom well in spring again. Pruning needs vary in the life of plants.

GARDENING

Prune French hydrangea in summer after flowering. Buds will form at tips of this season's shoots.

The peegee hydrangea blooms on current season's shoots. Cut its annual growth back every spring.

cut out as many old flowering growths as can be spared. With varieties that are free in producing new growths prune out all the old flowering wood. With those that produce but few new growths it is often necessary to retain a few of the previous year's canes.

If you do this be sure to cut their side branches back close to the main cane.

Shrubby species roses are pruned by thinning them out after flowering.

Fruit Trees and Grape Vines.

Prune fruit trees in late winter or early spring. Avoid summer pruning except with dwarf trees which should have their annual growths pinched back to six or seven leaves in July. Until fruit trees reach bearing age prune lightly with the objective of developing a sound framework of well spaced branches. Cut out weak and interfering branches and dead or diseased wood. Keep the centers of the trees fairly open to admit light and air and to make pest control easier. Keep the trees moderate in height to facilitate spraying and harvesting. Avoid

For cutting trees, line A to B is best. Others leave undesirable stubs or scars which may rot.

A pole pruner in use on branches of sapling. Of cuts shown in solid lines (left) use middle one.

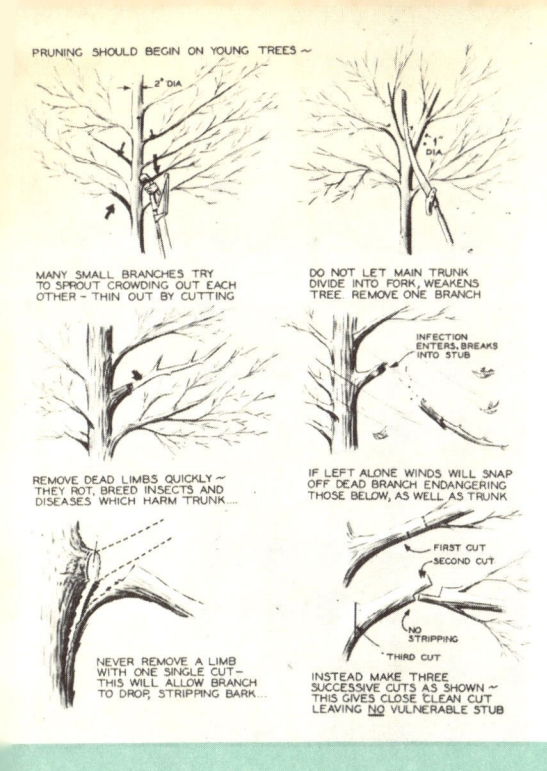

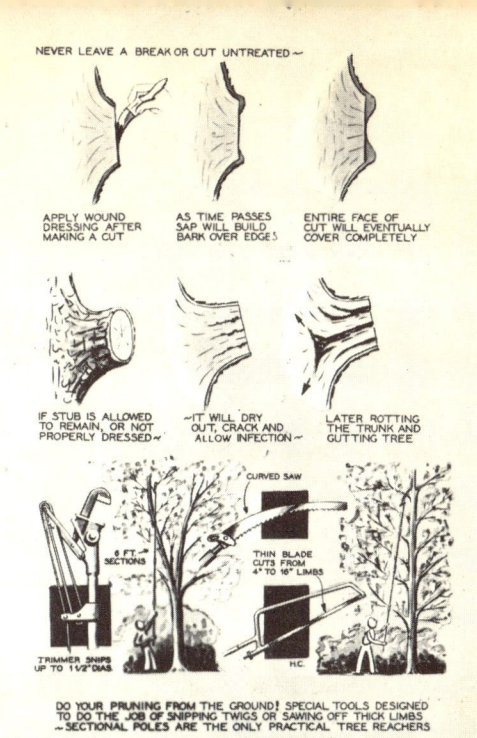

Pruning Should Begin on Young Trees.

the development of sharp V crotches. Most bearing trees need annual pruning.

Apples and pears produce most of their fruit on short side growths called spurs on older wood. Prune these fruits by thinning out crowded shoots. Avoid excessive cutting back (except possibly when rejuvenating neglected trees). Never prune pears more than absolutely necessary. To do so encourages the dread fire blight disease.

Peaches and apricots need more pruning than other fruits. They bear along shoots produced the previous year. After the

Never Leave a Break or Cut Untreated.

framework of the tree is formed prune to force the production of strong young growth each year. Cut out weak branches and twigs and cut back severely one third to one half of all the previous year's shoots that exceed a foot in length.

Cherries need no pruning other than corrective thinning once the framework is established. Pruning of established plums consists of judicious thinning to keep the top from becoming dense. No more of this should be done than absolutely necessary, however. •

To remove branch expertly, make undercut 2 feet out, tie branch to higher limb for safe lowering.

Overcut is then made farther out, branch is out of way and pruning can be made without danger.

ROSES

A long term undertaking, the rose needs ample soil and sunlight.

TWO requirements above all others make for the successful cultivation of roses—plenty of sunshine and a deep, rich, well drained soil. With these you are far more than half way along the road to exhibition-quality flowers.

Once planted you expect roses to stay put for a long time. During those years you can add to the surface soil but you can't directly modify the underlayers—where most of the roots are. Therefore, do the very best job possible *before* you plant. Make sure of good subsurface drainage. Condition the soil to a depth of two feet. Add plenty of humus, preferably in the form of half rotted cow manure. Use bone meal liberally.

Soils on the heavy side are preferred to light sands or gravels. Don't interpret this to mean that infertile clays are suitable.

Roses need good air drainage. Low-lying pockets and places closed in by dense shrubbery, or buildings provide conditions favorable to their arch enemy, the black spot disease, and to mildew. Shelter from high sweeping winds is desirable.

Ascertain which types and which varieties thrive best in your locality. There are tremendous differences in the adaptability of the particular roses. Get the best plants possible. Don't fall for bargain-priced offers by concerns not known to be thoroughly reliable. A good rose bush is a long time investment.

Plant in fall or early spring. Set budded or grafted plants (unless they are trained in tree form) so that the union of the bud or graft is just below the surface. Work good soil around the roots; pack it firmly.

If planted in the fall, prune moderately then severely the following spring. If spring-planted prune hard at planting time.

Routine care of established roses consists of: (1) Pruning (see chapter "How to Prune"). (2) Fertilizing. A spring application of a complete fertilizer or of sheep manure, wood ashes and bone meal cultivated into the surface followed by a dressing of complete fertilizer about midsummer is sufficient on fertile land. On poorer soils fertilize once a month but not later than August. (3) Watering. Never let roses suffer from lack of moisture. Soak the soil thoroughly at weekly intervals during dry weather. (4) Spraying and Dusting. You *must* persist with this if you want good roses. In early spring give a dormant spray of lime-sulphur. Keep the foliage covered with a fungicide throughout the entire summer. Watch for red-spider and other insects. (5) Winter covering. •

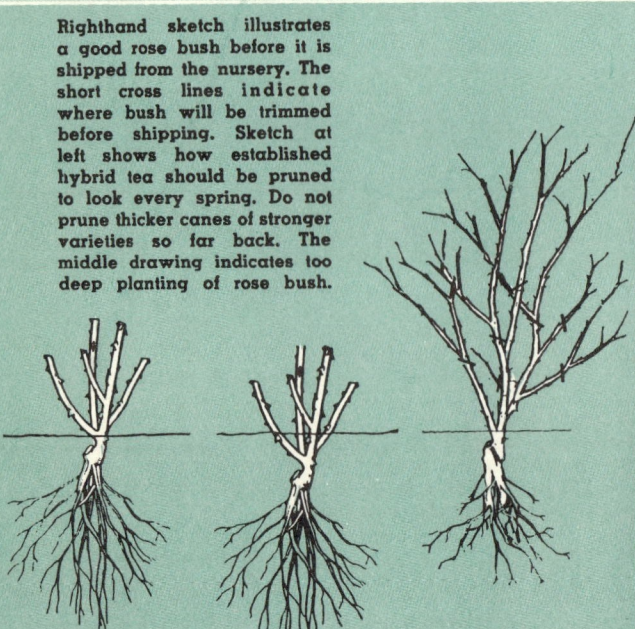

Righthand sketch illustrates a good rose bush before it is shipped from the nursery. The short cross lines indicate where bush will be trimmed before shipping. Sketch at left shows how established hybrid tea should be pruned to look every spring. Do not prune thicker canes of stronger varieties so far back. The middle drawing indicates too deep planting of rose bush.

For show blooms selective disbudding is recommended. All faded flowers should be removed promptly to make for tidiness.